the
new nations
of
AFRICA

by Ben Wattenberg
and Ralph Lee Smith

Maps by Rafael D. Palacios

HART PUBLISHING COMPANY • NEW YORK CITY

CONTENTS

CONTENTS

CONTENTS

ACKNOWLEDGMENTS

Grateful acknowledgment is made to the following sources, which have generously provided photographs for this work. The photos appear on the enumerated pages.

ARAB INFORMATION CENTER,
120 East 56th Street, New York, N. Y.
201, 205, 212, 265, 269, 272

BELGIAN GOVERNMENT INFORMATION
CENTER, 630 Fifth Avenue,
New York, N. Y.
50-51, 52, 53, 54, 55, 111, 116, 122-A,
124, 130, 316 (2), 318, 319, 320-321,
322

BRITISH INFORMATION SERVICES,
45 Rockefeller Plaza, New York, N. Y.
382 (2), 385, 387 (2), 392-A, 427,
428-B, 429-B, 431, 432-433, 436, 437
(2), 438, 439

CENTRAL AFRICAN DELEGATION TO THE
UNITED NATIONS, 386 Park Avenue
South, New York, N. Y.
76

THOMAS COOK & SON, WAGONS-LITS
INC., 587 Fifth Avenue, New York,
N. Y.
106, 118-119, 129, 434-A, 440

DELEGATION OF NIGER,
125 East 72nd Street, New York, N. Y.
281, 284

EAST AFRICA TOURIST TRAVEL
ASSOCIATION, 6 East 45th Street,
New York, N. Y.
158, 221-A, 376 (3), 377 (2), 378,
379, 394, 430, 434-435, 435-A

EMBASSY OF THE REPUBLIC OF IVORY
COAST, 46 East 74th Street,
New York, N. Y.
193

FRENCH CULTURAL SERVICES OF THE
FRENCH EMBASSY, 972 Fifth Avenue,
New York, N. Y.
182

FRENCH EMBASSY, PRESS & INFORMA-
TION DIVISION, 972 Fifth Avenue,
New York, N. Y.
23, 59, 60, 61, 62 (2), 63, 64, 66,
72 (2), 81, 82-83, 88, 92, 99, 100, 101,
105, 136, 137, 138, 142, 147, 148, 149,
173, 174, 177, 178, 181, 183, 186, 187,
188, 189, 191 (2), 194, 216, 218, 220,
221-B, 222, 224 (2), 225 (5), 230, 231,
233, 234, 235, 239-A, 244, 250, 251,
255, 260, 261, 262 (2), 264, 277 (2),
278 (2), 282, 283 (3), 293 (3),
327 (2), 328, 329 (2), 330, 332, 399,
400, 410, 415, 421, 422, 446-447, 448,
450-A

EWING GALLOWAY, 420 Lexington
Avenue, New York, N. Y.
18-19, 21, 22, 24-B, 27, 28-29, 31, 38-39,
153, 200, 202, 203, 206, 209, 210.

GHANA INFORMATION SERVICE,
605 Fifth Avenue, New York, N. Y.
160, 162-163, 165, 168

GHANA MISSION TO THE UNITED
NATIONS, 144 East 44th Street,
New York, N. Y.
161

MINISTRY OF INFORMATION, FEDERA-
TION OF NIGERIA, 575 Lexington
Avenue, New York, N. Y.
288-289, 291, 296, 298-299, 304, 306,
307, 311, 312-A

MOROCCAN MISSION TO THE UNITED
NATIONS, 342 Madison Avenue,
New York, N. Y.
270, 271

8

NIGERIAN CONSULATE GENERAL,
575 Lexington Avenue,
New York, N. Y.
290, 292 (2), 293-D, 294, 300, 302 (3),
303, 309, 310, 312-B

OFFICE ALGERIE D'ACTION
ECONOMIQUE ET TOURITSTIQUE,
40-42 Rue D'Isly, Algeria.
24-A, 25, 34-35, 36, 40 (2), 41 (2),
42 (2)

PERMANENT MISSION OF THE ISLAMIC
REPUBLIC OF MAURITANIA TO THE
UNITED NATIONS, 150 East 52nd Street,
New York, N. Y.
245, 246, 248, 249-A, 249-B

PERMANENT MISSION OF MALI TO THE
UNITED NATIONS, 111 East 69th Street,
New York, N. Y.
238

PERMANENT MISSION OF THE REPUBLIC
OF TOGO TO THE UNITED NATIONS,
801 Second Avenue, New York, N. Y.
401, 404

PERMANENT MISSION OF SIERRA LEONE
TO THE UNITED NATIONS, 30 East 42nd
Street, New York, N. Y.
340, 345, 347

PERMANENT MISSION OF UGANDA TO
THE UNITED NATIONS, 801 Second
Avenue, New York, N. Y.
428-A, 429-A

PERMANENT MISSION TO THE UNITED
NATIONS OF THE REPUBLIC OF CHAD,
150 East 52nd Street, New York, N. Y.
89-A, 89-B, 91, 94

PICHONNIER, BY COURTESY OF
U. A. T. FRENCH AIRLINES,
2 Broadway, New York, N. Y.
70-71, 75, 82, 83, 86, 93, 95, 103, 104,
135, 140, 141 (3), 150, 236-237, 247,
253, 445, 450-B

PROVISIONAL GOVERNMENT OF THE
REPUBLIC OF ALGERIA,
236 East 46th Street, New York, N. Y.
32

*Scenes from Julien Bryan's film
"Tropical Africa"*
INTERNATIONAL FILM FOUNDATION,
INC., 1 East 42nd Street,
New York, N. Y.
232, 239-B

SOMALI MISSION TO THE UNITED
NATIONS, 236 East 46th Street,
New York, N. Y.
355-B, 356-A, 358

SUDAN MISSION TO THE UNITED
NATIONS, 144 East 44th Street,
New York, N. Y.
366-A, 367-B, 373

TANGANYIKA MISSION TO THE
UNITED NATIONS,
205 East 42nd Street, New York, N. Y.
381, 386 (2), 389, 390-391, 392-B

TUNISIAN TRADE & TOURIST OFFICE,
543 Madison Avenue, New York, N. Y.
408, 411, 413, 414-B, 417, 418, 423

UNITED NATIONS, PHOTO LIBRARY,
Room 994, 1st Avenue and 42nd Street,
New York, N. Y.
123-A, 123-B, 123-C, 123-D, 259, 266,
350, 351, 352, 353, 355-A, 363, 365,
366-B, 367-A, 368, 369, 370, 372, 380,
388, 398

WESTERN NIGERIA INFORMATION
SERVICE, 385 Madison Avenue,
New York, N. Y.
297

WIDE WORLD PHOTOS, INC.,
50 Rockefeller Plaza, New York, N. Y.
33, 47, 112-113, 115, 122-B, 128, 157,
166, 198, 339, 342, 344, 356-B, 414-A

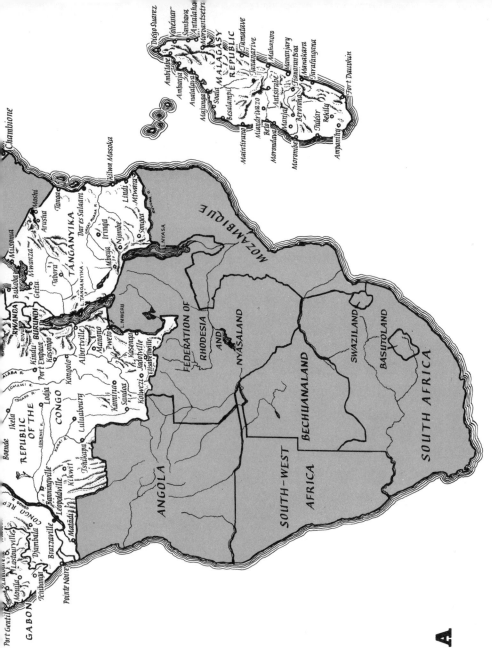

MAP OF AFRICA

The shaded areas are not part

of the 29 new nations of Africa.

FOREWORD

Not very long ago, the continent of Africa was the special preserve of colonial powers. Lands were administered primarily for exploitation. Except for the people directly involved, few others knew what was going on in this vast area.

In the last few years, the world has witnessed a dramatic turn of events. Young Africa has emerged from its chrysalis—exultant, virile, hopeful. Since 1956, twenty-nine new governments have taken their seats in the council of nations. These new African polities have become a new force in international affairs.

Despite internecine conflict here and there, the picture on the wide screen is that of vibrant peoples who are eager to take their rightful place in the society of nations; and, through dint of hard work, to realize the full potential of their human and natural resources.

Illiteracy is regarded as a scourge which must be eliminated as quickly as possible. Educational facilities are burgeoning; industries are growing by leaps and bounds. The leaders of the new countries are quite aware that economic viability can only be attained through unremitting effort and dedication.

Africa is leapfrogging from the 14th century to the 20th century, from the bullock-drawn cart directly to the jet plane. The transition is so radical and so rapid that whatever faults and failures there be should be regarded with some understanding. If there is a lack of sympathy for the fledgling nations of Africa, it is because only a handful of the American public knows anything about these new countries. Little is known of the history of these peoples, less of their former glories, and but little more of their art, and of the intellectuals in their midst today. If the bare facts are not known, how can their problems be understood?

THE NEW NATIONS OF AFRICA presents the main facts relative to each of these countries: its history, ethnology, industry, politics, economic conditions, form of government, educational facilities. An exhaustive, or even a thorough coverage of each of these aspects, would be impossible in a single volume. This book will serve well as an introduction to the continent. The authors have tried to impart to the reader the special character of each country, and to point out its unique problems and aspirations.

To dramatize the text, a great many photographs have been gathered. A great deal of time and care has been expended in researching these pictures. In this interesting task, the diplomatic corps of the nations covered have been most cooperative.

Great difficulty was encountered in compiling the statistical matter for this book, for the statistics available from such sources as the U.N. and the African embassies reveal great disparities; and both of these have, at times, differed from data obtainable from other standard sources. In one instance, as many as four different figures have been encountered for the area of a single country.

This is understandable when one takes into focus that many of the new African nations have little administrative machinery available for such research, and that many of the nations are so young and so new that the only statistics available are those compiled by the former colonial power for an area which in many cases, does not correspond to the boundaries of the country as it exists today.

At the least, THE NEW NATIONS OF AFRICA must impress the reader with the enormous diversities of culture on the African continent. Dramatic differences exist—not alone between nations—but between the different ethnic groups within each nation. People tend to regard Africa, in one big blur, as a welter of underdeveloped people. Not alone is there a haze in most minds about names and boundaries, but until very recently, there has been but little awareness that each of the nations of Africa—like every other country on the globe—is guided, to a large extent, by dominant personalities. In this volume, you will be introduced to most of the important leaders of Africa.

Recent headlines in the newspapers make it mandatory for everyone who wants to know what is going on in world affairs to get to know these men, and to get to know the peoples they represent; for the problems of any continent, no matter how seemingly remote, in this day and age become the problems of world civilization.

The material in this book covers events up to February 1, 1963.

Harold H. Hart
Publisher

The publisher wishes to acknowledge his heartfelt appreciation
to Arlette Brauer, Helen Gerson, and Esther Weinberger,
who have participated so conscientiously
in the picture research of this book.

the
new nations
of
AFRICA

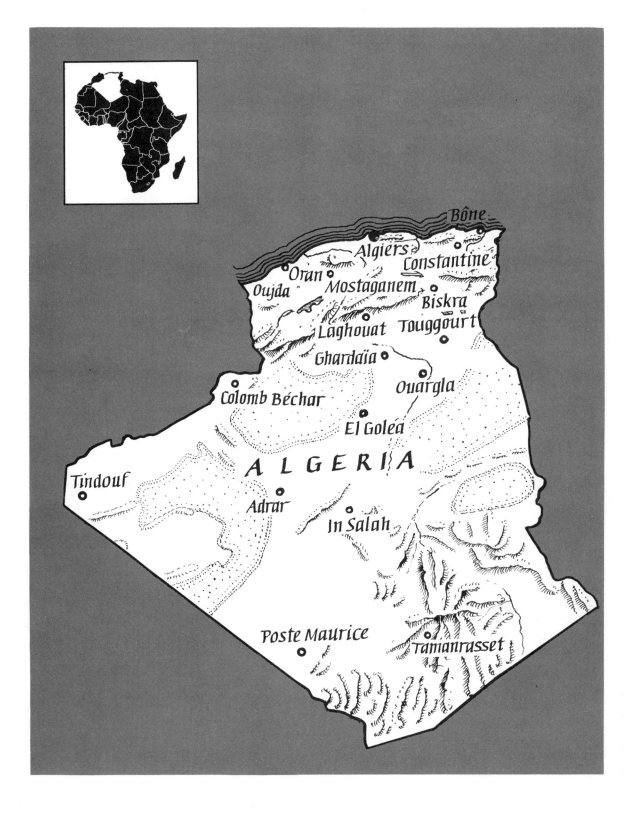

ALGERIA

Splendid Cities and Saharan Wastes

Algeria has had the most violent and protracted struggle for independence of any country on the African continent. One hundred and fifty thousand Moslems were slain; many executed in city streets, many anonymously chosen for reprisal, others haphazardly slaughtered during the accidents of strife. Ten thousand Europeans were also killed; some in battle—others victims of terrorist tactics.

The Algerian cities, made over in the image of Metropolitan France, were but facades. Beyond appearances and behind the gorgeous boulevards were the great masses of Arabs and Berbers, with their own traditions and their steadily increasing sense of national identity. Under the pressure of their insistent demands for independence, the façade cracked.

Although Algerian law did not provide for residential segregation, settlers and Moslems tended to reside in different sections of Algerian cities. There is a striking contrast between the broad boulevards of the European part of the capital, Algiers, and the squalor of the Casbah, the old city whose narrow streets are crowded with Moslems.

Like every Algerian city, Algiers has its *bidonvilles*—shantytowns built of any material at hand, including gasoline cans or *bidons*. Hundreds of thousands of Algeria's poor live in such slums.

THE HISTORY OF ALGERIA

First settled by the Phoenicians, the coastal towns of Algiers, Bône, and Phillipeville were originally trade outposts of these seafarers. Algeria shares the history of North Africa with Libya, Tunisia, and Morocco. Here the Carthaginians, a people of Phoenician stock, held sway until the Romans levelled Carthage in the last Punic War.

The Vandals, a north European tribe of the fifth century, sacked Rome; and then crossed over to Africa where they brought an end to the remnants of Roman culture on the North African shore. Algiers and the other coastal cities were despoiled.

In the seventh century, the westward movement of the Arabs brought Algeria into the Moslem empire. The invading Arabs intermingled with the nomadic Berbers of the desert who adopted Mohammedanism; their descendants have remained the basic native population of Algeria.

Although the Ottoman Turks invaded Algeria in the sixteenth century, the land retained virtual independence under the local rule of the Dey of Algiers. The inland areas were never completely subjected to central rule by the Turks, but continued to be the scene of tribal conflicts that kept the borders of Algeria uncertain.

The coastal cities operated as strongholds for pirates and were occasionally subjected to punitive raids by foreign powers, including one

18

HARBOR OF ALGIERS   As one looks up from the bay to this city built on hills, the houses seem to rise in ordered tiers. There is an elevated highway along the harbor front, which has been laid on a structure of beautiful arches. This busy seaport contains 870,000 people.

by the United States, led by the redoubtable Stephen Decatur, in 1815.

ERA OF FRENCH CONTROL

In 1830, France invaded Algeria and conquered Algiers. Years of bitter warfare, against Arabs and Berbers, followed. France's recent struggle with the Algerian people had its roots in the wars that raged one hundred and thirty years ago. A romantic patina, tinted with adventure tales of the French Foreign Legion, has discolored the true nature of

19

these wars, but they were marked by great brutality on both sides.

In 1848, the region was declared a portion of France itself; but it wasn't until after World War II that all Algerians legally became French citizens, with all the implicit rights and privileges. The official reason given by the French for the withholding of citizenship was that the Arabs and the Berbers lived under Moslem religious laws, under which for example, polygamy, illegal in France, was legal in Algeria. But even the granting of citizenship to the Arabs did not operate to make an appreciable change in their lives. Frenchmen continued to rule.

Many French families now came to settle in Algeria, establishing farms and businesses, building cities and transportation facilities. For these French settlers, Algeria was part of France; to the Moslems, France was still the alien conqueror. There were serious uprisings by native Algerians in 1870 and 1880; and the Sahara region, in the south, was not brought under effective French control until 1909.

The land remained deceptively quiet until 1954. In November of that year, a revolution began that only ended with independence, eight years later, on July 1, 1962.

CAUSES OF UNREST

French colonialism was no more repressive than that of most other European powers. The French were in Africa as exploiters. However, they also built roads, improved health and sanitation, dug wells, and even built some schools. Unfortunately, despite all these beneficent works, many Moslems remained in virtual peonage.

Many French immigrants built farms; most of them prospered. But as the per capita French income moved up, that of the Moslems kept almost stationary. In 1955, the average annual income was $115 per individual. But during the same year, the average income for Moslem natives engaged in agriculture was only $38 per person. This was one of the lowest figures in all Africa.

Much of the arable land, including most of the best land, was owned by Europeans. Much of this land had been confiscated from the Moslems by the French colonial power, *without compensation,* to make room for new European settlers, to the outrage of the natives.

"Land" became an issue with the Moslems. In 1960, there were some 17 million acres tilled and planted, and almost a third of this acreage was owned by approximately 20,000 Europeans. The land hunger and poverty of the Moslems was constantly aggravated by their great increase in population.

The Moslems felt they benefited but little from Algeria's agricultural prosperity. They resented the conversion by the settlers of much of the best land from food crops to export crops, a move which made food more expensive for the poor. In addition, much of the land was given over to viniculture; wine, Algeria's main export, was produced in defiance of a Moslem religious ban on intoxicating drinks.

A SENSE OF BELONGING

When the first French settlers arrived, they found a country of 855,000 square miles; more than twice the area of all England, France, and West Germany combined. To a depth of 150 or 200 miles, the

BOO SAADA   Irrigation has created a fertile farmland and a prosperous modern town on an arid plain in the Atlas Mountains.

ELKANTARA   Each day, the children of this oasis village drive small flocks of sheep to scant desert pastures.

Mediterranean coastal area has a pleasant climate, similar to southern France. It was in this area they settled.

The Algerian settlers, whatever their national origin, felt themselves to be *Algerian,* sons of the soil. The name which they gave to themselves, *pieds noirs,* meaning "black feet," was chosen to proclaim to the world that Algeria's earth clung to their feet.

There were considerable differences between the *grands colons,* the big settlers who owned large farms, industrial enterprises, transport lines, etc., and the "little men," who owned small stores or who were office clerks. But settlers, big and little, united when their interests were menaced by the Moslem majority. This unity came all the easier because a very large proportion of the "little men" were employed in the Algerian civil service. For them, independence meant certain loss of their livelihood.

The Europeans, numbering about 1 million in 1960, were not an immigrant group. Many were third- and fourth-generation Algerians, roughly 80 percent born in Algeria. The fear of being dispossessed of their rich land and prosperous shops turned many into desperate men.

THE BEGINNINGS OF REBELLION

The French government ruled Algeria with a strong hand; so much so that the first organizations of Moslem nationalists sprang up among the hundreds of thousands of Moslem Algerians working in France. This happened in the 1930's.

Algeria itself remained quiet until 1945. Then, on V-E Day, an uprising occurred against the French in the inland district of Setif. The revolt was very severely repressed, the Moslem casualties running into tens of thousands. For the next nine years, the country remained quiet on the surface but simmered with repressed hatreds.

Some attempt was made to improve Algeria's agriculture by introducing modern methods and modern machinery in the interior. Millions of people were resettled as a preventive measure against the spread of rebellion, and to effect a more even distribution of the population. Whatever French intentions were, this resettlement caused very considerable hardship to the people involved.

In the fall of 1954, open rebellion broke out in Algeria.

STREET SCENE IN ALGIERS
This Moslem woman, wearing veil and high heels, and perched atop a motor scooter, vividly portrays the impact of new ways on the Arab community.

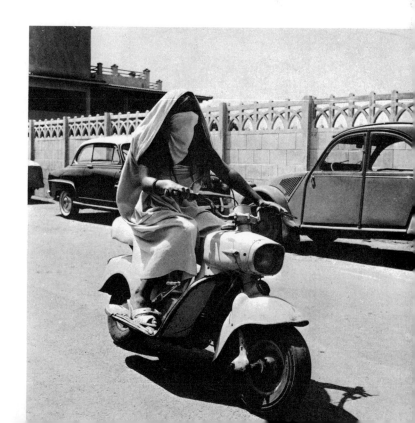

SHEEP MARKET *The village of Sidi-Aissa lies in a region of high plateaus and excellent pasture land.*

NEGRESS AND CHILD *From the neck of this woman from Southern Algeria, there hang a number of square pouches, which contain charms against evil spirits. These amulets are sometimes inscribed with magic incantations.*

TYPICAL STREET *This thoroughfare leads to the Casbah, the native quarter of Algiers.*

THE FRENCH DILEMMA

Though Algeria was a severe drain on her economy, France, because of national pride, felt impelled to maintain dominion. Moreover, there were strong ties of kinship between thousands of Algerian colonists and thousands of families in France. Consequently, the mother country was incapable of dealing rationally with Algeria. Attempts to solve the intricate problems had resulted in the fall of various French post-war governments.

From 1954 to 1962, nearly 800,000 French troops—more than half the French Army—were sent to Algeria to maintain public order.

REVOLT OF THE FRENCH GENERALS

When it appeared that a settlement might be reached with the Moslems, the Algerian-based French generals were thoroughly disenchanted with the French home government. They feared loss of privilege for the French settlers. On May 13, 1958, they staged a coup. Led by most of the General Staff, the rightist forces, in and out of France, brought General Charles de Gaulle to power. They believed that de Gaulle would not tolerate a loss of French prestige in Algeria.

They were soon disillusioned. De Gaulle, driven by inexorable forces and supported by a large part of public opinion, soon expressed a desire to negotiate with the Algerian Moslems. By September, 1958, a cease-fire was agreed to between the Algerian provisional government and France.

On January 24, 1960, General Massu and General Salan led an insurrection of the French Army in Algeria, and threatened France it-

STREET IN THE CASBAH   A bewildering tangle of huddled buildings and narrow winding streets, this small native quarter of Algiers has long been a symbol of the traditional ways that were retained during the long years of French rule. But the people in European dress and the insulators and telephone wires overhead testify that the 20th century has had some impact on these ancient streets.

self with civil war. Popular as this move was with the conservative elements in France and with the French Army, most of the French generals and their forces in Algeria and in France remained loyal to de Gaulle. The coup was quickly put down. De Gaulle, with increased public support and greater international prestige, resumed negotiations with the Algerians.

INDEPENDENCE DECLARED

In March, 1962, an agreement was signed at Evian by the representatives of the French government and the National Liberation

THE ETERNAL SAHARA This desert, the largest on earth, extending over 3 million square miles, is the decisive force in many countries of Africa. The terrain varies between high sand dunes, plateaus of denuded rock, and beds of gravel. There are enormous massifs, and huge depressions which run as much as 100 feet below sea level. The prevailing barrenness, broken only intermittently by date-bearing oases, yields a climate of utter extremes. At times, nights are bitter cold; and during some days, the heat sears like a furnace. Today, the Sahara is linked by telegraph stations, and by a network of air and automobile routes.

Front. This pact provided for Algerian independence, if such independence was approved by a plebiscite both in France and in Algeria. Algeria was to receive sovereignty over the Saharan territories with their rich oil resources. The rights of the European settlers who chose to remain in Algeria were to be guaranteed; and France was to secure recognition of her military and economic interests.

Shortly after the armistice, Ben Bella, leader of the Algerian extremists, who had been kept prisoner by the French for several years, was released.

On April 8, a French plebiscite approved the Evian agreement. On July 1, 1962, Algeria voted 99.7 percent in favor of independ-

ence. More than 70 percent of the five million possible voters cast ballots. Even the majority of Europeans who voted backed independence.

ARAB POLITICS

Prior to 1954, the Moslems had been composed of several different parties. Most of these groups merged in 1954 to form the revolutionary *Front de Libération Nationale* (F.L.N.). It was F.L.N. that negotiated the establishment of a provisional government and the cease-fire with de Gaulle. With the promise by de Gaulle that the Algerian question would be settled, the F.L.N. ceased, for the most part, its terrorist campaign. Yet many members of this organization remained in French prisons until the day of independence.

The F.L.N. named Ferhat Abbas, a highly respected moderate, as Prime Minister. Ahmed Ben Bella was named First Deputy Prime Minister; and Belkacem Krim, a moderate who controls the Kabylia region, Minister of Defense and Deputy Prime Minister. Ben Youssef Ben Khedda, another moderate, was nominated as Minister of Social Affairs, and later became Prime Minister.

The well-educated Ferhat Abbas maintains a stout admiration for French culture. He originally favored the complete cultural assimilation of Algeria with France. He married a Frenchwoman, and enlisted in the French army at the onset of World War II. But late in the 1930's, French colonial policy disheartened him. By 1943, he openly advocated Algerian independence, and was promptly jailed by the French. Favoring peaceful negotiation, he was a strong force in keeping the Moslem extremists under control. However, his love of French culture weakened him politically. Despite the people's respect for his integrity, Abbas was replaced by Ben Khedda.

Ben Youssef Ben Khedda, also a moderate, and not as bound to French culture as his predecessor, sought to continue relations with France and the West.

Ben Khedda was opposed by Ahmed Ben Bella, leader of the extremist party. Ben Bella was a militant opponent of French ties. He repeatedly declared that independent Algeria would be a socialist state. The suspi-

RUE D'ISLY *Signs in French, the traffic jam, and the balconied archi-tecture, all testify that the city of Algiers is "The Paris of Africa."*

cion that he was pro-Communist was reinforced in October, 1962, when, soon after becoming the first Prime Minister of independent Algeria, he thumbed his nose at American public opinion and paid a state visit to Castro in Cuba, where he declared great friendship for the Communist leader.

However, Ben Bella, in contradiction to his actions, claimed to be a moderate, and made an appeal for United States aid, proclaiming neutralism and insisting that his objective was the establishment of a society in Algeria based on social justice.

POWER STRUGGLE FOLLOWING INDEPENDENCE

After the declaration of Algerian independence, Ben Bella and Ben Khedda were in a power struggle for control of the country. The result was a breakdown in business and government administration.

Extremist Algerian forces and the French groups opposed to Algerian independence continued their terrorist activities through the spring and summer of 1962. The S.A.O. (the French Secret Army Organization), staffed by dissident French generals, carried on a campaign of terror in Algerian cities and captured sectors of Algerian territory that had to be retaken by loyal French troops. Algerian nationalist forces raided European sectors of Algerian cities; the S.A.O. raided Algerian sectors. Curfews were imposed by the government, but violated by the contending armies.

ALGERIAN REBELS   A group of Maquisards in a winter hideout have covered their uniforms with native garments to protect themselves from the cold. These were soldiers of the F.L.N.

BEN BELLA   In October, 1962, Ahmed Ben Bella, unyielding leader of the dissident anti-French, pro-Soviet National Liberation Front, was selected Premier of independent Algeria.

During the summer of 1962, all urban life was in chaos. Fearful of their lives, many of the remaining Europeans fled. By May, 1962, 15,000 heads of families had registered with the authorities for repatriation to France, which received about 500,000 refugees. Once numbered at about one million, less than one-half of the European population remained.

Not all settlers went to France, for only 50 percent of the Algerian European population was French. People of Spanish origin constituted 35 percent of the European population. Jews, Greeks, Italians, and Maltese made up the remainder. Many had no homeland to which to return.

Hundreds of thousands left Algeria in a panic. Most of the *pieds noirs* went to France, where they are being absorbed under considerable difficulties. Many Algerian Jews, distrusting Ben Bella's proclamations of friendship because of his violent attacks on Israel, have also departed for Israel and for France, swelling the Jewish population of France by 50 percent.

CREATION OF THE POLITICAL BUREAU

On August 8, 1962, the provisional government formally transferred power to a so-called Political Bureau. Immediately, the Political

MARKET AT AÏN-BOUCIF   This is a seasonal market in which Sahara nomads from the north of the desert come to sell their wares to the Arabs who come down from their mountains. Aïn-Boucif means Fountain of the Sandman. This is the major social event of the season. In this market, the nomads set up lean-tos, and offer camel hides, gourds, shoes, pouches, mats, rugs, and dates. Donkeys, mules, and sheep also are a most important part of the fair. Each section of the market specializes in trading a particular kind of animal. Because of the scarcity of pasture lands, there are no cows. The nomads wear pointed straw hats to protect themselves from the sun. The mountain Arabs wear white turbans.

Bureau ordered an end to property seizures and announced agreements with various guerilla forces, by which these rebel groups became part of the national army.

By September 5th, Ben Bella was able to announce a cease-fire pact with the few remaining guerrilla forces. The Political Bureau's forces, renamed the National Popular Army, took over Algeria peacefully.

The new government, under Ben Bella, moved swiftly on the international front. Ben Bella announced that the establishment of a socialist state was the immediate objective of the new nation. A pact was signed with France, defining French aid to Algeria.

A cargo of wheat arrived from the U.S.S.R.

THE FIRST NATIONAL ASSEMBLY

The first national elections, on September 25, 1962, brought into office the unopposed candidates proposed by the Political Bureau. Ferhat

THE AMENOKAL   The Chief of Chiefs of the Tuaregs and his chieftains meet in Tamanrasset in the Hoggar Mountains. The Amenokal wears the traditional silver Tuareg cross. The Tuaregs are known as the "blue men," because their blue veils impart a blue tinge to their skins.

Abbas was elected Speaker of the first National Assembly. The Vice-Presidents included Hadj Ben Alla, a member of the Political Bureau, Beyag Ahkammouk, the amenokal, or chief, of all the Tuareg tribes, and Roger Roth, Vice-President of the Transitional Executive Council and one of the sixteen European deputies in the National Assembly.

On October 8, 1962, Algeria joined the United Nations. Ben Bella visited President Kennedy in Washington.

By November, 1962, Ben Bella was having difficulties with the Algerian Communist Party. Although numerically weak, the party had gained influential positions in such key organizations as the General Union of Algerian Workers, the General Union of Moslem Students, and the Union of Algerian Women. Ben Bella, in response to criticism by these groups, declared there was room for only one party in Algeria. He warned the Communists that he would act if they did not stop their activities outside the National Liberation Front. Ben Bella insisted that although administrative autonomy for the General Union of Algerian Workers was acceptable, political activity would not be tolerated.

DETERIORATION OF THE ECONOMIC SITUATION

Towards the end of 1962, there were ample indications that the Algerians had become weary of slaughter and of the unsettled conditions that followed the chaos of war. A crisis developed between the Ben Bella government and some radical army units led by 28-year-old Colonel Si Hassan, which threatened, towards the end of September, to degenerate into a civil war. Both factions refrained from radical action, because it was realized by everyone involved that the Algerian people had become fed up with conflict, both military and political, and would lend support only to a movement for economic betterment. The popular slogans became "Work, Not Blood!" and "Work, Bread, Houses!" The catchword of the day was "Seven Years of War is Enough!"

As the economic conditions worsened, Ben Bella was forced to seek further aid from the French and from the United States. Under the Evian agreement, French aid was due to end on December 31, 1962.

The pressure was on. The extreme leftist groups attacked Ben Bella as a traitor to the revolution. Leaflets denouncing him, printed by the Marxist Party of the Social Revolution, were the last straw. In December, 1962, Ben Bella banned the Algerian Communist Party, and put lock and shutters on their daily newspaper, *Al Hourya.*

Negotiations were conducted with France to extend the sorely-needed aid. In a turnabout not uncommon in the Levant, Ben Bella's Minister of Foreign Affairs, Mohammed El Khemisti, who was conducting negotiations with France to extend the aid, came out in favor of "a healthy co-operation with France."

AN AFTERMATH OF REVENGE

When the de Gaulle government and the negotiators of the F.L.N. met in Evian, France, to conclude an arrangement for peace, they in-

cluded in their agreement a clause which guaranteed all participants immunity from either prosecution or persecution for any action committed during the years of the Algerian War for Independence. In Algeria, this clause was ignored by the Algerians in their treatment of the 80,000 Moslem auxiliaries—the *harkis*—who had fought with the French Army. The harkis became open targets of savage revenge.

Directly after the War of Independence, some 10,000 harkis and their relatives were murdered by vengeful mobs. In Tizi-Ouzou, six harkis were doused with gasoline and set aflame; there was the case of a sergeant whose skin was stripped off him with pliers, in a village square; the eyelids of other harkis were sewn together, and thousands of others were subjected to horrible reprisal. This stark parade of barbarity marched on, unchecked by the authorities.

MARKET PLACE OF EL OUED
This oasis village, 120 miles south of Biskra, is deep in the Algerian Sahara. The thick walls of these one-story dwellings provide protection against the fierce sun.

TAILOR OUTDOORS In *Aflou, a small town in the mountainous region of Djebel-Amour, an elder craftsman sits in front of his home, embroidering a decorative edge on a burnous. He unwinds the embroidery thread from the spindle at his side.*

SPINNING THREAD In *Michelet, a town about 100 miles from Algiers, a Kabyle woman spins wool. The thread wound around a large spindle, is used in the home-weaving of the rugs and tapestries. A wide sash ties her child to her back.*

RUG-MAKING IN TLEMCEN *Young girls, some from orphanages, are finishing rugs in a small carpet-making establishment. This traditional handicraft is taught in a vocational school. Apprentices receive token payment during training.*

WOMEN OF TIOUT *In the poor Berber region of the Aurès Mountains, the ornate, multiple strand of necklace of the smiling woman is common.*

THE UNIVERSITY OF ALGIERS *Established at the turn of the century, this institution has an enrollment of 2,600 students, the majority of whom are Algerians. One of the best-known of its graduate schools is the School for Colonial Medicine. The university's main problem is to find new teachers from Canada, Switzerland, and other French-speaking countries to replace the former French faculty.*

HAND SPINNING *This old woman still practices the ancient art of hand-spinning. She twirls the wool held on a distaff, and winds the wool onto a spool supported on her thigh. This wool, bleached over a sulphur fire, will be woven into the traditional white burnous.*

Some 32,000 harkis found refuge in France; while 6,000 others were waiting, at the end of 1962, to be transported from Algeria under the protection of French troops. But even in France, these men cannot be deemed to be safe from the long, vindictive arm of their 300,000 countrymen who work in French cities.

THE OUTLOOK FOR ALGERIA

At the close of 1962, the loyalty to the Ben Bella government of Kabylia, a largely Berber region in the interior, remained in doubt. Its leaders, Belkacem Krim and Mohammed Boudjaf, yielded to him, but remain resentful.

An even greater threat to Ben Bella are the military commanders who control certain *milayas* (military zones) and do not want to incorporate their units into the National Army. Their leader, Colonel Houari Boumédienne, does not feel that Ben Bella is radical enough to properly promote Algerian interests, and confided to a foreign ambassador, "I'm going along with him for a bit of the way. After that, we'll see."

At best, without French aid, the future for Algeria would be precarious. However, France has a solid interest in maintaining ties; it needs the Sahara for the testing of atomic weapons and it hopes to exploit Saharan oil. Moreover, France cannot dispassionately face the total abandonment of Frenchmen in Algeria, which might result if France permitted the new state to collapse economically.

THE LAND AND ITS RESOURCES

Algeria is bordered on the east by Tunisia and Libya, and on the west by Morocco. Beyond the coastal area lies a vast desert, occasionally broken by clusters of oases.

This region, south of the Sahara Atlas Mountains, represents about 80 percent of the total area of Algeria and is populated by the nomadic Tuareg and other Berber tribes. Huge oil reserves exist in this vast, sandy wasteland, and are already being worked. This territory was formerly governed by the French as a separate entity. Today, these deserts serve as a proving ground for French atomic weapons.

The fertile areas produce rich harvests of wheat and barley. Livestock numbers in the millions. Vineyards and citrus fruit orchards flourish. Most of the grain is used for home consumption; but wine and citrus fruit are major exports.

Some minerals, including iron, phosphate, and zinc, have been discovered. In 1960, iron ore accounted for 10 percent of Algeria's exports; while in the same year, wine accounted for 50 percent of the total exports. However, oil holds the greatest promise for Algeria's future. Although oil exports have amounted to only 8 percent of the total out-of-country shipments, when the Sahara is tapped, oil exports should rise steeply.

Algeria shares the unfortunate characteristic of all the Saharan lands: limited natural resources. The country has always had to be subsidized by France to make up its trade deficit. In 1960, exports totalled $394,300,000, while imports were a massive $1,275,300,000. The budget requirements of Algeria were always beyond Algeria's capacity, and France has always footed the bill. In 1959, France supplied two-thirds of the Algerian budget which totalled about $300,000,000.

A FANTASTIC BIRTH RATE

In 1960, the population of Algeria was about 11 million, of which 10 million were Moslems. In 1954, the birth rate of the Moslem population increased by almost 3 percent. This meant an increase of approximately 300,000 Moslems from 1954 to 1955; and in each succeeding year thereafter, an increase by a proportionately larger number. It is estimated that 55 per cent of the Moslem population are children and adolescents.

THE CITY OF ALGIERS

Among Algeria's riches are its large seaports and industrial centers. Algiers, the capital, with a population of 870,000, is the chief port with an excellent harbor on the Mediterranean. The European sectors are splendidly laid out, with wide boulevards which have led some to refer to the city as "The Paris of Africa." Algiers has extensive rail and air services, and is a re-fueling station for international shipping.

Algiers is a flavorsome city, redolent with the culture of France, Arabia, and Turkey. It has gorgeous mosques, beautiful churches. There are magnificent palaces, rich gardens, beautiful parks and terraces, and a university. Alongside of these fine, urbane and sophisticated establishments, there is the Casbah, the Arab section with its steep, tortuous streets, its small, intimate cafés, its tiled patios, and its bits of Arabian Nights' atmosphere. Walking in this quarter, it is hardly possible to realize that, not too far away, there are race tracks, yacht basins, golf courses, tennis courts, bathing beaches, and vivid 20th-century activity.

THE CITY OF CONSTANTINE

Constantine (population 217,000), is a trade and commercial center, connected by rail with its port at Phillipeville, 40 miles to the north. In the second century, the city, then called Cirta, was the capital of the Numidian kings. Near Constantine, there stand interesting ruins of elaborate Roman fortifications.

This city, perched on top of a steep rock, is surrounded by chasms that rendered it well-nigh impregnable. The French captured Constantine in 1837, and built access bridges over the surrounding canyons. These ingenious architectural structures lend enormous interest to Constantine and greatly enhance the sight-seeing aspects of a city, which are definitely the most considerable on the North African Coast. Knowing travellers rank Constantine as one of the most fascinating cities in the world.

BÔNE AND ORAN

Bône, birthplace of St. Augustine, has a population of 144,000 which throng its animated sidewalk cafés. An old Roman city, it contains interesting relics of former grandeur.

Oran, the second largest city (population 430,000), and a Mediterranean port, was founded by the Arabs a thousand years ago. It has extensive industries, including foundries, canneries, metal and glass works. Two colleges grace the city.

IN BRIEF

AREA	855,000 sq. miles. Larger than Alaska and Texas combined.
TERRAIN	The northern area is a coastal plain about 150 or 200 miles deep. Two ranges of mountains—the Maritime Atlas and the Saharan Atlas—running east-west parallel the coast. The desert region south of the Saharan Atlas constitutes 80% of the country. It is a low irregular plateau about 1,500 feet high. There are no navigable rivers.
CLIMATE	The northern coastal portions have a Mediterranean climate, similar to that of southern France or Italy. Winters are mild with a fair amount of rainfall. Summers are hot and dry. The desert area is hot and arid; night temperatures drop to freezing.
CAPITAL	Algiers, population 870,000. In this city, 40% of the people were European, but the majority have left.
OTHER CITIES	Oran, 430,000; Constantine, 217,000; Bône, 144,000; Sidi bel Abbas, 115,000.
POPULATION	11,000,000 (1960); about 250,000 Europeans.
ETHNIC GROUPS	Between one and two million Kabyles (a Berber People); the majority are Arabs (an Arab-Berber group).
LANGUAGES	Arabic is the predominant language. Berber languages are spoken by over 1,500,000 people. French, used in commerce, is spoken by the European community.
RELIGION	Arabs and Berbers are Mohammedan. Most Europeans are Christian. There are an estimated 100,000 Jews.
DATE OF INDEPENDENCE	July 1, 1962.
FORM OF GOVERNMENT	A Constituent Assembly, elected on the one-party slate of the F.L.N. Premier is appointed.
EDUCATION	Most Europeans are literate. Less than 10% of the Moslem community can read and write. Over 17,000 primary schools with about 750,000 pupils, about 90% of them Moslems. About 20,000 pupils in vocational schools. Algiers University

FERHAT ABBAS *A strong leader of the F.L.N., Ferhat Abbas was a natural choice as first Prime Minister of the Provisional Government, set up late in 1958. In October, 1962, he became the first speaker of the National Assembly of the new nation of Algeria.*

has 5,500 students. 1,000 pupils attend teachers' colleges.

CURRENCY Algerian Franc (same value as French franc).

INDUSTRY Milling, leather processing, carpet weaving, and manufacture of matches.

CROPS: Wheat, barley, oats, grapes, tobacco, corn, vegetables, flax, silk, figs, dates.

STOCK: Sheep, cattle, goats, camels.

MINING: Phosphates; iron ore; oil.

TRADE

1960: IMPORTS	$1,275,300,000
EXPORTS	$ 394,300,000
DEFICIT	$ 881,000,000

MAJOR IMPORT: Petroleum, machinery, motor vehicles. (80% supplied by France).

MAJOR EXPORTS: Wine, iron ore, citrus fruits. (76% taken by France).

TRANS-PORTATION Algeria has about 2,800 miles of railroad, most of it runs east-west along the coast. Some short lines to south. There are over 8,000 miles of main roads for motor vehicles. Algiers has an international airport used by 400,000 passengers per year.

47

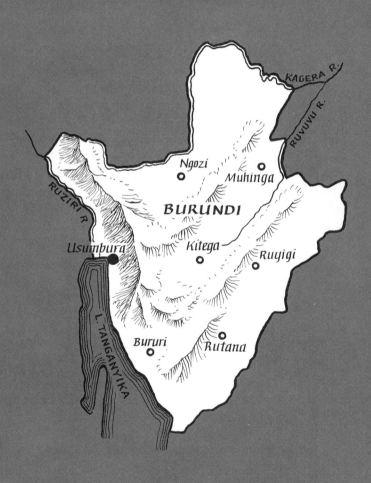

BURUNDI

Overpopulation in a Feudal Land

This tiny country, bordering Congo (Leopoldville), was formed from the southern half of the U. N. Trust Territory of Rwanda-Urundi, and until its independence, was administered by Belgium. Although Burundi shares the history of its sister state to the north *(See page 315)*, Burundi can look forward to somewhat greater political stability than Rwanda, for the Burundese are intensely loyal to their Mwami, or king.

Mwami Mwambutsa, of the Watusi tribe, is held in great affection by the Bahutu tribe who form five-sixths of the population. The Watusi, the giants of the country, have kept the Bahutu in servitude for 400 years; but despite this, the present Mwami is a highly respected figure— and with good reason. The Mwami takes his responsibilities very seriously. After independence was achieved, the Mwami toured the country addressing his people, telling them that freedom could only be enjoyed if they were mindful of the duties of citizenship.

On July 1, 1962, against the advice of most of the influential leaders of Africa, Burundi became a sovereign state, severing its connection with Rwanda. There had been a traditional separation even while both countries constituted a U.N. Trust Territory. The Burundese, who considered themselves under the headship of their respected Mwami, understandably chose autonomy.

OVERPOPULATION AND A TOTTERING ECONOMY

Burundi is a land of 10,000 square miles, approximately the size of Vermont. With 2,200,000 inhabitants, the density of population exceeds 200 persons per square mile. This is populous by world standards, and Burundi is one of the most crowded countries in Africa.

Agriculture is meager; famine, a constant threat. Only because food has been supplied by relief agencies, by the U.N., and by the U.S., has the country been able to stave off starvation.

The only crop that brings in revenue is coffee. Gold, tin, tungsten, and tantalum are mined in small quantities. No sizable reserves have been discovered.

Herds of cattle are numerous, but they are of poor quality. As elsewhere in Africa, the possession of a great number of cattle is a mark of social prestige. Grazing ranges are overstocked with emaciated beasts, since the Burundese are reluctant to part with even the most sickly animals.

Most economists do not believe that Burundi can develop a viable economy. Financial aid is essential if the country is not to founder.

Burundi has ordered almost all of its former Belgian administrators out of the country. It is considered neutral in international politics.

WASWAHILI SCHOOLROOM   Waswahili natives of the Moslem faith attend a school, in Usumbura, reserved for them. Long in contact with the Arabs, these people write Swahili in Arab script. The board also shows some Swahili written in Roman script. The man with the fez on head is the teacher. The class consists of both adults and children, for all ages attend the same class. Most learning in this type of school is a study of the Koran; and probably most of the books in the classroom are copies of the holy book. The school shown is far superior to most schools in this part of the country, for desks, benches, and white-washed walls are unusual. Most schools are just a clearing in the bush, with mounds of earth for seats.

MWAMI MWAMBUTSA, KING OF BURUNDI *Mwambutsa IV*
succeeded to the throne in 1915. At Kitega, he presides at the High Council
of Burundi, numbering 32 members. He no longer makes decisions himself,
as he did before the Constitutional Monarchy was established in 1961, but
depends on the council to direct native administration. The Mwami and his
drum are considered divine sources of power. He is surrounded with a very
strict protocol whose significance is both magical and religious. He will be
succeeded by one of his sons chosen by a council, known as the Biru. Since
the eldest son is not the heir apparent,but only one of the pretenders to the
throne, most reigns start with lively competition among the sons of the
defunct Mwami.

IN BRIEF

AREA 10,747 square miles; slightly larger than Vermont.

TERRAIN Most of the country is an undulating plateau, 3,000 to 6,000 feet high. Near the western border runs a chain of mountains, 6,000 to 10,000 feet high. The country is landlocked, over 600 miles from the nearest coast.

CLIMATE Pleasant, temperate climate due to its elevation, despite proximity of the equator. The mean temperature is 66°F. and varies little throughout the year. In a usual day, temperature range is 55° to 77°. Annual rainfall is 44 inches (slightly more than New York City); but there is a three-month dry season (June through August) with almost no rain.

CAPITAL Usumbura (population: 48,000).

POPULATION About 2,200,000.

ETHNIC GROUPS The Bahutu and Bantu make up about 83% of the population. The Watusi about 16% of the total. The Twa, a pygmy group, less than 1%; perhaps some 18,000 in all. There are very few outsiders in the country.

MAIN STREET IN USUMBURA Hotel Paguidas, built in 1941, is at right. Hotel Olympia, opened in 1948, is at left.

LANGUAGE   The Bahutu language is spoken by most of the population. Also, Swahili.

DATE OF INDEPENDENCE   July 1, 1962.

FORM OF GOVERNMENT   Monarchy. Legislature elected under UN supervision in September, 1961. Mwami or king, is executive leader. Legislative Assembly of 32 members elected by universal suffrage. Cabinet headed by Premier. Member of the United Nations.

CANDIDATES AT ELECTION   Because of widespread illiteracy, candidates are identified by numbers or colors, which voters use to associate with the proper ballot boxes, which likewise, are numbered and colored to match. Since some voters cannot even read numbers, the numbers serve only as symbols. During the elections, illiterates vote by dictating their choices to school children, who fill in the ballots for their elders. The voting booths are placed along corridors near which candidates are seated.

VOTING The picture of each candidate is posted on a ballot box. Since most of the people cannot read, this method of identification assures that the voter is casting his ballot for the candidate he wants to vote for.

EDUCATION About half the children of school age are currently enrolled in primary schools. In 1960 less than 3,000 pupils were receiving secondary school or technical training. No university.

CURRENCY Unit is the Congolese franc. (50 francs = U.S. $1.00 official rate of exchange).

INDUSTRY Almost none except for some minor dairy processing.

CROPS: Mostly subsistence farming. Cassava meal is important. Coffee is major export crop; some palm oil, tobacco.

STOCK: Large numbers of undernourished cattle of poor quality. Also sheep, and goats.

MINING: Small quantities of tin, gold, tungsten, tantalum, mined. No important mineral deposits discovered as yet.

TRANS-PORTATION ROADS: The basic road system is one of the densest in Africa. There are 6,080 surfaced roads in former Ruanda-Urundi.

COMMUNI-CATIONS 1,814 telephones known to exist in former Ruanda-Urundi (1960).

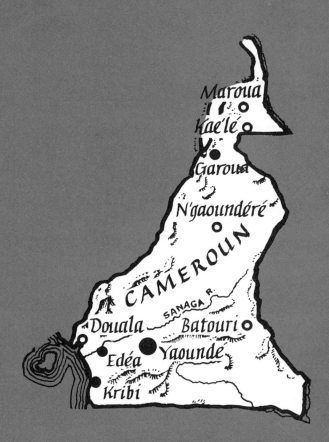

Maroua

Kae'le

Garoua

N'gaoundéré

CAMEROUN

SANAGA R.

Douala

Batouri

Edéa

Yaounde

Kribi

CAMEROUN

The Racial Crossroads of Africa

Stamp collectors will recall various issues of stamps that reflect the changing history of Cameroun. In the nineteenth century, Germany issued a series of pictures of a German battle cruiser with the name "Kamerun" printed at the bottom of the stamp.

In 1884, the German explorer, Gustav Nachtigal, negotiated protectorate treaties with the local chief of Cameroun. British missionaries had been in the area somewhat earlier; but Britain recognized Germany's claims and Cameroun remained a German protectorate until the First World War.

At the close of World War I, by the terms of the armistice, one-fifth of the German colony was assigned to Britain; the other four-fifths to France. Both parts of Cameroun were then administered as mandates under the aegis of the League of Nations.

When the German stamps disappeared, they were replaced by British stamps that read "Cameroons," and by French stamps which were marked "Cameroun." The French stamps were used until Cameroun became an independent nation in 1960.

The British stamps were issued until 1961, when a plebiscite was held in Cameroun. The northern section of British Cameroons voted to join the Federation of Nigeria. The southern section voted to become part of the Republic of Cameroun. Cameroun, of course, now issues its own stamps.

A NATION OF DIVERSITIES

Though it is only a little larger than the state of California, Cameroun has four markedly distinct geographic regions. The southern part of the country is covered by part of the dense equatorial rain forest. (*For a description of Africa's forest, see chapter on Gabon*) The central region is high plateau country. The north is essentially one vast, flat plain. The west is mountainous, rising to the 13,354-foot peak of Great Cameroun.

The weather of the country varies greatly. The coastal area has a rainfall that is over 150 inches a year; in the drier north, the annual rainfall is about 31 inches.

Politics are complicated by the existence of eighty-four legally constituted political parties.

Sixty-eight newspapers and periodicals circulate in the nation.

Cameroun's population of 4 millions is so diverse that the country has been called the "Racial Crossroads of Africa." Bantu tribes live in the south, and semi-Bantu in the west. The center and northern sections are principally inhabited by Semitic and Hamitic groups. There is also a group of pygmies. Over 500,000 persons are listed as unclassified.

Although French is the official tongue, a great many languages and dialects are spoken.

Twenty percent of the people are Catholics; 16 percent,Protestants; 16 percent,Moslems; the remainder are animists.

THE FRENCH COMMUNITY

In its economic and social development, Cameroun, a member of the French Community, has received substantial assistance from France. The Brazzaville Conference of 1944 laid the foundation for a new relationship between France and her colonies. "The aim of our colonial policy," said a French statement issued at the conference "must be to develop the production potential and increase the wealth of the overseas Territories; thus, by raising their purchasing power and their standard of living, we shall assure the Africans of a better way of life."

The French Constitution of 1946 gave complete French citizenship to Africans, assured them of voting powers, and provided for territorial representation in the French Parliament. At the same time, an economic development fund called FIDES (*Fonds d'Investissement pour le Développement Économique et Social*) was established. In 1958, with the creation of the French Community, FIDES was replaced by FAC (*Fonds pour Aide et Coöperation*), a French government agency offering economic and technical assistance to those African states electing to become part of the French Community.

HOW THE COMMUNITY WORKS

The French Community is somewhat similar to the British Commonwealth of Nations. A common language and historical ties characterize both groups. The British "sterling area," involving, among other things, preferential trade agreements among the Commonwealth nations, has its counterpart in the "franc area" of the French Community.

These two large international groupings have many differences. The Commonwealth has no formal structure, no centralized direction of foreign or economic policy, and no mutual security and defense policy. Even monetary unity is not complete in the British Commonwealth, for Canada is not a member of the sterling bloc. By comparison, the French Community has a formal structure, calling for periodic conferences of the heads of state, a court of arbitration for its members, and a consultation board that makes major policy recommendations. Be-

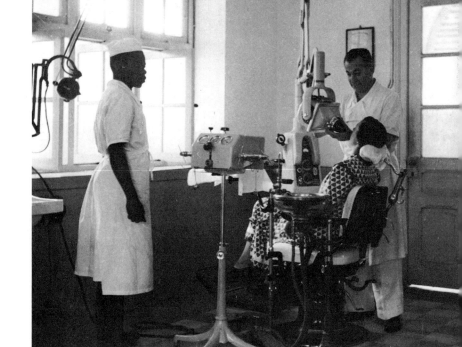

DENTAL CLINIC Native aide assists a European dentist at the General Hospital at Douala.

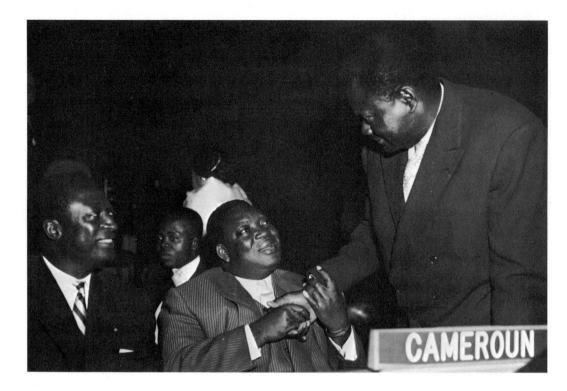

SCENE AT U.N. Charles Okala (seated), Minister for Foreign Affairs of Cameroun, is being greeted by Stephane Tchichelle (standing), Vice-President of the Council of Ministers of Congo (Brazzaville), in the Assembly Hall of the United Nations.

cause of this formalized structure, France has a larger role in matters affecting the mutual security of member nations in the French Community than Great Britain is permitted in concerns of the Commonwealth.

Many of the differences between these two international groupings can be explained by the types of nations involved. The British Commonwealth includes a number of modern, advanced nations, many with populations exceeding that of the mother country. By contrast, France is the most populous nation of the French Community; and it is the only member that ranks as a highly developed country. This means that members of the French Community must rely heavily on France for development and international trade.

FRENCH AID AND MODERNIZATION

The help that Cameroun receives from FAC (formerly FIDES) is typical of the assistance France gives to French Community members. Between 1948 and 1958, FIDES made the equivalent of $200 million available to Cameroun, earmarking the money for two four-year plans. The first plan focused on strengthening the basic economy, concentrating primarily on transportation, industrial development, and necessary equipment for public works. The second plan provided for development of the rural economy; funds were granted to diversify agriculture, stimulate internal trade, and provide training and better working conditions for laborers and farm workers.

BAMOUN DANCERS   *The white-robed elder holds a native rattle.*

COFFEE CULTURE *Man-
led zebus pull a disk-harrow
on a plantation.*

KAELE AIRPORT *Natives flock to see the big bird which Air France has
just landed in north Cameroun.*

STRAW VILLAGE   *Conical huts of mud and straw are fenced off to protect village dwellers from wild animals and marauders. The smaller huts are for storage.*

The two plans have improved many areas of Cameroun's industrial and social life. In the medical field, from 1948 to 1958, Cameroun doubled the number of its hospitals. In education, the number of pupils enrolled in primary and secondary schools rose from 45,000 to 270,000.

In 1946, the principal port of Douala had a serious shortage of drinking water. The completion of a modern water supply system for this city was one of the projects of the first four-year plan. Now the city no longer suffers periods of drought. Similar improvements were introduced in other drought-ridden urban centers.

A major project of the first four-year plan was to build a transportation network that would link the northern, eastern, and southern areas of the country to the port of Douala. Shortly after the Second World War, a number of mineral deposits were found, but their development was delayed for lack of adequate transportation. Since that time, roads suitable for heavy vehicles have been built, connecting the major portion of the country with Douala. At the same time, the port itself has been expanded; its shipping capacity has increased four times from the 200,000 tons of freightage in 1946. The country's two railway lines have been modernized and have been provided with new diesel engines.

THE LEADERS OF CAMEROUN

Yaoundé, the capital, a city of 55,000, is in the interior. The President, Ahmadou Ahidjo, is a Moslem who was formerly a postal clerk. He is a skillful politician and a middle-of-the-roader.

The Vice-President, John Foncha, is a Catholic.

AHMADOU AHIDJO   The son of a Fulani Chief, he was born in 1922. He attended a secondary school in Yaoundé, and became a postal radio operator in 1941. After many years in politics, Ahidjo was elected President of the Republic, in 1960.

DEVELOPMENT OF AGRICULTURE

Cameroun's major cash crops include bananas, timber, cocoa, coffee, and cotton. Production of all these commodities has been greatly expanded by the introduction of modern agricultural methods, another example of great achievement through French Community assistance. During the ten-year period from 1947 to 1957, total agricultural exports have been tripled.

Cameroun's modernization program is still in an early stage, but its impressive success thus far shows what can be accomplished through intelligently applied mutual assistance.

IN BRIEF

AREA
166,796 square miles; a little larger than California.

TERRAIN
Situated in middle Africa with range of all varieties of African geography. Northern savanna gradually rises to plateau region, with maximum height of 4,500 feet. South is dominated by rain forest, with small coastal plain along Gulf of Guinea. Entire western section is high, with forested Cameroun Mountains. Two main rivers: Benoué and Sanaga; the latter is not navigable.

CLIMATE
Two extremes of climate: the north is temperate with a mean temperature of 73°, rainfall of 31.2 inches, and a dry season from October to April. The south is tropical, with an average annual rainfall of 152.5 inches. Two short dry seasons: December to February and July to September.

CAPITAL
Yaoundé (population 55,000).

OTHER CITIES
Douala, 120,000.

POPULATION
4,097,000; about 16,000 Europeans.

ETHNIC GROUPS
Hamitic peoples in the north, Bantu in the south, semi-Bantu in the west, some Pygmies.

LANGUAGE
French is official language. Each ethnic group has its own language or group of languages.

RESIDENTIAL SECTION OF DOUALA   This city, chief port and commercial center of Cameroun, lies in the shadow of Mount Cameroun, a 13,000-foot peak of volcanic origin. The city lies on the estuary of the Wouri River. Douala has some fine public buildings, squares, open-air cafés, and a very busy waterfront.

RELIGION	500,000 Protestants, 622,500 Catholics, and 600,000 Mohammedans (1956 estimate). More than half the population is either animist or pagan.
DATE OF INDEPENDENCE	January 1, 1960.
FORM OF GOVERNMENT	National Assembly of 100 members and President are elected every five years. President appoints Prime Minister and Cabinet members, who are responsible to Assembly. An Economic and Social Council, and an independent judiciary. Member of French Community and United Nations.
EDUCATION	In 1958 more than 65 percent of school-age children attended school. There were 2,463 primary schools (293,977 students) and 50 secondary schools (6,645 students). In addition there were 64 technical schools (3,344 students), plus teacher-training and other special schools. No universities.
HEALTH FACILITIES	12 hospitals, 40 medical centers, 256 dispensaries, 20 pharmacies, 3 mental institutions, 28 leprosy centers, and 28 mobile health units.

CURRENCY	Unit is the French Community franc (247 francs = U.S. $1.00).
INDUSTRY	Major industrial enterprise is an aluminum plant at Edéa. Other industries include cotton gins, sawmills, manufacturing of household articles, metal furniture, building materials, soap, and clothing; also, processing of peanut and palm oil, tobacco, rubber, and cotton oil.

CROPS: 90 percent of all exports are agricultural, including cocoa, coffee, bananas, palm oil, palm kernels, rubber, wood, tobacco, and peanuts. Cotton, yams, plantains, cassava, and millet are grown for domestic use.

STOCK: Cattle, sheep, goats, pigs, and horses for domestic use and export.

FISHING: Fresh and salt fish, processed for domestic consumption.

MINING: Gold, cassiterite (a tin ore), rutile, and bauxite.

TRADE

1960:	EXPORTS	$97,000,000
	IMPORTS	$83,000,000
	SURPLUS	$14,000,000

MAJOR IMPORTS: Machinery, cotton fabrics, vehicles, petroleum products, chemicals, and pharmaceuticals.

MAJOR EXPORTS: Agricultural (*see* Crops).

TRANS-PORTATION

ROADS: 350 miles surfaced (1958); 5,465 miles unsurfaced, all-weather (1956).

VEHICLES: 9,000 passenger cars; 18,900 commercial vehicles (1959).

WATERWAYS: Ocean ports are Douala and Kribi; river port is Garoua.

AIR TRAFFIC: 15 airports, largest at Douala.

RAILROADS: 323 miles of track.

COMMUNI-CATIONS

Radio-telephone service from Douala to Europe. Three local radio stations, and 82 post offices. Telephone service in five urban centers. In 1958, 68 newspapers and periodicals were published regularly.

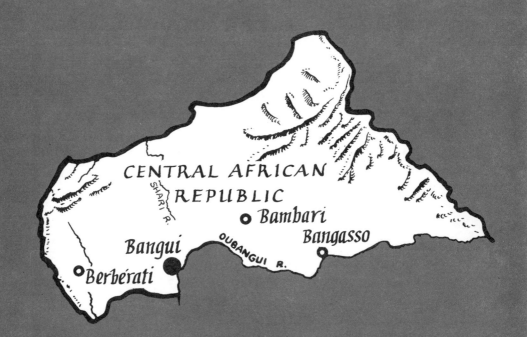

CENTRAL AFRICAN
REPUBLIC

SHARI R.

Bambari

Bangasso

Bangui

OUBANGUI R.

Berbérati

CENTRAL AFRICAN REPUBLIC

Young Leaders in a Poor Land

David Dacko was thirty years old when, on August 12, 1960, he sat beside André Malraux, French Minister of State, and signed the document that officially converted the colony of Ubangi-Shari into the independent Central African Republic. The next day, Dacko became the first President of the new nation.

In Africa, many of the new countries have young leaders. This is because during colonial rule but few opportunities for education were accorded to the natives. After World War II, educational facilities were enlarged; but by the time independence arrived, even the accelerated program had not produced a significant number of graduates. The pool from which truly qualified leaders can be drawn is still woefully small.

The cabinet in many of these countries has been compared to a small group of graduate students. Many young Africans now serving their countries in high governmental posts are virtually neophytes in both foreign affairs and administrative experience.

THE RISE OF DAVID DACKO

David Dacko is typical of many of the new leaders of Africa He was born in the Central African Republic (then called Ubangi-Shari), in 1930. He aspired to a teaching career, which he believed was the best way he could further the growth of his country. In 1957, he was abruptly thrust into politics when the people elected him to the new Territorial Assembly, a representative body that had just been established by the French. Within two months of his election, he was named Minister of Agriculture; and in 1959, he became Minister of the Interior. When Barthelemy Buganda, the very energetic and popular governor of the territory was killed in an airplane crash in 1959, the Legislative Assembly chose David Dacko, Buganda's cousin and right-hand man, to head the government

A POOR LAND

Central African Republic is poverty stricken and landlocked. Though it covers more than 238,000 square miles—an area only slightly smaller than Texas—its 1,227,000 people constitute an extremely sparse population. The country is predominantly agricultural; 90 percent of the people are rural. The density of population is but five persons per square mile. Bangui, the capital and only large city, contains only 80,000 inhabitants, less than that of Lexington, Kentucky, or Glendale, California. There are no railroads; and only 1,350 miles of hard-surface roads. In 1956, the net income per capita was under $100 per year.

Somewhere between 95 and 99 percent of the population are illiterate. There are less than 6,000 European residents in the entire country; most of these are French.

The country's principal exports are cotton, coffee, diamonds, and peanuts. Under preferential trade agreements in effect in the French

Community, France purchases most of the agricultural goods at a price that ensures a profit to the growers. In most instances, this represents a subsidy, since France pays more than world market prices. The United States purchases most of the diamonds that are mined in the country.

Despite the fact that the government of Central African Republic has kept all development programs at very modest proportions, in 1959, the country had a trade deficit of close to $2,000,000. This deficit severely limits the types of goods that can be purchased. Financial aid from France, Great Britain, the United States, and the United Nations helps make up the deficit, but a better solution depends on diversifying and ameliorating the agricultural products.

AFTER THE MARKET   After attending a market day or a funeral, the people are apt to break into a dance. The dancers can be seen in the back in an informal grouping. The woman in the forefront is joining in the rhythm.

DRUMMERS In Bozoun, the Kare, members of the Baya tribe, dance to the rhythm of tom-toms, carved from tree trunks and covered with well-stretched antelope skins.

BOY SCOUTS ON MARCH   Each town has its Boy Scout troop.

Young men like David Dacko have huge problems confronting them. Only by great courage and endless concentration can these dedicated leaders compensate for their limited background of experience in government and the pitiful lack of a seasoned corps of trained officials.

CUSTOMS UNION

In 1959, four of the former territories of French Equatorial Africa—Central African Republic, Chad, Congo (Brazzaville), and Gabon—signed an agreement establishing a customs union. This economic federation permits merchandise, property, and capital to move freely across the borders of these four nations. An authority was set up to administer the ports, railways, river navigation, telephone and telegraph communications of the member states.

Needless to say, great benefit has flowed to each of these new nations through the establishment of this economic community. Substantial trade advantages will likely be derived through the ability of the union to bargain collectively for the benefit of its members.

THE PROBLEM OF EDUCATION

Central African Republic is one of the five nations that was formed out of the huge former colony of French Equatorial Africa. During a half century of rule in this area, the French devoted less than 1 percent of the budget to education for the native population. As late as 1946, only 5 percent of the children in the territory were attending school. With the formation of the French Community of Nations (*See chapter on Cameroun*) about 15 percent of aid funds, granted by the French to members of the French Community, was allotted to education. By 1958, the number of children attending school in the Central African Republic had increased to 27 percent.

Education beyond the secondary-school level remains a major problem. Central African Republic now has several technical schools, and several small teacher training colleges, but no college or university at the general European level. It is not easy for students from Central African Republic to attend accredited colleges. South African universities are not open to them; and in West Africa, only the University of Dakar, University College of Sierra Leone, the University of Ghana, and Ibadan College in Nigeria, maintain standards that are on a par with colleges in the United States and Europe. But so many students clamor for attendance at these institutions, that none of these colleges can hope to accommodate more than a few students from neighboring countries.

A few students from Central African Republic are now enrolled at the University of Paris. As the number of secondary-school graduates in Central African Republic increases, more will seek education in foreign lands. With the assistance of major foundations, a few American colleges and universities are inviting hundreds of African students to study in the United States.

A WEALTH OF FAUNA

The nation Dacko heads was once named Ubangi-Shari, after its major rivers. The country is a showcase of the flora and fauna of tropical Africa. Nearly every species of African animal is found in the area. Elephants were once very common; but, by now, ivory hunters have depopulated the herds.

The great equatorial rain forest, the largest of the fabled rain forests of Africa, and the least affected by civilization, stretches across most of the southern half of Central African Republic. These forests contain more than five hundred different types of vegetation.

HUMAN DISFIGURATION

The people of the country are of great interest to anthropologists. The eight chief ethnic groups are divided into numerous sub-tribes. Some cut large areas of their skin, to form intricate patterns by incision. Color is introduced into the cuts, leaving the epidermis covered with elaborate tattoo-like designs.

The area in which Central African Republic lies is probably best known for the custom, among certain tribes, of using huge discs to extend the lips of their women. It has been thought that originally this disfigurement was effected so that Arab slave traders would become dis-

PYGMY HUT *In the very dense forest region around the village of Lobaye, African pygmies (Negrillos) have lived since 2500 B.C. They were probably the first inhabitants of Central African Republic. Their huts are made of slats with a roof of leaves, a construction seen only in forest regions. The pygmies are the only people in Africa who hunt elephants without guns, depending on their knowledge of the elephant's habits. Pygmies trade salt with taller Negro tribes. Their culture is rudimentary, and the small groups in which they live are sometimes ruled by women.*

enchanted by these grotesque faces, and would not carry the women off. However, among the tribes neighboring the Ubangi River, the custom became widespread and fashionable. Huge, plattered lips are now considered a mark of great beauty.

PRESIDENT DAVID DACKO
*Born in 1930, David Dacko was edu-
cated locally and then pursued his
studies in Congo (Brazzaville). He
became a teacher, and then got a
position as headmaster of an elementary school in Bangui.*

IN BRIEF

AREA
238,224 square miles, slightly smaller than Texas.

TERRAIN
Inland, average altitude of 2,000 feet. The nation is one large rolling plateau. Several rivers: major ones are the Ubangi and Shari, but navigation is often difficult.

CLIMATE
Dry season lasts six months; heavy rains fall during wet season, June to October; tornadoes are common at start of rainy season.

CAPITAL
Bangui (population, 80,000 in 1960).

POPULATION
1,227,000 (1961); about 6,000 Europeans.

ETHNIC GROUPS
The eight major groups are Mandija, Banda, Zandi, Banzin, Sara, M'Baum, Pambia, and Bounga—all Negro tribes. There are many sub-tribes.

LANGUAGE
Official language is French. Sangho is used throughout the nation. Also many tribal languages.

RELIGION
Mostly animists; many Mohammedans along the Northern border with Chad. Some Christians.

DATE OF INDEPENDENCE
August 12, 1960.

FORM OF GOVERNMENT
Parliamentary democracy with Legislative Assembly of 50 members popularly elected every 5 years. Prime Minister is

elected by majority party. He selects a six-member Cabinet. An independent judiciary. Member of Union of Central African Republics, French Community, and United Nations.

EDUCATION Rate of enrollment increased from 8 percent of the school-age population in 1948 to 27 percent in 1958. A total of 47,400 students enrolled in 243 primary, 15 secondary, and 17 technical schools. No universities.

HEALTH FACILITIES 2 hospitals and 109 other health facilities of various kinds.

CURRENCY Unit is French Community franc (247 francs = U.S. $1.00).

INDUSTRY Processing of timber, palm oil, peanut oil, and soap. Bangui, the capital, has a brewery and two clothing factories.

CROPS: Coffee, peanuts, sisal, and cotton are major crops; also, some rubber, palm oil, rice, grain, and sesame seeds.

STOCK: Cattle and sheep.

FISHING: Only small-scale.

MINING: Gold and diamonds.

TRADE

1959:		
IMPORTS	$17,150,000
EXPORTS	15,230,000
DEFICIT	$ 1,920,000

MAJOR IMPORTS: Food, beverages, cotton cloth, fuel, cement, iron, steel, sheet metal, and strip iron.

MAJOR EXPORTS: Diamonds, wood, and agricultural products (see *Crops*).

TRANS-PORTATION ROADS: 1,350 miles surfaced; 9,565 miles unsurfaced, many usable only during dry season.

VEHICLES: No statistics available.

WATERWAYS: 370 miles; not always navigable.

RAILROADS: None.

AIR TRAFFIC: Major airports at Bangui, Berbérati, and Bouar.

COMMUNI-CATIONS Radio-telephone from Bangui to Brazzaville and Paris. Local telephone systems and a telegraphic network. One radio station.

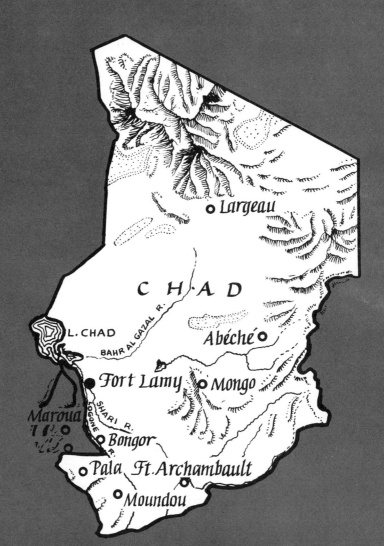

Largeau

C H A D

L. CHAD

BAHR AL GAZAL R.

Abéché

Fort Lamy   Mongo

SHARI R.

LOGONE R.

Maroua

Bongor

Pala   Ft.Archambault

Moundou

CHAD

A Land in Search of Water

Half of Chad is desert. In this sterile area—part of the Sahara—an area of over 200,000 square miles—almost as large as France—there dwell but 40,000 people. More than 95 percent of the people of Chad are illiterate.

The entire country, which is larger than Spain, Sweden, and Italy combined, has a total population of less than 3,000,000. Less than 4 percent of the people of Chad live in towns or cities, just about the same number to be found in Albany, New York.

There are no forests in Chad.

RELIGIOUS AFFILIATIONS

Only one out of one hundred inhabitants is a Christian.

Early in its history, a number of invasions from the Arabic north brought to Chad the Islamic faith. Thus, most of the people of northern Chad are Mohammedans, while the people of the south are principally animists. Animism, the name given to many primitive religions, holds that inanimate things are alive, or have souls. Most of the indigenous religions of tropical Africa are animistic, and involve the use of fetishes (carved representations of humans, animals, or other objects in which a spirit is believed to reside, and which are thought to possess potent magical powers).

A LONG MILITARY HISTORY

The tribes of Chad, living in an indefensible terrain of desert and open plain, have fought valiantly against subjugation. During the era of colonial expansion, the fierce tribal chiefs of Chad so strenuously opposed French control that all tribes were not subjugated until 1900. The territory was finally pacified by France in 1913, and a series of treaties was drawn up between the French representatives and local sultans. France has remained keenly interested in Chad for military reasons, and a popular saying among French generals was "Whoever holds Chad, holds Africa."

The French estimate of Chad's military importance was fully borne out during the Second World War. Chad, under the leadership of its distinguished colonial governor, Félix Eboué, aligned itself with General de Gaulle against Vichy France. Chad's stand rallied other territories of French Equatorial Africa to de Gaulle's side. Eboué's courageous action, taken at the risk of his career and his life, opened a new route for Allied communication to Cairo and the Middle East just when Rommel and his panzer divisions were threatening all Africa. Fort Lamy, the capital of Chad, became an important air base. It was from here that General Leclerc's famous desert troops departed to fight in the North African campaign.

Chad received its autonomy within the French Community in 1958, and full independence within that Community on August 11, 1960.

President François Tombalbaye, a Protestant is a member of the Sara tribe. His cabinet includes Moslems, Catholics, and animists. The President was formerly a schoolteacher. He has set himself the task of training efficient civil servants and spreading modern working habits among his people.

LIVESTOCK RAISING

The raising of livestock is ideally suited to the characteristics of the territory. Chad, a nation of almost 2.7 million people, has 4 million cattle, 4.5 million sheep, 2 million goats, 300,000 camels, and 150,000 horses.

In traditional African society, the principal value of cattle was social rather than economic. A man with much cattle was regarded as a man of wealth and prestige. The physical condition of the animals did not seem to matter—it was the *number* that counted. They were specially important as part of the transaction of the marriage contract. A man with many sons had to have enough cattle for each of them to buy one or more wives. A man with many daughters hoped to receive a substantial number of cattle each time he gave a daughter in marriage. It was most important to maintain and, if possible, to augment the accumulated capital of cattle that a man inherited.

Because more cattle meant greater community power, some tribes kept more animals than they could possibly use, and more than their grazing lands and water supply could support. They had no inclination to trade cattle for goods with their crop-raising neighbors.

More often than not, the animals from these poorly-pastured herds turned out to be poor specimens. Thus, despite the large number of cattle in Chad, the economic return from livestock raising is very low.

FORT LAMY   This city lies along the Shari River. The star in the center of the town is the Place de l'Étoile, the heart of the residential area.

What the country needs is scientific breeding, proper grazing lands, and water.

PROBLEMS OF DEVELOPMENT

Livestock production has always been the backbone of the economy; cattle, meat, hides, and skins have long been exported. In recent years, cotton has accounted for an increasing share of the exports. Chad's livestock products and cotton are but a tiny factor in the world market; and therefore, the economy of Chad is extremely vulnerable to fluctuations in world market prices. Since Chad has no forests and no known mineral resources, the development of a diversified economy presents a great challenge to the government.

RAISING THE LEVEL OF EDUCATION

Because many sheep-raising tribes are nomadic or semi-nomadic, the government has been seriously hindered in its effort to raise the level of literacy and education.

CATTLE MARKET Long-horned cattle and oxen are traded at this market in Fort Lamy. Beyond the market fences are private dwellings whose walls of beaten earth are studded with rows of tile and metal pipes to provide drainage for the flat roofs.

POTTERY MARKET *In this market at Fort Lamy, cigarettes, chewing gum, sweets, figs and dates are also sold. The showcases that are used here are large woven baskets or flat trays.*

MARKET IN ABÉCHÉ   In this city of 13,000, milk, meat, peanuts, dates, clothes, and a variety of wares are sold in the daily market. Dates are spread out on woven mats, and peanuts are displayed in gourds. Woven palm leaves provide shelter. The people here are mainly Ouäddaï.

FISH MARKET AT FORT LAMY   *A Cotoko woman is selecting smoked makalele, a kind of large sardine, from a fish stand. Dried carp lie on the torn straw matting.*

Along with other members of the French Community, Chad has been receiving French assistance to expand its educational system. Between 1955 and 1958, enrollment in the primary and secondary schools of the nation doubled. By 1958, there were 154 primary schools in Chad, with an enrollment of 32,610 students. However, there were only 485 students enrolled in secondary schools. The percentage of children attending schools rose from 1.4 percent in 1945 to 8.4 percent in 1958.

Most of the school development has been in the southern part of the country, particularly in several small urban areas. The problem of bringing education to nomadic people in sparsely settled areas has yet to be solved. Another reason for the retarded development of a public school system in Chad is the fact that Christian missionary activity there has been very limited. In many other African nations, a substantial network of Christian missionary schools laid the foundation for the ultimate establishment of a public school system.

THE TERRAIN

Lake Chad is a large, unusual body of water, lying on the intersecting boundaries of Chad, Niger, Cameroun, and Nigeria. Its strangest characteristic is that it is only three to four feet deep. Fed chiefly by the Shari River, it is situated at the bottom of a long, sloping plain, and gradually merges with a series of great marshes that spring back toward the lake in the dry season. Some geographers believe that the lake is slowly drying up, as windblown sand from the Sahara Desert continues to settle along its bottom.

TRANSPORTATION

In Chad, air travel is developing more rapidly than travel by river, road, or rail. Chad has no railways and only 188 miles of hard-surfaced roads; but it has five airports, including one at Fort Lamy that can accommodate the largest airplanes in international service. Among French Community nations, Fort Lamy handles a volume of freight second only to that of Orly Airfield in Paris.

In Chad the transportation problem is particularly severe because waterways are navigable only part of the year. Nevertheless, at this stage of the country's development, even the limited use of waterways is economically important. As commercial activities grow, the government of Chad plans to devote increasing attention and funds to the development of all phases of a modern transportation network.

THE SEARCH FOR WATER

Because of the seven-month dry season in the semi-arid, stock-raising regions of the country, the country's water problem is a constant concern. At present, many flocks and herds move south during the dry season in

WRITING CLASS   In addition to learning script, the pupils are studying how to select metal type for printing, and how to set up such type in a holder.

BOX SEAT *The three women on the camel are from the district of Moussoro in the north of Chad. They are watching dances and ceremonials being performed at a tribal festival.*

PAPYRUS PIROGUE *This native craft, made of dried reeds, is a common mode of travel and transport on Lake Chad. The grasses from which the canoe is made grow along the banks of the lake.*

search of water. An active prospecting effort is currently being made to find water below the earth's surface, and in a number of areas these attempts have been successful. The development of more adequate water resources is a key step toward the introduction of systematic ranching methods, which the government is encouraging.

IN BRIEF

AREA 495,794 square miles, about the combined size of Texas, Wyoming and Colorado.

TERRAIN From valleys of the Shari, Logone, and Bahr al Gazal Rivers, land gradually slopes upward to 5,000 feet in the Wadai Mountains and to over 10,000 feet in the northern volcanic Tibesti Mountains. Northwest lies a great stretch of Sahara Desert. Lake Chad is at the southwestern corner.

CLIMATE Desert region in the north; tropical rainy region in the south (seven-month rainy season averages 35-47 inches a year); between the two lies a drier tropical area with only four or five months of summer rain.

CAPITAL Fort Lamy (population 58,179).

POPULATION 2,675,000; about 5,000 Europeans.

ETHNIC GROUPS Two major groups: one in the north is mainly Caucasian; in the south, predominantly Negro. The Caucasians are Arabs, Fellata or Peuls, Hausa, Kanebou, and Toubou. The Negro peoples in the south are Saras, Hakka, Massa, and Moundang.

BOUM DANCERS The dancers are 14-and 15-year old girls from the Baibokoum area. They are expert in the difficult regional dance called the Boum. Their bracelets are made of silver and copper; the other adornments are brightly colored beads.

FRANÇOIS TOMBALBAYE The President of Chad is a Protestant. Born in a small village in 1918, he qualified as an assistant teacher after a few scant years of elementary schooling. He bears on his face the tribal markings of the Sara-Madjingaye group from which he stems.

LANGUAGE	Official language is French; many Moslems speak Arabic; but they and the Negro peoples have their own languages.
RELIGION	Most of the northern peoples are Mohammedans; in the south, animists are found. Less than 1% converted to Christianity.
DATE OF INDEPENDENCE	August 11, 1960.
FORM OF GOVERNMENT	Parliamentary democracy; the National Assembly is directly elected for five years; leader of majority party is designated Prime Minister, and selects a fifteen-member Council of Ministers. There is an independent judiciary, and an Economic and Social Council. Member of Union of Central African Republics, French Community, and United Nations.
EDUCATION	Percentage of children attending school increased from 1.4 percent in 1945-1946 to 8.4 percent in 1957-1958. In 1958, there were 154 primary schools with 32,610 students; 485 students in four secondary schools; and 215 students in four technical schools. No universities.
HEALTH FACILITIES	One polyclinic hospital and five urban dispensaries in Fort Lamy. In the bush: 62 dispensaries, 4 mobile health units, 14 infirmaries, 12 medical centers with maternity wards, and 35 private dispensaries.
CURRENCY	Unit is French Community franc (247 francs = U.S. $1.00).

INDUSTRY   Processing of cotton, meat, rice, and peanut oil. Carbonated beverage plant in Fort Lamy.

CROPS: Cotton is chief crop, mostly grown for export; rice, millet, peanuts, chick peas, wheat, dates, sweet potatoes, cassava, and corn are also grown.

STOCK: Cattle, sheep, dromedary camels, donkeys, horses, goats, and pigs.

FISHING: Fresh and dried, for domestic use and export, catch coming from the Chad basin.

MINING: None.

GRINDING PEANUTS *To extract oil, a camel pulls the crudely-hinged logs which crush peanuts in a large wooden mortar.*

TRIBAL CHIEF   This headman hails from the Kanem area.
His shirt, his embroidered ceremonial costume, and the sheep-
skins draped over his horse, are marks of his rank. The Chief
has come to town to celebrate a feast day.

*ARCH OF WELCOME   As you drive into town from the airport
of Fort Lamy, you are greeted by this trellis which spans the highway.*

TRADE

1959: IMPORTS $24,587,000
       EXPORTS   16,471,000
       DEFICIT $ 8,116,000

MAJOR IMPORTS: Capital and consumer goods; semi-finished products.

MAJOR EXPORTS: Cottonseed, peanuts, livestock, meat and fish, leather and hides.

**TRANSPOR-
TATION**

ROADS: 188 miles are hard-surfaced. 300 miles are unsurfaced, but all-weather.

VEHICLES: No figures available.

WATERWAYS: Navigation possible only at height of rainy season.

RAILROADS: None.

AIR TRAFFIC: Five main airports and three smaller airfields. In 1958, 38,420 passengers and 17,000 tons of freight were carried.

**COMMUNICA-
TIONS**

Radio and telegraph network are government-owned. No local press or daily newspapers existed in 1962.

95

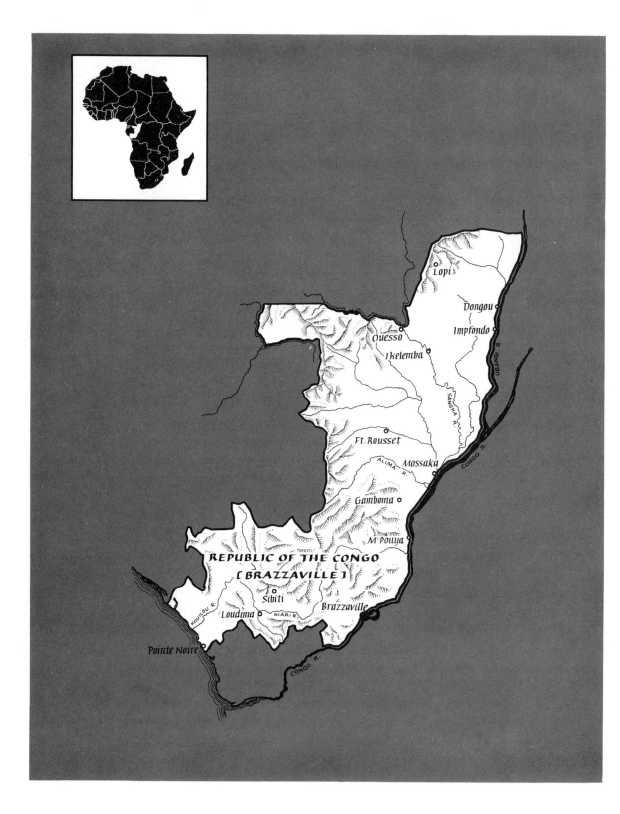

REPUBLIC OF THE CONGO
[BRAZZAVILLE]

Lopi

Dongou

Impfondo

Ouesso

Ikelemba

UBANGI R.

SANGHA R.

Ft. Rousset

ALIMA R.

Mossaka

CONGO R.

Gamboma

M'Pouya

Sibiti

Loudima

NIARI R.

KOUILOU R.

Brazzaville

Pointe Noire

CONGO R.

CONGO (BRAZZAVILLE)

French Orientation in Equatorial Africa

The former Belgian colony in Africa, of which the chief city is Leopoldville, is officially known as Republic of the Congo. The former French possession, with its capital at Brazzaville, is officially known as The Congo Republic. To avoid confusion, we shall adopt current newspaper usage and refer to the former Belgian colony as Congo (Leopoldville). We shall refer to the former French colony as Congo (Brazzaville).

THE FRENCH CONSTITUTION OF 1946

In February, 1944, General de Gaulle went to Brazzaville to meet representatives of the French territories that had supported the Free French Movement. Their loyalty to the Allied cause had been a major factor in preventing Nazi infiltration into Central Africa. In recognition of this aid, the Brazzaville Conference initiated a new French policy toward the colonies. Recommendations were adopted for giving the people of the French territories "an ever-larger share in the life and democratic institutions of the French Community."

These principles were reflected in the French Constitution of 1946, which provided for universal suffrage in the territories. Deputies were to be elected from the colonies within each territory.

INDEPENDENCE ACHIEVED

When, in 1958, General de Gaulle became President of France, he offered each of the French territories a choice as to future status. Each nation had the option of remaining a republic within the French Community or seeking complete independence. With the exception of the Republic of Guinea, all the French colonies of tropical Africa voted to remain within the French Community; and the people of what is now

Congo (Brazzaville) voted four to one in favor of this status.

In November, 1958, the Congolese Territorial Assembly officially proclaimed the creation of The Congo Republic. In 1961, Fulbert Youlou was elected to head the government.

FULBERT YOULOU

Fulbert Youlou was born in 1917, and completed his secondary studies at the Catholic seminaries in Brazzaville and in Akono, in Cameroun. Ordained as a priest in 1946, he served for ten years in his parish.

In 1956, Youlou founded the *Union Démocratique de Defense des Intérêts Africains* (UDDIA), and he was defrocked for devoting himself to politics. Nevertheless, he is strongly supported by the large Catholic group which comprises one-third of the population; and in that same year, he was elected mayor of Brazzaville. The Matswai tribe regards Youlou in mystical awe; and he also draws support from the Bakongo tribe from which he stems. Kasavubu, head of Congo (Leopoldville), on the other side of the river, is also a Bakongo.

THE BRAZZAVILLE BLOC

In December, 1960, the representatives of twelve of the former colonies of France met in Brazzaville to form the "Brazzaville Bloc." These nations aimed to coordinate their foreign policy and to cooperate on economic matters. To achieve this result, they set up an economic secretariat, and jointly sponsored an inter-territorial airline which was called *Air Afrique*. The Brazzaville group is strongly French in orientation. It has come out openly against Communism.

In May, 1961, eight other nations of Africa—Ethiopia, Liberia, Libya, Nigeria, Sierra Leone, Somalia, Togo, and Tunisia—met in the city of Monrovia, the capital of Liberia. Two of the original sponsors of the Brazzaville group, Mali and Guinea, did not attend. The eighteen heads of state agreed to promote their mutual interests through cultural and economic cooperation. To this end, in July of that year, experts of the group met in conference in Dakar. The Brazzaville Bloc is not a union of states—it is merely a very loose federation of independent nations, mostly new nations, whose interests are akin.

Guinea and Mali withrdew from the Brazzaville Bloc, and joined the Casablanca Bloc, a group of nations consisting of Ghana, Morocco, and the U.A.R., a more leftist group than the moderate, pro-Western Brazzaville Bloc.

PHYSICAL FEATURES AND POPULATION

The great Congo River, and its principal tributary, the Ubangi, form the boundary between Congo (Brazzaville) and Congo (Leopoldville). The equatorial rain forest covers half the land with all but impenetrable jungle.

The climate is tropical. Lying athwart the equator, Congo (Brazzaville) has high humidity, two wet and two dry seasons, and an average

GRINDING MANIOC   This root food is something like the sweet potato. The house is a typical middle-class home of brick and cement. Such homes are occupied by families who earn $60 or more a month.

TRAINING CENTER AT POINTE-NOIRE These apprentices are
learning railroad maintenance in a machine shop.

temperature ranging between 80 and 90 degrees.

In the Congo basin, the annual precipitation amounts to nearly
98 inches.

Congo (Brazzaville) contains approximately 790,000 people. In
the area of the city of Brazzaville, the density is 44 persons per square
mile, while the forest zones of the north are practically uninhabited.

NATURAL RESOURCES

As in all African nations with rain forests, the wood products of
Congo (Brazzaville) account for more than one-third of the nation's
exports. Production of okoume wood (a rare fine-grained wood) increased from 5,000 cubic meters in 1947 to 56,000 in 1957, while that
of other exotic woods increased from 50,000 to 428,000 cubic meters.
Exploitation of these resources is carried on by firms under government
concessions. Replanting by lumber companies and other conservation

100

measures are strictly enforced, to insure forest preservation.

The country appears to have various mineral deposits. These include copper, lead, zinc, and phosphate. Oil prospecting is now being carried on.

Substantial hydro-electric resources are available; although, at present, comparatively little electric power is produced. Where the Kouilou River flows through a magnificent gorge about 60 miles from Pointe-Noire, work on a 360-foot-high dam was begun in March, 1961. This project, when completed, will yield 7 billion kilowatt-hours annually. Since the country's phosphate deposits are located near this site, the development of power could be the beginning of an electro-chemical industry for Congo (Brazzaville).

A BIG LITTLE RAILROAD

Despite the difficulties imposed by climate and terrain, Congo (Brazzaville) has a relatively well-developed transportation system. Brazzaville's excellent location at the mouth of the Congo River makes

MODERN APARTMENTS   At Pointe-Noire, second largest city of Congo (Brazzaville), stands this upper-class, new apartment house. Rents run about $120 a month for a two-bedroom apartment.

it a natural terminus for trade between the seacoast and cities in the interior.

For some time, the state has had a strategically located railroad. The single track Congo-Ocean Railroad runs 320 miles between the Congo River port of Brazzaville and the Atlantic Ocean port of Pointe-Noire. It is one of the most remarkable short hauls in the world.

This railroad line plunges into the equatorial rain forest and travels through some of the most difficult terrain in tropical Africa. Descending to the sea, it twists and turns down the Mayombé Escarpment, crossing ninety-two bridges and going through twelve tunnels.

Congo (Brazzaville) also has over 4,900 miles of permanent roads which, because of the tropical climate, require constant and expensive upkeep. Most of these roads connect with the Congo-Ocean Railroad at the Brazzaville terminal. Thus, both river and road traffic converge upon Brazzaville.

From 1948 to 1958, the freight traffic on the Congo-Ocean Railroad doubled. Traffic at Pointe-Noire rose from 169,400 tons to 560,000 tons.

OUTLOOK FOR INDUSTRIAL DEVELOPMENT

The country now possesses a number of modern plants. Industrial activity has been steadily progressing, even though hampered by certain human and physical factors—a sparse population, a limited domestic market, and a lack of capital. Under such circumstances, a significant increase in production is difficult. The balance of trade remains unfavorable, the deficit being offset by foreign aid, mostly from France.

However, despite the drive toward industrialization, the economy is still primarily agricultural, with 80 percent of the arable land being owned and farmed by Congolese. Seventy-five percent of agricultural products are grown for home consumption.

A STRONG EDUCATIONAL ESTABLISHMENT

In Congo (Brazzaville), almost 75 percent of school-age children are enrolled in primary schools. One-third of these children are girls, an unusually high percentage for Africa, where females are not generally accorded an education. In the city of Brazzaville and its environs, the enrollment exceeds 90 percent of the child population.

However, there are only 10 secondary schools, with an attendance of under 4,000 boys and girls; but the country has a teacher-training college, two large vocational schools, and many apprenticeship centers. There are plans for building a university in the city of Brazzaville.

CHURCH OF ST. ANNE   *This unusual edifice is one of the architectural showpieces of Brazzaville.*

POLITICAL STABILITY

Congo (Brazzaville), since independence, has been a rather stable country. Its leaders feel that they are building for a new day. The attitude, perhaps, was best expressed by Fulbert Youlou at the ceremonies celebrating the proclamation of independence, at which the President said:

"This, gentlemen, is what the Congo is and what it must be: a harmonious synthesis of two civilizations, one of which is rooted deep in this Africa—eternal, massive, but so varied nonetheless—land of broad savannas, deep forests, immense rivers that cause us to live close to the very sources of our life; the other is French civilization, which has itself sprung from the various origins out of which modern France has grown. . . .

"At the very time that our independence is proclaimed . . . we . . . reaffirm our attachment to the renovated Community in order that France may continue to give us her technical and material assistance and that we may harmonize the broad lines of our policies within a great ensemble, with a common language, culture, and sentiments."

DONGOU FISHERMAN   *About 200 miles north of Brazzaville, this fisherman repairs his net. A small brazier in the dugout canoe is used to warm a meal or smoke a fish.*

ABBE FULBERT YOULOU
Born in 1917, Youlou became
a Catholic priest and still, al-
though no longer an official in
the church, maintains his ec-
clesiastical title. He was elected
President in 1961.

IN BRIEF

AREA	132,047 square miles, slightly larger than Montana.
TERRAIN	Low, treeless coastal plain extends inland for about 40 miles to the mountain region of the Mayombé Escarpment, which has sharp ridges 1,600 to 2,600 feet high. Niari Valley north of this region is a savanna. Plateau region covering more than 50,000 square miles is between Congo and Ogoué river basins.
CLIMATE	Tropical, with two wet and two dry seasons, except for Congo River basin, which has rainfall throughout the year.
CAPITAL	Brazzaville (population, 100,000).
OTHER CITIES	Pointe-Noire, 57,000.
POPULATION	795,000; about 10,000 Europeans.
ETHNIC GROUPS	Major group is the Bakongo people in the southwest, who account for 45 percent of population; also Batehes, M'Bochi, Savgha, and Pygmies.
LANGUAGE	French is official language; many tribal languages spoken.
RELIGION	Mostly animist. Substantial Christian minority.
DATE OF INDEPENDENCE	November, 1958.

ELEPHANT AT WORK   *The forests of equatorial Africa use trained elephants for the arduous tasks of pulling down trees and hauling logs.*

FORM OF GOVERNMENT
Parliamentary democracy; National Assembly of 61 members elected for five-year term with majority leader as Premier, who selects ten-member Council of Ministers. An independent judiciary and an Economic and Social Council; member of Union of Central African Republics, French Community, and United Nations.

EDUCATION
In 1960, almost 75 percent of school-age children were enrolled; just under half were girls. There were 495 elementary schools with an enrollment of 99,400; 10 secondary schools with 3,370 students; and 30 technical schools with 1,365 students. A university is being built at Brazzaville.

HEALTH FACILITIES
2 hospitals, 13 medical centers, 20 infirmaries, 78 dispensaries, a Pasteur Institute in Brazzaville, and a malaria-prevention center in Pointe-Noire.

CURRENCY Unit is French Community franc (247 francs = U.S. $1.00).

INDUSTRY Cane-sugar refining, sawmills, production of soap, peanut oil, palm oil, rice processing, fish canning, manufacture of clothing, carbonated beverages, cigarettes, beer, liquid air, shipbuilding, building construction, and metals.

CROPS: Cassava, plantains, sweet potatoes, yams, rice, sugar cane are grown for domestic consumption. Pineapples, oranges, tangerines, and grapefruit are exported; also palm kernels, palm oil, peanuts, tobacco, and cocoa. Other crops are rubber and coffee.

STOCK: Cattle, sheep, goats, hogs.

FISHING: For local consumption.

MINING: Lead ore, tin, gold, phosphates, diamonds, copper, zinc.

TRADE 1959: IMPORTS $55,477,600
          EXPORTS   14,119,200
          DEFICIT $41,358,400
(Deficit is offset to a large extent by foreign aid.)

MAJOR IMPORTS: Capital and consumer goods.

MAJOR EXPORTS: Wood, foods, vegetables, oil products, ores, and agricultural products (*see* Crops).

TRANS- ROADS: 238 miles surfaced; 4,900 miles unsurfaced all-weather
PORTATION (1956).
VEHICLES: No figures available.

WATERWAYS: River traffic on Congo and Ubangi rivers.

RAILROADS: 320-mile Congo-Ocean Railroad to ocean port at Pointe-Noire via Brazzaville.

AIR TRAFFIC: Large airports at Brazzaville and Pointe-Noire, plus 12 local airports.

COMMUNI- Two weekly, one monthly, and one quarterly newspaper.
CATIONS Telecommunications and a radio system in Brazzaville.

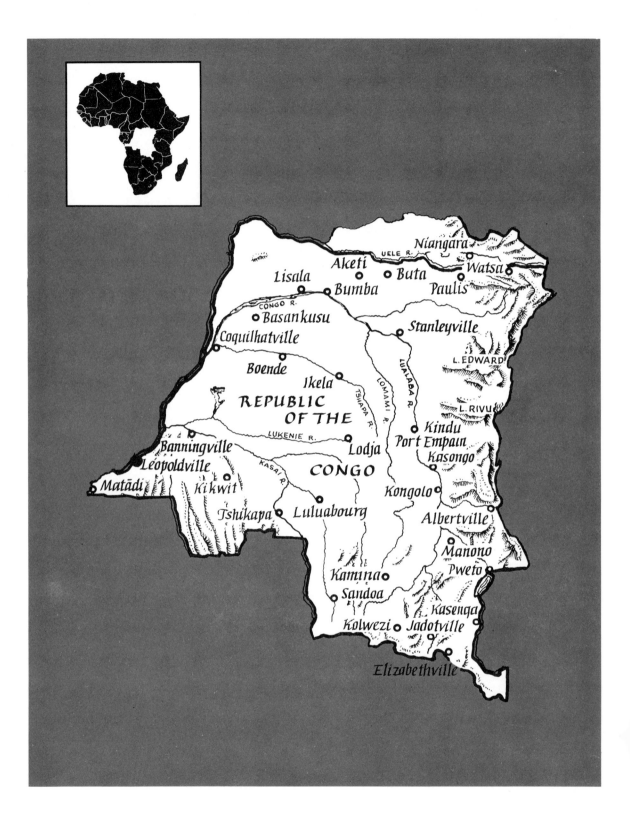

CONGO (LEOPOLDVILLE)

African Tinderbox

On June 30, 1960, the Republic of the Congo (Leopoldville) proclaimed its independence from Belgium. Wearing the maroon sash of the Order of the Crown, Belgium's highest decoration, which he had received the previous night, Patrice Lumumba, Premier of the new nation, addressed the assembled diplomats and guests, including Belgium's King Baudouin. They listened in stunned silence as Lumumba recapitulated the sufferings of the people of the Congo and of all Africa at the hands of the Europeans.

Recalling the "glorious history of our struggle for liberty," Lumumba said that only independence could put to an end the "humiliating slavery which had been imposed upon us by force." Colonialism, he said, had "left wounds too keen and too painful to be wiped from memory." He reminded his hearers of the "ironies, the insults, the blows that we had to submit to morning, noon, and night because we were Negroes." Lumumba's words may not have been diplomatic, but they were historically accurate. His strong language foreshadowed the disturbances that followed.

The colonial history of Belgian Congo had been extraordinarily grim. Lumumba was right in saying that colonialism had left deep resentments that would lead to grave trouble.

THE EARLY COLONIAL PERIOD

Just one hundred years before Lumumba's historic speech, the use of the wheel had been unknown in the Congo interior. There were no written languages. Cannibalism and witchcraft were common. However, the tribes of the Congo had a civilization of their own. Their art, especially their sculpture, roused the interest of European artists such as Picasso and Modigliani, and Congo art came to influence modern art.

The site of the present capital, Leopoldville, was a dense jungle. The interior of the Congo had been inaccessible to Western man until the great expeditions of Sir Henry Morton Stanley traced the sources of the Congo River in the 1870's.

After finding Dr. Livingstone in 1871, Stanley traversed Africa from east to west, exploring, in a three-year expedition, the course of the Congo River. Returning to Europe, he tried unsuccessfully to interest England in his discoveries. Later, King Leopold II of Belgium sent Stanley back to the Congo as his personal agent.

BELGIAN CRUELTIES IN THE CONGO

In 1884-1885, a conference was held at Berlin to parcel out spheres of influence in Africa. Leopold II succeeded in having himself recognized as sole master of the Congo Free State. The country did not become a Belgian colony: it was given to Leopold, personally, to administer. He treated the land as his personal fief; despite the fact that one of the prime intentions of the Berlin Conference was to give Leopold the administration of the Congo for humanitarian purposes, especially to effect the abolition of slavery.

From 1885 to 1908, he exploited its principal resources of rubber and ivory. The process involved great cruelty to the natives, who were mutilated or shot if they failed to fulfill work quotas. Labor-gang bosses brought in basketfuls of human hands as evidence of how they handled recalcitrant workers. The Belgian officers made their soldiers prove that they had not wasted any cartridges. A soldier was obliged to bring in part of a human body for every cartridge he was issued. These and other atrocities were revealed to the outside world by some courageous British journalists, the most prominent of whom was E. D. Morel. Authorities estimated that Leopold's twenty-three year rule of Congo (Leopoldville) took between five and eight million African lives.

International protests against these atrocities caused Leopold to relinquish his personal rule in 1908, and to turn Congo (Leopoldville) into a Belgian colony. Murder and mutilation ceased, but forced labor continued. Enormous mineral resources were discovered, and commercial mining was undertaken. This proved highly profitable.

BELGIAN PATERNALISM

After the Second World War, Belgium gave increased attention to the needs of the Congolese people. A ten-year plan, launched in 1950, involved a substantial financial investment in the economic development of Congo (Leopoldville). However, Belgium, unlike England and France, avoided taking any steps that might have prepared Congo (Leopoldville) for self-rule.

"The essence of the Belgian system," John Gunther said after his visit to the Congo in 1954, "is to buy off African discontent by giving economic opportunity, widespread social services, and a comparatively high standard of living."

PEST CONTROL   *Machines with insecticides are steaming injections into a sewer in Leopoldville.*

The Belgians believed that if the Congolese people were given sufficient economic advantages they would not demand independence. Steps were taken to prevent the growth of a Congolese professional group that might have led to political activity. Gunther in *Inside Africa* (1955) noted the professional lines above which Africans were not permitted to rise: "A Congolese Negro can become a first-class carpenter or mechanic, but not an engineer. He can be a bishop, a journalist, an accountant, a medical assistant, a teacher, a civil servant, or a pharmacist, but not an architect or an attorney. There are thousands of Negro lawyers in British and French Africa, but not one in the Congo."

The Belgians also tried to keep Congolese from going to Europe. Hundreds of students from the French and British African colonies attended European universities during the colonial period, but only a handful of Congolese ever achieved this goal. The Belgians tried to keep from the Congolese knowledge of such things as *habeas corpus*, a free press, elections, and trial by jury.

Fewer racial barriers existed in the Belgian Congo than in such areas as the Rhodesias and the Union of South Africa. Under Belgian rule there was no racial segregation in shops, elevators, banks, post offices,

or in local transportation. Mixed crowds attended sporting events and other public functions.

During the 1950's, economic opportunity for Africans was often substantial—within the spheres of activity allotted to them. In Elisabethville, capital of copper-rich Katanga, at least 8,000 Africans owned their own homes. Additional thousands were highly skilled workers. A few Africans in Leopoldville earned $20,000 or more a year.

Joseph Kapenda Tshombe, father of Moise Tshombe, the President of the secessionist province of Katanga, is an example of how a few Congolese made use of the economic opportunities offered by Belgian rule. The elder Tshombe owned a string of 16 village stores, a saw mill, a hotel, a fleet of trucks, and several cotton plantations, and became a millionaire.

CONFERENCE OF CONGO LEADERS   *In 1961, Congolese leaders met at Tananarive, in Malagasy Republic, for a round-table conference. In the front row, from left to right, Cleoface Kamitatu of Leopoldville Province; Jean Bolikango of Equateur Province; Joseph Ileo, Prime Minister; Joseph Kasavubu, President; Albert Kalondji of South Kasai Province; Philibert Tsiranana, President of Malagasy Republic; Moise Tshombe of Katanga Province; and Barthelemy Mukenge of North Kasai Province.*

RISE OF NATIONAL AWARENESS

It was the visit of a few selected Congolese to the Brussels World Fair, in 1958, that had such a shattering impact on the Congo (Leopoldville). When these men returned home, they started agitating. The political picture changed overnight; and a number of political parties sprang up.

Among the new politicians were two men who were to figure prominently in coming events: Joseph Kasavubu and Patrice Lumumba. Kasavubu was a member of the Bakongo, a tribe concentrated at the mouth of the Congo. He wanted to revive the old glories of the Congo kingdom; and for this purpose, he started the Abako Association, which was formed as a cultural club, and later became a political party. Because Kasavubu was strongly attached to his tribe and believed in tribal autonomy, the Abako Association supported federation of the several provinces with local autonomy.

Lumumba, a young man from the eastern part of the country, had no such tribal loyalties. He was a townsman who worked as a postal clerk. He advocated a centralized Congo, with a strong national government which would override tribal powers.

When the neighboring French Congo became a sovereign state under General de Gaulle's new constitution of 1958, nationalist feelings were stirred. Riots developed and events moved swiftly. By January, 1959, Belgium decided to withdraw. Independence was granted on June 30, 1960.

THE FRUITS OF BELGIAN POLICY

The policy that by-passed self-rule for Congo (Leopoldville) had serious consequences. At the time of independence, there were only fourteen university graduates in Congo (Leopoldville). The 25,000-man Congolese army had no African officers. Only twelve Congolese had risen to administrative positions in the colonial government. By comparison, Ghana had 1,500 British-trained civil servants when it achieved independence in 1957. In September, 1960, United Nations officials

PARLIAMENT *Chamber of Deputies in session on opening day,
June 17, 1960.*

estimated that it would take a generation of intensive effort to train
enough Congolese to man the nation's administrative and technical services.

IGNORANCE OF ADMINISTRATIVE TECHNIQUES

The concept of office routine was non-existent. Premier Lumumba
did not even have a secretary. A U.N. administrator reported that the
Congolese Minister of Agriculture had asked permission to sit in the
office of a U.N. agricultural official—just to learn how an office operates.

The stage had been set for economic chaos. Fearing the worst, many
Belgians withdrew their assets from Congo (Leopoldville). The government's liquid treasury assets slumped from $150 million at the start of
1959, to $13.6 million early in 1960. (The government had previously
enjoyed a substantial surplus, but had incurred a $50 million deficit in
1959.) Belgian technicians and administrators fled *en masse*. Airplane
flights from Leopoldville to Brussels were booked up weeks in advance.

BOULEVARD KING ALBERT PREMIER   This is the main street of Leopoldville, a city of 400,000 people. The building in the center is the "Au Petit Louvre" department store.

SECESSION OF KATANGA AND SOUTH KASAI PROVINCES

In Katanga Province, Belgian officers were still in control of Congolese troops; and Belgian commercial interests continued to exercise power in local politics.

On July 11, 1960, under the leadership of its president, Moise Tshombe, Katanga Province seceded from Congo (Leopoldville) and declared that it was an independent state.

116

Tshombe's reasons were more complex than most journalists assumed. He was not merely an unconditional servant of his Belgian masters, as his enemies assert. In Katanga, the rivalry between the Lunda tribe and the Baluba tribe had caused considerable bloodshed. Tshombe's declaration of secession was motivated not only to defend the Belgian mining interests, but also to forestall his rival tribe, the Baluba, from taking power in Katanga. Tshombe had also won considerable loyalty from among white Belgian officials and soldiers of fortune, who had come to Katanga from all parts of the world.

The immediate spur for Tshombe's secession was the general election held in May, 1960, in which the Congolese National Movement —Patrice Lumumba's Centralist Party—won the largest number of seats. Tshombe and his supporters concluded that Katanga would be back-seated, and they believed they had to act fast.

In the absence of firm central controls from Leopoldville, simmering tribal animosities boiled over into action. By August, armed clashes and riots had spread throughout the nation and threatened the peace of Africa.

On August 9, 1960, at the request of President Kasavubu, the United Nations authorized an international force to enter Katanga to prevent armed conflict that might lead to world war.

On August 23, 1960, Albert Kalonji, leader of South Kasai Province, announced that mineral-rich South Kasai Province had also seceded to become an independent state.

The economic situation worsened. In December, 1960, hundreds of people perished of famine in South Kasai Province. In Leopoldville, of every two workers employed in June, one was out of work in October. Consumer goods became increasingly scarce as the cost of living rose.

POWER STRUGGLE OF RIVAL LEADERS

Joseph Kasavubu, President of Congo (Leopoldville), and Premier Patrice Lumumba found their differences irreconcilable. In September, 1960, Kasavubu declared Lumumba's premiership ended; and announced that Lumumba had been replaced by Joseph Ileo, President of the Senate. The turn of events augered conflict.

Lumumba defied Kasavubu. In his attempt to retain authority, Lumumba was backed by a considerable armed force, and by the open support of Ghana, Guinea, and India. But the U.N. forces prevented Lumumba from extending his military control.

During this impasse, Colonel Joseph Mobutu, 29-year old leader of the Congo (Leopoldville) National Army, declared himself strong man of Congo (Leopoldville), and created a government of young intellectuals under President Kasavubu.

Lumumba insisted he was still Premier, and continued his attempts

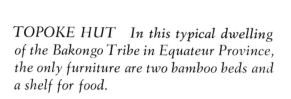

TOPOKE HUT   In this typical dwelling of the Bakongo Tribe in Equateur Province, the only furniture are two bamboo beds and a shelf for food.

to take control. He was brutally assassinated on February 12, 1961. Lumumba's mantle was quickly assumed by Antoine Gizenga, who had set up his own government in Stanleyville, capital of Oriental Province, the Lumumba stronghold.

THE TANANARIVE CONFERENCE

After Lumumba's death, Joseph Ileo was recognized as Premier in Kasavubu's government. But civil disturbances grew worse. The U.N. did not succeed in completely suppressing the conflict between warring

partisan forces. In March, 1961, the important political leaders held a full-scale conference at Tananarive, capital of the Malagasy Republic. It was agreed that the Republic should be dissolved and replaced by a loose federation of eight or nine autonomous states. This plan was never put into effect.

ADOULA NAMED PREMIER

In May, 1961, Kasavubu proposed a federation of twenty states under a strong central government. Tshombe then paid a visit to Kasavubu in Leopoldville, and was arrested by the national government. Some time later, Tshombe agreed to accept the authority of the new central government and he was released on June 22, 1961.

In August, 1961, Kasavubu named Cyrille Adoula, thirty-nine-year-old former labor chief, and one-time opponent of Patrice Lumumba, as the new Premier. Adoula formed a forty-two man cabinet to assist him, thus providing representation for all parties and groups. He invited Antoine Gizenga, in Stanleyville, to join him as Vice-Premier of the government. When, in September, 1961, both Adoula and Gizenga attended the meeting of neutralist nations in Belgrade, their joint presence offered some hope for political stability in Congo (Leopoldville).

U.N. forces, meanwhile, attempted to deal with the Katanga secession, but their efforts precipitated a new crisis. In August, 1961, U.N. soldiers arrested many of the Belgian officers of the Katanga army, and sent them back to Belgium. On September 12, U.N. forces attempted to seize Elisabethville, capital of Katanga, and thus end the secession. Katangan troops vigorously resisted the attack. After eight days, the fighting ended in an uneasy truce. During this truce period, U.N. Secretary General Dag Hammarskjold, flying from Leopoldville to Ndola in northern Rhodesia, to confer with Katanga President Tshombe, was killed in a plane crash.

DEFEAT OF KALONDJI AND GIZENGA

The central government unseated the autonomous regimes which had been set up by Kalondji, and by Gizenga; but despite a second

U.N. military intervention, Tshombe managed to prevent effective incorporation of Katanga into Congo (Leopoldville).

Fighting was resumed in December, 1961; and, this time the United Nations forces were successful.

In January, 1962, Tshombe accepted the Kitona Pact under which Katanga was to become incorporated into Congo (Leopoldville) on a federal basis. But later, Tshombe refused to carry out the agreement on the ground that the Katanga Assembly had not ratified it.

ECONOMIC DIFFICULTIES

When Adoula took office in 1961, inflation was rampant. The U.S. dollar, officially rated at fifty Congolese francs, was bringing one hundred francs on the black market. The government was operating with a monthly deficit of $12 to $15 million. The Congo Central Bank, by issuing new money, made further currency devaluation inevitable. Adoula invited U.N. advisers to study Congolese financial problems and develop a sound fiscal policy.

Congolese trade fell behind. Plans were made to double the $7 million monthly imports. Luxury goods were to be banned; materials to expand factory output favored. The U.N. provided a $10 million loan, and the United States granted $12.9 million in aid.

Various major resources remain underdeveloped; for example, Congo (Leopoldville) has the greatest untouched potential of hydro-electric power in the world. But Congo (Leopoldville) must build additional roads and improve river facilities to realize its rich promise.

GEOGRAPHY AND MINERAL WEALTH

Congo (Leopoldville) is as large as the United States east of the Mississippi. Its great lifeline is the Congo River, which runs 2,700 miles through the jungles to the Atlantic Ocean. Most of the northern half of Congo (Leopoldville) lies in the equatorial wet region, and half the country is covered by the great equatorial rain forest.

The potential wealth of this giant forest is matched by the great mineral wealth of the country. Eight percent of the world's copper is

NKUNDU HUNTER Metal-tipped, wooden spear, a carved, wooden shield, and a knife with a large circular handle, studded with nails, are the weapons of this primitive hunter.

ART CLASS In the Fine Arts Academy of Leopoldville, students with plaster molds, assemble the separate parts to form a large statue.

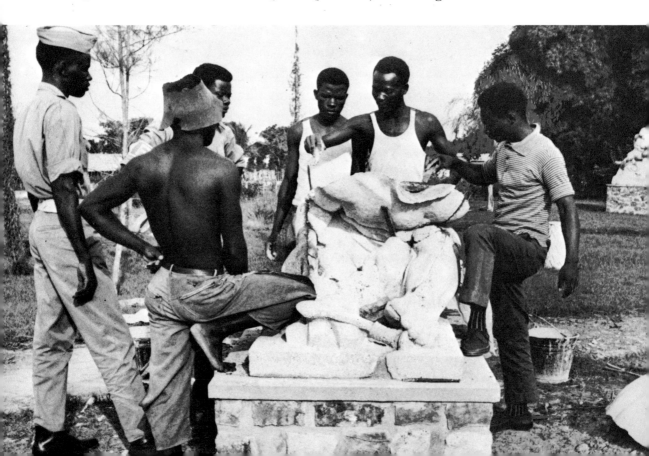

JOSEPH KASAVUBU   He studied for the Catholic priesthood, but became a schoolteacher and then an administrator in the Colonial Government. When Congo (Leopoldville) became independent in 1960, Kasavubu was elected President.

MOISE TSHOMBE   Related by marriage to the Chief of the Lunda tribe, the main tribe in Katanga, he enjoys wide popular support, and is undisputed leader of the province. He is personable; speaks excellent French.

PATRICE LUMUMBA   When 31, he was arrested for embezzlement and sentenced to prison. Lumumba was extremely able, but his lack of tolerance made him enemies among the other leaders and plunged the Congo into chaos.

CYRILLE ADOULA   Born in 1921, Adoula was educated as a devout Catholic. Named Prime Minister in August, 1961, he has strong Socialist leanings. He hails from Equateur, the least developed province.

supplied by the rich mines in Katanga Province.

UNION MINIÈRE

Union Minière, a giant corporation, owned by many European investors, and in part by the government of Congo (Leopoldville), controls the vast mineral wealth of Katanga.

Union Minière, ranking third among the world producers of copper, produces more than 60 percent of the world's supply of cobalt, 16 percent of the world's supply of germanium, 5 percent of the world's supply of manganese, and virtually all of the world's supply of radium.

Eighty percent of Katanga's revenues derive from Union Minière. Before independence, mining accounted for two-thirds of the value of all exports of Congo (Leopoldville), and Katanga Province was responsible for 80 percent of this total. Union Minière itself accounted for 20 percent of the Congo's gross national product, and provided 45 per-

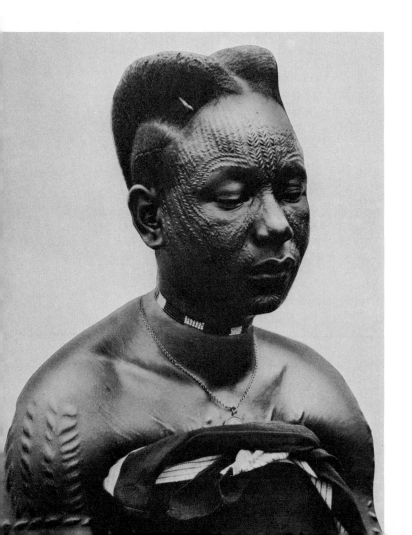

BUDJA WOMEN Lacerations are made on the face, in a traditional design, by scarifying the skin and rubbing ashes into the wounds.

cent of the Congo's revenues. Because of the paternal interest of Union Minière, the Katangan mine workers were given exceptionally fine medical care and have been accounted as the healthiest African group on the continent. Fifty-six percent of Katanga's adult males are salaried employees, an unheard of figure in Africa.

U. N. POLICY STIFFENS

In the fall of 1962, the United Nations policy toward Katanga hardened. While Britain and Belgium continued to buttress the Tshombe regime, there was a definite shift in American policy, motivated by a growing fear that, unless the position of the Leopoldville government was strengthened by a substantial share of the Katanga mine royalties, the shaky central government of Cyrille Adoula might collapse and be replaced by a more radical set-up.

Early in December, the United States agreed to supply the U. N. forces in the Congo with arms and equipment. Brigadier Ronald Noronha, the Indian officer in charge, readied his troops for action.

By year's end, fighting broke out in the mining town of Lubumbashi, with a shooting affray between Katanga gendarmes and the Ethiopian troops of the United Nations. Soon U. N. troops occupied Elisabethville, and went on to take the important mining center of Jadotville. Tshombe, who had fled to Southern Rhodesia, returned to Katanga to lead the resistance.

THE THREAT TO THE MINING INSTALLATIONS

While the fighting ravaged Katanga, Tshombe, with his back to the wall, threatened to dynamite the key mining center of Kolwezi. This town, located 150 miles northwest of Elisabethville, produced 75 percent of Katanga's hydro-electric power, and is the main seat of its mining plants. During the week of January 20, 1963, the wily leader of Katanga was persuaded that it would be useless to continue resistance. Tshombe announced that "Katanga's secession is ended."

Tshombe guaranteed that Kolwezi would not be damaged; and in return, exacted a guarantee from the United Nations for his own personal liberty. This guarantee was underwritten by Premier Cyrille Adoula. The U. N. ordered Tshombe to repair to Kolwezi and prevent destruction of industrial installations, and to have his troops hand over their weapons to the U. N. forces.

A few days later, Kolwezi was under the control of the U. N. forces and out of danger. Joseph Ileo was named as Resident Minister of the Central Government in Katanga. At the end of January, 1963, it appeared that the crisis in the Congo was over.

NEW ECONOMIC DEVELOPMENT

While the fighting was going on in the Congo, negotiations were carried on in Brussels which could herald a new development, not only for the Congo, but for 17 other new nations of Africa. A treaty was being negotiated between the European Common Market and 18 of the former colonies of Belgium, France, and Italy. The objective was to establish a new Eurafrican Association. If these 18 African nations were admitted as associate members in the Common Market, they would export agricultural and mining products to the Common Market; and in return, they would receive capital equipment and other industrial aids. (For participants, *see* New Eurafrican Association in *Glossary*.)

THE CITY OF ELISABETHVILLE

Elisabethville, the city that copper built, has broad jacaranda-lined streets. It has dial telephones, twenty-three hotels, two daily and three weekly newspapers, two moving picture theaters, a public library, an academy of music, a zoo, a museum, a cathedral, four banks, a publishing house, a sports' stadium, nearly a dozen foreign consulates, restaurants, night spots, clubs. It is the seat of Congo's State University.

THE CONFLICT BETWEEN ELISABETHVILLE AND LEOPOLDVILLE

Elisabethville lies almost one thousand miles distant from Leopoldville. In Africa a continent where communication was very primitive, this distance rendered the Province of Katanga remote and alien to Leopoldville, the only real bond between the two cities being the overlordship of the Belgian Government. The language, the culture, the climatic conditions, the tribal loyalties, and the economy of Katanga differ from those of Leopoldville. The differences, in fact, are far greater than the bonds. When the ties with the colonial power were severed, many Katangans felt that their province, too, should be independent.

There were a number of African leaders who saw eye-to-eye with this contention. Nations like the United States, opposed to Katanga independence, based their opposition on the ground that Congo (Leopoldville), without Katanga, would not be economically viable. They feared that, lacking the resources of Katanga, the government at Leopoldville would prove unstable, and that this instability would invite interference by the Soviet Bloc, who might wish to take advantage of the turmoil, and promote a Communist movement.

Some African leaders, notably Nkrumah, who had supported Pan-Africanism and the formation of large stable governments, feared that the fragmentation of the Congo would, by repercussion, imperil their own regimes, and lend some strength to the separatist movements, that were simmering in their own countries. However, most impartial observers were of the opinion that Katanga's secession was grounded in wide popular support. Had the United Nations held a plebiscite in Katanga, there is little doubt that an overwhelming majority would have supported Tshombe and the secession of the province. Had there been no support of the Kasavubu government on this issue by the United Nations, it is held likely that the resolutions of the Tananarive Conference would have been controlling, and that no military action on the part of either Leopoldville or Elisabethville would have followed. Of course, these conclusions are conjectural.

Toward the end of January, 1963, Prime Minister Cyrille Adoula announced a policy of "no victors, no vanquished," and asserted that a general amnesty would be granted to all participants in the Katanga secession.

VIEW OF LEOPOLDVILLE   Boulevard Albert Premier, which runs through center of the city, is the principal business thoroughfare.

IN BRIEF

AREA	905,381 square miles, as large as the entire area of the United States east of the Mississippi.
TERRAIN	The Congo River and tropical rain forest dominate the geography. About half the country is covered by the rain forest. Low-lying central plateau is surrounded by higher land, with mountain ranges rising from 6,000 feet to the 16,795 feet of Mount Ruwenzori. Largest lakes include Tanganyika, Edward, Albert, Kivu, Mweru, and Leopold II. Most of the smaller rivers drain into the Congo, which flows 2,700 miles through the country.
CLIMATE	Hot and humid in low-lying regions, frequent, heavy rains from October through May south of the Equator, and from April to November in the north. Higher eastern regions have fairly temperate climate.
CAPITAL	Leopoldville (population 400,000).

OTHER CITIES	Elizabethville, 184,000; Stanleyville, 127,000.
POPULATION	14,150,000 (1961); about 115,000 non-Africans.
ETHNIC GROUPS	Mainly Bantu; also Sudanese, Nilolu, Pygmy, and Hamitic peoples.
LANGUAGE	Official language is French. Lingala, Swahili, and other native tongues.
RELIGION	Mainly animist, with about 4,000,000 Catholics, 800,000 Protestants, and 150,000 Mohammedans.
DATE OF INDEPENDENCE	June 30, 1960.
FORM OF GOVERNMENT	Parliamentary democracy headed by President and Premier. Two chambers in the legislature: House of Representatives and Senate. Member of United Nations.

MULUNGU-TSCHIBINDA VILLAGE These mud-brick, white-washed huts, built to resemble the native habitations of the area, are a government housing project. There is a crude fireplace in each for cooking. An air vent is provided by a hollow pipe which protrudes from the dome.

YANGAMBI TRIBESMAN
His necklace is made out of ivory beads and leopard's teeth. The headdress is made by inserting feathers into a skull cap of leopard skin.

EDUCATION

In 1957, all elementary school education was free, and 29,537 primary schools had an enrollment of 1,640,070; 271 secondary schools had 16,486 enrolled, while 600 technical schools had 28,278. There is a state-controlled university at Elisabethville. There is a state-aided independent Catholic university near Leopoldville.

HEALTH FACILITIES

In 1958, 332 general and maternity hospitals; 99 institutions for sleeping sickness, leprosy, and tuberculosis; plus 2,483 rural dispensaries, all services solely for Africans. For Europeans: 127 general and maternity hospitals.

CURRENCY   Congo franc (50 Congo francs = U.S. $1.00).

INDUSTRY   Sawmills; manufacturing of textiles, shoes, metal drums, bags, bottles, paints and varnishes, metal frames, furniture, copper wire, and nails; production of cement, soap, cigarettes, beer, soft drinks, palmetto oil, and cottonseed oil.

CROPS: 93% of agricultural exports in 1956 were coffee, palm products, rubber, and cotton. Cassava, plantains, corn, sweet potatoes, rice, peanuts, peas, and beans are grown for domestic use.

STOCK: Cattle, pigs, sheep, and goats.

FISHING: Both fresh- and salt-water, mostly for domestic use.

MINING: Industrial diamonds, uranium, cobalt, and copper, all in great quantities; also gold, tin, zinc, manganese, silver, cadmium, tantalium, tungsten, bismuth, radium, beryllium, and germanium.

TRADE   1958: EXPORTS $411,625,000
           IMPORTS   350,606,100
           SURPLUS $ 61,018,900

MAJOR IMPORTS: Vehicles, machinery, food, fuels, textiles, iron and steel, chemicals, and pharmaceuticals.

MAJOR EXPORTS: Mineral and agricultural products (*see* Crops and Mining).

**TRANS-
PORTATION**   ROADS: 21,000 miles, hard-surfaced in urban areas (1957). VEHICLES: 33,800 passenger cars (1957); 23,500 commercial vehicles (1957).

WATERWAYS: 8,518 miles navigable and in service in 1957.

RAILROADS: 3,182 miles of tracks.

AIR TRAFFIC: 8 international airports, 34 other principal airports, and 112 local airports in 1958.

**COMMUNI-
CATIONS**   Postal, telephone and telegraph services are government-owned. In 1958 there were 12 radio stations, 7 daily newspapers, and over 300 other publications.

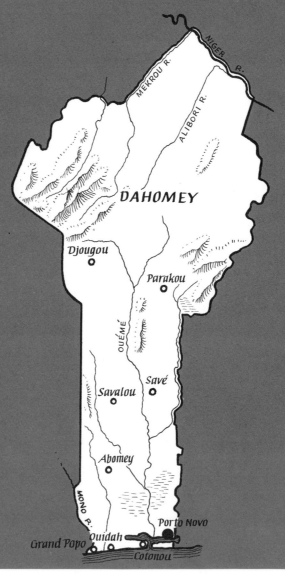

DAHOMEY

Museum for Anthropologists

Dahomey, a former French colony, one of the smallest of the new African nations, is a narrow strip of land lying between Togo and Nigeria. It runs due north from a tiny coast on the Gulf of Guinea where Porto Novo, the capital, and such port cities as Cotonou and Ouidah bustle with the activities of its one-crop economy.

About the size of Pennsylvania, Dahomey has a population of 1,935,000, of whom more than 95 percent are illiterate. The density runs 43.4 per square mile.

ONE-CROP ECONOMY

The one substantial cash crop is the oil palm (*elaeis guineensis*). The yellowish-orange to brownish-red oil, pressed from the fruit of this palm, is used chiefly in making soaps and candles; mixed with other oils it provides a superior grease for metals and machines. The kernel is doubly useful. Its white oil, because of its pleasant odor and flavor, is widely used in making margarine; the palm kernel cake that remains after the oil is extracted is excellent cattle fodder.

But when the market for palm oil and palm kernels is depressed by fluctuations of world prices, Dahomey suffers severely. This is the familiar problem of nations dependent on a single cash crop offered for export.

SOME PROJECTED SOLUTIONS

Two classical solutions are possible: Dahomey can strive for greater diversification of agricultural products and raw materials for the export market; or Dahomey can undertake a program of industrialization.

For some African nations, prospects for diversifying agricultural and raw material production are rather good. Gabon, for example, so long dependent on forest products, recently discovered substantial deposits of various minerals. Her chances for breaking out of a one-crop economy now seem bright. Unfortunately, Dahomey seems to have little likelihood of finding the same kind of solution. Mineral production is negligible. Prospecting thus far has produced no hopeful discoveries; and though cotton, kapok, coffee, and tobacco are being grown experimentally in the search for export crops, it appears that for the immediate future the oil palm will continue to be the mainstay of Dahomey's one crop economy.

As for industrialization, prospects for the expansion of small manufacturing activities do not seem promising. Industrial expansion would be hard to achieve while the country's economic pattern is ruled so completely by one crop.

POPULATION GROWTH

The average density-of-population figure masks the wide regional differences. Sparsely settled districts in the north have as few as 10 persons per square mile; the crowded south, particularly near the coast, contains nearly 300 persons per square mile.

It is an axiom of contemporary demographic studies that as modern public health techniques are introduced to underdeveloped areas and epidemic diseases are controlled, population figures climb very steeply.

MEDICAL CARE AND ECONOMIC STRESS

Yellow fever and other epidemic diseases that were rampant hazards a few decades ago, have practically disappeared from Dahomey. Sleeping sickness, once prevalent in the north, has been brought under control, largely through the unceasing activity of mobile health units. In the outlying districts, the populace is periodically given injections against various diseases. Cerebro-spinal meningitis, formerly annually epidemic in the north, has become rare. While there is no immunization against leprosy, it may soon disappear completely from Dahomey through the effectiveness of preventive measures. Yaws, long one of the most common diseases of tropical Africa, can now usually be cured by penicillin injections. Malaria and tuberculosis are rapidly being brought under control.

But progress in elimination of disease, and the subsequent rise in

MUSEUM AT ABOMEY   In this Historical Museum are displayed embroidered hangings which trace the history of royal dynasties, which date back to the 17th century. On display are relics from the reign of each king—clothing, personal objects, sculpture—as well as the spoils of successful wars.

population, intensify the economic problem. Dahomey currently suffers from an unfavorable balance of trade. Imports are 20 to 30 percent in excess of exports. To better the standard of living of a rapidly increasing population while coping with the handicap of a one-crop economy, is the difficult and urgent issue facing the leaders.

A FASCINATING CULTURE

Although a young nation, Dahomey's cultural traditions and remarkable history have long fascinated anthropologists and historians. Art connoisseurs greatly esteem the native sculpture—particularly the small bronzes which represent a tradition centuries old, and which are regarded as among the finest African art objects.

135

BOY SCOUTS   *A parade in celebration of a national holiday.*

The African custom of scarring the skin and working color into the wounds is elaborately developed by some Dahomey tribes. Often the process is extended until, in some individuals, large sections of the body resemble patterned textiles. There are a number of well-known African personages who bear such scarification on their faces, a dramatic reminder that present-day Africa is removed but a short time from the primitive Africa of yesterday.

SOME HISTORICAL ODDITIES

Before colonization by the Europeans, Dahomey was ruled by well-established dynasties of powerful kings. As a consequence, there is much more historical information available about Dahomey than there is for most other African states.

A great ruler of recent times was King Gezo, whose 40 years' reign began in 1818. He led his warlike subjects in successful campaigns against neighboring tribes, and united many of them into a powerful and respected dominion. Gezo's military enthusiasms were paralleled by his interest in national problems. His administrative reforms were substantially greater than those of other native kings. But he apparently did not abolish some of the most savage aspects of Dahomey tribal rites, including that of human sacrifice at the burial of kings and tribal rulers. It is known that Gezo's palace was decorated with human skulls, and legend reports that his sleeping chamber was paved with the heads of vanquished enemies.

Dahomey was long famous for its extensive use of professionally trained women soldiers. In the mid-nineteenth century, there were as many as 18,000 of these Amazons in the nation's armies. These female soldiers were not administrative aids, like the Wacs and Waves of recent

IMPROMPTU MUSIC   *Natives wait for the beat of the tom-toms to spring into a dance. The musicians and the audience combine native and western dress.*

history, but front-line fighters who invaded and conquered neighboring territories, and who, on various occasions, even succeessfully fought off colonizing French troops.

RECENT POLITICS

Dahomey became a republic in 1960. Its President, Hubert Maga, who comes from a poor family, studied at Dakar, became a teacher, and then moved into politics. A skillful politician, he became Under-Secretary of State for Labor in the French cabinet of Félix Gaillard. After serious riots had broken out in Dahomey in 1960, he assumed the political leadership of his country and won the presidency by a large majority.

The country operates under one-party rule. The *Parti Dahoméen*

de l'Unité (PDU) won all sixty seats in the National Assembly in the general election of December, 1960.

The country's budget is heavily subsidized by France.

IN BRIEF

AREA
44,696 square miles, about the size of Pennsylvania.

TERRAIN
From south to north, the country has four major geographical areas. To the south, the coast is a low sandy strip, one to three miles wide, with no natural harbors; landing on sandbars is extremely difficult. Inland, the lagoons are gradually being filled with drifting sand. Lagoons are interconnecting but have only two outlets to the sea, at Grand-Popo and Cotonou. Next northward is the region of clay, which is the main palm-tree area; this area is intersected by a large swampy depression, stretching cross-country, east to west. Then the Atakora Mountains, running diagonally cross-country, rise from 1,000 to 3,000 feet. Region also includes the fertile plains of Borgou and Kandi. Major rivers are the Oueme, Mono, Couffo.

CLIMATE
Two zones: south and north. South is hot and humid, temperatures from 72° to 93°. Four seasons: major dry season November to April; shorter one July to September. In between are heavy rain periods. In the north are greater temperature variations, less humidity; two seasons, a dry October to April and a rainy April to October. Progressive decrease in rainfall from south to north.

CAPITAL
Porto Novo (population: 32,000).

OTHER CITIES
Cotonou, about 30,000.

POPULATION
1,935,000; about 5,000 Europeans.

BARIBA HORSEMAN   Horses are the pride of the Bariba tribe of Upper Dahomey. The Bariba, proud of his horsemanship which is displayed at official celebrations, measures his importance by the number of horses which he owns. The Baribas grow shea trees and kapok.

STILT VILLAGE   *Natives of Ganvié paddle to the floating-boat market of Ganvié, "The Venice of Dahomey." The stilt houses are made of bamboo frames on palm branches tied together and supported by tree trunks. Later the roofs will be thatched with grass or palm leaves.*

DOCK-TO-DOOR SERV-ICE *A woman fish peddler delivers fresh fish to a Ganvié housewife.*

FISHING AT GANVIÉ *Fishermen cast home-made nets in Noukoué Lake.*

CANOE FISHING *On the Noukoué Lake the fishermen rig sails on poles on their dug-out canoes.*

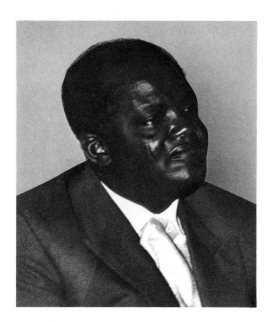

HUBERT MAGA Born in 1910, Hubert Maga was educated in Senegal and became a teacher. He was elected President when he was 51 years old.

ETHNIC GROUPS   Largest are the Fon peoples, to whom the Adjas and Aizos are related.

LANGUAGE   Official language is French; tribal languages are spoken.

RELIGION   Majority are animists; a fetish cult still exists in the south. About 163,000 Catholics and 18,000 Protestants.

DATE OF INDEPENDENCE   August 1, 1960.

FORM OF GOVERNMENT   Parliamentary democracy; President, Vice President, 70 members of the National Assembly are elected for a five-year term by direct universal suffrage. There is an independent judiciary and an Economic and Social Council with purely consultative functions. Member of the French Community and the United Nations.

EDUCATION   29.1 percent of school-age children were enrolled in 1960. In 1958 there were 430 primary schools with 75,410 students; 12 secondary schools with 2,260 students. No universities.

HEALTH FACILITIES

In 1954, there were 2 hospitals, 74 other medical centers and infirmaries.

CURRENCY

French Community franc (247 francs = U.S. $1.00).

INDUSTRY

Light industry only; palm-oil mills, cotton, peanut, and coconut-fiber-processing plants; factories for soap, furniture, and cotton fabric.

CROPS: Palm products are the basic cash crop. Some export of peanuts, coffee, castor-oil seed, cotton, and tobacco. Main food crops are corn, yams, rice, millet, and cassava; also fruits such as oranges, tangerines, pawpaws, guavas, and bananas are raised for local consumption.

STOCK: Cattle in the north, hogs in the south, poultry, sheep, and goats throughout the country.

FISHING: Fresh and dried fish for domestic use and for export.

MINING: Small quantities of gold.

TRADE

1959:	IMPORTS	$15,800,000
	EXPORTS	9,700,000
	DEFICIT	$ 6,100,000

MAJOR IMPORTS: Automobiles, petroleum products, iron and steel, machinery, sugar, cotton cloth and piece goods.

MAJOR EXPORTS: Palm kernels, peanuts, palm oil, cotton, steel, machinery, sugar, cotton cloth and piece goods.

TRANS-PORTATION

ROADS: 343 miles surfaced. 2,482 miles unsurfaced, but all-weather.

VEHICLES: No statistics available.

WATERWAYS: None.

RAILROADS: 360 miles of track.

AIR TRAFFIC: Five relatively small airports, at Cotonou, Fandi, Natitingou, Cana, and Parakou.

COMMUNI-CATIONS

Publicly owned telegraph and telephone services. Two monthly and three bi-weekly publications.

GABON

Jungle Country with Forest Wealth

Gabon lies directly on the equator and is covered by jungle—perhaps the most impenetrable jungle in all Africa—a rain forest with many varieties of moisture-loving trees, vines and shrubs, all evergreens, growing thickly together.

Dank and moist, dark and forbidding, where rainfall keeps the terrain a lush green throughout the year, the rain forest is one of the great natural wonders of Africa. In the forests of Gabon, midst a primeval depth of trees and vines, live the Pygmies, barely touched by civilization. Here, too, live the Bantu, famous for their carved religious figures.

In the rain forests, trees sometimes attain a height of almost 200 feet. Their trunks are often covered by heavy vines and various types of parasitic growths. The foliage of most of the trees is near the top. In the heavier forests, the leaves form a high roof and the ground is frequently in heavy shadow.

Much of Africa's virgin forest has been destroyed. The custom of burning the savanna grasslands in order to clear the land decimated many forests when the fires spread out of control. In spite of such rampant deforestation, the rain forests continue to have a profound effect on the culture and economy of every country that they cover.

THE WOODS OF GABON

From the forests of Gabon come African walnut, coralwood, satinwood, zebrawood, and the famous okoume, treasured the world over. Commercial cutting has sharply reduced forest acreage. As early as 1930, the French colonial government estimated that unless scientific reforestation was promptly begun, the forest of Gabon would disappear within 25 years. Since then, all lumber companies have been under government control; reforestation and limitations on cutting have been enforced.

NEWLY DISCOVERED MINERAL DEPOSITS

Gabon's forests are the mainstay of her economy, but Gabon has recently discovered a new source of wealth.

Recent prospecting activities have revealed that Gabon is one of the richest of the equatorial republics in known mineral deposits. Oil, potash, uranium, manganese, and iron have all been found, and additional prospecting will probably reveal other minerals. The Mekambo iron field is considered to be among the richest in the world; reserves are estimated as high as a billion tons of ore, of which at least 63 percent is iron. Unfortunately, the ore fields are 280 miles from Owendo, the nearest port, and the intervening terrain is so rough and hilly that it will be necessary to build a 400-mile railroad to transport the ore. The scheduled completion date for the railroad is 1965.

Despite the inaccessibility of many of its mineral deposits, the discovery of this underground wealth has already made Gabon one of the few African nations with a favorable balance of trade. In 1960, the value of exports exceeded the value of imports by 30 percent. Gabon is spending this trade surplus on metal products and machinery to expand her mining industry in order to create a basis for industrialization.

HISTORY OF GABON

Portuguese navigators landed on the coast of Gabon around 1470. Trading posts were established, and Portuguese missionaries followed. English, Dutch, and French ships came to Gabon to engage in the lucrative slave trade that was not abolished until the Congress of Vienna (1814-1815).

Gabon's present capital, Libreville, the nation's principal city, was founded in 1849. The city fathers were slaves who had been freed from a contraband slave-running vessel. France secured control of Gabon in the late nineteenth century, and incorporated the country into French Equatorial Africa in 1910. In a referendum held on September 28, 1958, the nation voted to become an autonomous republic with the French Community.

In 1961, Leon M'Ba, a businessman then 59, was elected as the country's first President. Leon M'ba had formerly served as the elected mayor of Libreville.

IMPROVING HEALTH CONDITIONS

Gabon is one of the world's most sparsely populated countries. Only 440,000 people live in an area of 103,000 square miles—approximately 4 persons per square mile. Very large areas are uninhabited.

The death and infant mortality rates are very high. Common diseases include bilharziasis (a parasitic blood disease), leprosy, malaria, tuberculosis, and yaws. At the end of 1959, Gabon had 51 doctors—one for every 6,000 persons—12 registered midwives, and 450 nurses and

INDEPENDENCE DAY   Youths of the Libreville High School in gym uniform parade in celebration of Independence Day on August 17, 1960. The flags represent the popular Girl Scout and Boy Scout organizations.

health workers. A full-scale medical offensive to combat tropical diseases had been mounted by Gabon, which allots 15 percent of its annual budget for public health services.

ALBERT SCHWEITZER, HUMANITARIAN

Gabon's most famous resident is Dr. Albert Schweitzer, renowned clergyman, philosopher, musicologist, physician, and Nobel Prize winner. In 1913, Dr. Schweitzer came to the tiny village of Lambaréné, in the rain forest, to establish a clinic and hospital for the benefit of the natives of the area. Thousands of people from all parts of the world have made the pilgrimage to this clearing in the heart of the forest, to be inspired by the work of this great humanitarian.

FOREST WORKERS' HUTS *Temporary camps, like this one near Franceville, are customarily set up near each working area.*

LEON M'BA The President was born in 1902 at Libreville. He became an accountant, then a journalist; and in 1956 he was elected mayor of his home town.

IN BRIEF

AREA 103,088 square miles, slightly smaller than Oregon.

TERRAIN Almost all the land lies in the Ogoué River basin whose source is in the Congo Republic. River divides the country roughly into two equal parts; with tributaries it provides several hundred miles of navigable waterways. Coastal lowlands, never higher than 1,000 feet, extend eastward to valleys of the Ogoué and N'Gounié rivers. Beyond the lowlands rises a belt of plateaus of varying heights. There are several groups of mountains; the highest peak is Mount Iboundji—5,165 feet.

CLIMATE Temperature varies little, averaging about 80°. Two rainy seasons: a short season, October to mid-December; and a longer period, mid-January to mid-May. Average annual rainfall: Libreville, 98 inches, and Cocobeach, 157.5 inches (compared to New York State's 42 inches).

CAPITAL Libreville (population, 20,000).

FOREST CLEARING   Most of Gabon is covered by the rain forest, a dense jungle, seemingly impenetrable. From these forests come mahogany, kevazingo, ebony, and okume, the fine woods which Gabon exports, and which constitute the chief source of the country's income. Okume, the most valuable of these woods, is used for plywood. Along the crude road, lie huge trees which have been felled, and which await transporting to a processing center.

POPULATION   440,000; about 4,500 Europeans.

ETHNIC GROUPS   Pygmies, said to be the original native inhabitants, are now a small minority; Fang came from the north in the nineteenth century; Omiene, Bakota, and Eshira are the largest of nearly 40 Bantu tribes in Gabon.

LANGUAGE   French is the official language; Fang is spoken in northern Gabon; Bantu languages in other parts of the country.

RELIGION   About one-third are Christians; the remainder mostly animists.

DATE OF INDEPENDENCE   August 17, 1960.

FORM OF GOVERNMENT   Parliamentary democracy. National Assembly of 40 members elected for 5-year term, majority leader becoming Premier. There is a nine-member Executive Council, an independent judiciary with a Supreme Court, an Economic and Social Council, and an Administrative Tribunal. Member of French Community and United Nations.

EDUCATION   In 1959 there were 337 elementary schools, with almost 80 percent of school-age children attending, compared with 14.3 percent in 1945-1946. There were seven secondary schools, and two technical schools. No universities.

HEALTH FACILITIES   Four hospitals, thirty regional medical centers, two maternity and child-care centers, three centers for treatment of sleeping sickness, nine mobile health units, and several leprosy centers.

CURRENCY   Unit is the French Community franc (247 francs = U.S. $1.00).

INDUSTRY   Principal industry is processing timber in sawmills, and making plywood and veneers. Other light industries are oil processing, carbonated beverages, rice processing, soap manufacturing and palm-oil mills.

CROPS: Cocoa, coffee, rice, peanuts and palm products, for exports; bananas, cassava, taro, sweet potatoes, and corn raised for local use.

STOCK: None of any importance.

HUNTING AND FISHING: Fishing solely for the domestic market; whale and elephant ivory for export.

MINING: Manganese, iron, uranium, oil, potash, gold, and diamonds.

TRADE

1959: EXPORTS $43,708,000
IMPORTS   29,120,000
SURPLUS $14,588,000

MAJOR IMPORTS: Metal products and machinery, food, textiles, vehicles, fuels, and cement.

MAJOR EXPORTS: Wood, crude petroleum, cocoa, gold, peanuts and coffee.

TRANS-PORTATION

ROADS: 191 miles surfaced; 2,399 miles all-weather, unsurfaced (1959).

WATERWAYS: Two large ports, Libreville and Port-Gentil. Inland waterways are used mostly for floating logs.

RAILROADS: None.

AIR TRAFFIC: Two airports (Libreville and Port-Gentil), plus 120 small landing fields. Approximately 53,500 passengers were carried in 1958.

COMMUNI-CATIONS

Seven monthly journals or bulletins, each with a circulation of 200 to 500 copies. Postal and telegraph services. Radio station at Brazzaville in the Congo Republic serves Gabon.

HARBOR AT LIBREVILLE   This natural harbor on the Gulf of Guinea, is the principal port as well as the capital of Gabon. Excavation and improvement of this port have high priority in national economic planning. Libreville, meaning free town, was established in 1849. Today, it has a population of 20,000. The town lies astride the estuary of the Gabon River, close to the rain forest. This rain forest, if not checked, would soon overrun the city and grow right up to the water's edge—just as it did before the city was founded. Libreville has pleasant squares and fine government buildings.

Bawku

Navrongo

Lawra

Gambaga

BLACK VOLTA

WHITE VOLTA

Yendi

Bole

Tamale

Salaga

G H A N A

Kete krachi

Sunyani   Mampong

VOLTA R.

Kumasi

Obuasi

Ho

Dunkwa

Koforidua

Accra

Tarkwa   Cape Coast   Winneba

Takoradi   Sekondi

GHANA

Trailblazer in African Politics

Ghana, formerly the Gold Coast, a British colony, pioneered and set the pattern for independence for many of the new African nations.

Ghana was the first West African colony to be granted self-government, and the first to become completely independent. It chose as its name that of an ancient African empire which achieved greatness more than a thousand years ago.

Since gaining independence in 1957, Ghana has been in the forefront in advancing the cause of African nationalism, and has become one of the richest and most progressive nations in West Africa. Its per capita income is rapidly approaching $200 a year, the figure that economists use to distinguish developed from underdeveloped countries.

KWAME NKRUMAH

Perhaps, a good deal of the country's political orientation is due to the dynamism of its leader, Kwame Nkrumah.

Nkrumah is a Christian, though not a practicing one. He is the son of a goldsmith, and was educated by Catholic missionaries, and trained as a teacher. He continued his education at Achimota College in his native land, and then he worked his way through several universities in the United States. He earned doctorates in theology and philosophy; and at one time, he seriously thought of becoming a priest.

Kwame Nkrumah formed the Convention People's Party in 1949. The next year he was jailed by the British for sedition. But in 1951, he won an overwhelming victory in the first national election. He was escorted from his prison, directly to the British Governor General, and invested with the authority to build a new nation.

PREPARING FOR FREEDOM

From 1951 to 1957, Nkrumah and the British Governor, Sir Charles Arden-Clarke, worked together to train the Ghanaians for self-government. Their efforts were eminently successful. When Ghana became independent in 1957, a strong corps of educated and seasoned native leaders was ready to take control. In contrast with most of the other newly independent African nations, Ghana has many top-level executives, and thousands of adequately trained civil servants. Today, only a relatively few outsiders still hold positions of authority in the country.

OPPOSITION TO NKRUMAH

The Ashantis have formed a "National Liberation Movement," led by the chief of the Ashantis, Asantehene Prempeh II. This is the toughest opposition Nkrumah has to face.

Nkrumah is also opposed by the United Party, led by Dr. Busia. This party is composed of middle-class people of the coastland. The party rejects Nkrumah's dictatorial politics, and charges that the government is not democratic.

Nkrumah has jailed or exiled the opposition leaders. He has harassed opposition newspapers, and he has adopted many facets of a personality cult. His monuments are everywhere. Stamps and coins bear his image, and his many titles include the official title of Osagyefu, redeemer, bestowed upon him by the Ghanaian legislature itself.

After an unsuccessful attempt to assassinate him, Nkrumah has become very suspicious; and he has even jailed men who have long been his closest friends.

NATURAL WEALTH

Ghana's chief wealth lies in the cocoa crop, which provides over 60 percent of the value of all Ghanaian exports. Ghana is the largest cocoa producer in the world, and the revenue from this crop has supplied the Ghanaian government with funds for roads, schools, and hospitals. There is no plantation system in the country; the cocoa trees are owned by about 300,000 small, independent farmers.

In 1951, when Nkrumah's government took over practical control of the nation from the British, the cocoa crop was endangered by swollen

PARLIAMENT HOUSE *Statue of Ghana's first President, Kwame Nkrumah, stands prominently before Parliament House, seat of the government in Accra.*

shoot, a disease which destroys the cocoa-bearing trees. The native government waged a vigorous campaign against the disease. The diseased trees were cut out; the others sprayed; and farmers shown how to prevent the disease from spreading. Today, Ghana's cocoa crop is surpassing all previous records.

Other major sources of wealth in Ghana are gold and manganese. Ghana is the world's largest exporter of manganese. The Soviet Union produces more manganese, but exports less.

PAN-AFRICAN POLICY

Nkrumah's concepts of nationalism go beyond the present boundaries of Ghana. The Ghanaian President is a leader in the political effort to create larger African nations from the many existing smaller states.

Like many African leaders, Nkrumah is greatly concerned with the problems created by the arbitrary demarcation lines drawn between the new nations. The African leaders feel that such artificial boundaries handicap the development of the continent, by having created small, economically insecure countries that face great difficulties in the fight for national survival.

The Ghanaian constitution provides for the future transfer of Ghanaian sovereignty to a large union of states. Ghana inspired the Ghana-Guinea Union shortly after Guinea became independent from France; but in effect, this agreement was only a paper arrangement, and it merely signified Ghana's hope that some day it would become part of a larger, stronger state.

Genuine political independence, Nkrumah believes, can come only when real economic independence has been achieved. Nkrumah sponsors African socialism. He has often expressed himself in favor of "an African personality" and hopes for the formation in the future of "a United States of Africa."

GOVERNMENT BOTANICAL GARDENS   *Royal palm trees at Aburi.*

THE FIRST FIVE-YEAR PLAN

In 1951, Nkrumah initiated a five-year plan to revitalize the economy. Based on an earlier British plan, it concentrated on the improvement of basic services—communications, public utilities, education, and preventive medicine. Many roads were built, running water and electricity made more widely available, and the telephone and telegraph systems were modernized.

HYDRO-ELECTRIC POWER AND ALUMINUM

The most significant industrial development in Ghana will be the construction of the Aksosombo Dam on the Lower Volta. This giant structure, 2,000 feet long and 375 feet high, will provide Ghana with abundant electric power, a new and important industry (aluminum), and will facilitate the development of many subsidiary industries. While the electricity generated by the project will be available for wide industrial and private use, the chief consumer will be a large aluminum reduction plant to be built near the dam site, by Kaiser Aluminum

MASS EDUCATION   A mass literacy campaign, organized by the Department of Social Welfare and Community Development in the Accra area, proved an outstanding success. During the campaign, 25 classes were established at various points in the capital and these were run by 200 voluntary leaders. At the end of the campaign a Literacy Day was organized at which 817 new learners were presented with certificates. This picture shows a part of the Literacy Day celebration.

FRANCIS NWIA KOFIE KWAME NKRUMAH   From his name it is known that Nkrumah was born on a Saturday, for that is the name that mothers of the Akan tribe give to their children born on that day. The year was probably 1909.   Greatly influenced by Nigeria's Dr. Nnamdi Azikiwe's articles in the "African Morning Post," he became interested in politics.

Company and other companies. Rich bauxite deposits, located in western Ghana about 200 miles from the plant, will be used to produce 220,000 tons of aluminum annually.

THE VOLTA RIVER PROJECT AND IRRIGATION

The Volta River Project will provide water for irrigation and will open hundreds of thousands of new acres to agriculture. Moreover, this project will create an inland network of water transportation. It will convert Ghana's almost exclusively agricultural economy into an industrial frame. Ghana has no coal or oil deposits; the hydro-electric capacity of the Volta River Project will compensate for this basic lack.

THE NEW HARBOR OF TEMA

Aluminum produced at the Volta River Project will eventually be shipped from the new harbor at Tema, not far from the capital city of Accra. This recently completed harbor has 500 acres of enclosed water, compared to 220 acres of water in the older harbor of Takoradi, in the western part of the country. The Tema harbor will also have adequate shore space for extensive warehouses, railway sidings, and marshaling yards.

A separate fishing port and a modern town will be built adjacent

161

to the Tema harbor. Plans call for a well-housed population of 100,000. Fishing, now developing into a major industry, provides the Ghanaians with abundant protein, previously lacking in their diet. Government aid to fishermen has resulted in the purchase of 84 motorized fishing vessels to replace traditional small, oar-propelled boats and has greatly increased the catch.

ASSEMBLY OF CHIEFS *The Ashanti chiefs have gathered in honor of the occasion of the opening of Tema Harbor, early in 1962. The umbrellas are symbols of authority. As a matter of protocol, a chief can only be addressed through an intermediary—never by direct oral communication. The chiefs, for the most part, are clothed in hand-woven silks. The headband trimming of shells, stars, crescents, and other forms, as well as their shoulder straps, bracelet, anklet and sandal decorations are all gold-plated. The young boy is the grandson of Chief Annokwei, one of the dignitaries.*

NAVIGATION AND AVIATION

In 1957, Ghana, aided by the Zim Israel Navigation Company, founded a shipping fleet, the Black Star Line. The line is now wholly owned by Ghana, although Zim provides part of the operational and managerial direction. The Black Star line owns four vessels, charters others, and has eight refrigerated cargo ships on order.

Similarly, Ghana has established its own air line, Ghana Airways, owned 60 percent by Ghana and 40 percent by the British Overseas Airways Corporation. Ghana Airways numbers five Ghanaians among its pilots. All but 23 of the 250 employees are Ghanaians.

EDUCATION AND HEALTH

Between 1950 and 1955, school enrollment doubled. Educational facilities are being further improved. The University College of Ghana (424 students), the Kumasi College of Technology (536 students), and the Law School will be merged to form a new University of Ghana.

Ghana holds the distinction of being the first African country that is near the goal of universal primary education. Literacy classes for adults have been widely established; and the University College offers a program of adult studies, geared to enlarging the knowledge and capacities of the teachers of the nation.

Considerable gains have been made in the public health service. Of the 250 physicians in Ghana, 100 are employed by the government. A new medical school will be built in Accra; meanwhile more than 200 Ghanaians are studying medicine abroad.

THE MODERN CITY OF ACCRA

Accra has the advantage of a coastal location. Though the city is humid, the temperature rarely goes higher than 86 degrees.

In Accra, one can see how, with intelligent planning, a new modern city can replace a ramshackle town. Accra has fine department stores; wide, well-illuminated streets. Its night life is the liveliest in West Africa.

Ghana's University College, beautifully laid out, is affiliated with the University of London and serves more than 1,000 students. Accra's International Airport is used by most of the world's airlines.

This city of approximately half a million people, with handsome, well-kept government buildings, new office structures, and government-sponsored housing developments, dramatically foreshadows the face of the new Africa.

FOREIGN AID

Ghana receives economic and technical aid from the United Nations, the United States, and Great Britain; but has itself begun to give aid to less developed African nations. Ghana lent $28 million to Guinea when that nation became independent; and sent social development experts to help Nigeria during the first difficult days of its independence.

It may be noted that the Convention People's Party, though socialist, understands the need for private capital, and has encouraged private foreign investments. Nkrumah has made it explicit that his government is not communist, and that his ideal is a welfare state, based on socialist principles.

INAUGURATION OF PRESIDENT NKRUMAH   On July 1, 1960, Ghana declared itself a republic. In a solemn ceremony at State House, nationalist leader Kwame Nkrumah was inaugurated as the first President.

COLLEGE STUDENTS   *The youthful Republic of Ghana is a land of sharp contrasts. While it has retained the essentials of its own culture, it has adopted many Western characteristics. In this college group, men in Western style business suits chat with others who wear the colorful national garb.*

IN BRIEF

AREA 91, 863 square miles, about the size of Oregon.

TERRAIN Long sandy coastline, backed by plains and scrub, is intersected by several rivers and streams. Belt of tropical rain forest extends inland from the western coast, broken by heavily forested hills. To the north is rolling savanna. These plains are traversed by the Black and White Volta rivers.

CLIMATE Four regions: the eastern coast is warm and fairly dry; the southwest corner is warm but very humid; the forest region is also warm and humid; and the north is hot and dry. Two wet seasons in the south are March to July and September to October. In the north, there is one rainy season from April /May to October.

CAPITAL Accra (population: 391,000 in 1961).

OTHER CITIES Kumasi, 220,900; Sekondi-Takoradi, 121,000.

POPULATION 6,691,000 (1961).

ETHNIC GROUPS Mainly of the Akan family; also the Ga and Ewe peoples, with many linguistically related tribes.

LANGUAGE Official language is English. The predominant tribal languages are Twi, Ashanti and Fanti.

RELIGION Majority are animists, though there is general belief in a supreme deity. The leading Christian communities are Methodist, Presbyterian, and Roman Catholic; there is also a substantial Mohammedan element in the north.

DATE OF INDEPENDENCE March 6, 1957.

FORM OF GOVERNMENT Republican, with a President and a one-house legislature of 103 members elected for five years. There is a House of Chiefs for each major region. The President selects a Cabinet of at least eight ministers from among members of Parliament. There is an independent judiciary. Member of the British Commonwealth and the United Nations.

EDUCATION In 1958 there were 471,020 students enrolled in 3,634 primary schools and 152,997 students in 1,300 secondary schools.

SIR NANA AGYEMAN
PREMPEH II   He is chief of
the Ashantis. His headgear has
been wrought of pure gold shells
attached to a headband. The
necklace, too, is pure gold, as are
the bracelets, rings, talismans
around his ankles, and sandal
decorations. The gown is char-
acteristically Ghanaian. The
whisk in his left hand, made of
horsetail hair and leather, is a
symbol of authority.

The two institutes of higher education are the University College of Ghana and Kumasi College of Technology.

HEALTH FACILITIES

Thirty-six government hospitals, plus twenty-six hospitals maintained by mining concerns and missions. Nine health centers, and several medical field units.

CURRENCY

Unit is a Ghana pound (1 £ = U.S. $2.80).

INDUSTRY

Only light industry: printing and publishing, lumber, furniture, clothing, soft drinks, bakeries, beer, cigarettes, soap, and edible oils.

CROPS: Cocoa is the most important. Others include maize, millet, rice, peanuts, palm oil, limes, kola nuts, coconut oil, copra, and shea butter (fat used for food and lighting).

STOCK: Raised solely for local consumption.

FISHING: For domestic use only.

MINING: Exports of gold, manganese, diamonds, and bauxite are second only to cocoa in importance.

TRADE

1957: IMPORTS $270,480,000
       EXPORTS   256,760,000
       DEFICIT $ 13,720,000

MAJOR IMPORTS: Textiles, food, machinery and vehicles, manufactured goods, chemicals and fuels.

MAJOR EXPORTS: Forest and agricultural products (*see* Crops), and minerals such as gold, manganese, diamonds, and bauxite.

TRANS-PORTATION

ROADS: 1,645 miles are surfaced.

VEHICLES: 17,600 passenger cars. 16,400 commercial vehicles (1959).

RAILROADS: 750 miles of track.

WATERWAYS: A national shipping line; two deep-water seaports.

AIR TRAFFIC: An international airport at Accra, with three other smaller landing fields.

COMMUNI-CATIONS

Government-owned radio station at Accra. All major towns have telephone, telegraph and postal services. More than two dozen newspapers and periodicals.

GUINEA

Boké

Labe
Pita
Dalaba Dabola Kouroussa
Mamou

Kindia Kankan

Conakry

Siguiri

Kissidougou

Beyla

N'Zérékoré

GUINEA

Rebuff to the French Community

In 1958, the French government offered its African colonies two alternatives: accept the new French constitution and become a member of the French Community; or reject the constitution and gain full independence, but be prepared for immediate cessation of all French aid.

Referendums were held throughout French Colonial Africa. All the colonies, save Guinea, accepted the new constitution; and each subsequently became a republic within the French Community.

Guinea chose independence by an overwhelming 97 percent vote. The French departed in force, leaving the fledgling Republic of Guinea in dire financial straits. In an effort to relieve the urgent situation, Guinea quickly borrowed $28 million from Ghana. Technical assistance and further financial aid, primarily from the Eastern bloc of nations (Russia, Czechoslovakia, Poland, and China), put the new nation on its feet.

SÉKOU TOURÉ

President Sékou Touré is the leader of the Democratic Party of Guinea, the only party in the country. He is the son of a peasant. His grandfather, Samory, was a tribal chief who led an uprising against the French in the 1890's, and formed an extensive but short-lived empire.

Born in 1922, a member of the Malinke tribe of Guinea's interior, Touré was reared in a poor, backwoods family. A Moslem, he began his studies at a village Koranic school; and at ten, was sent to a primary school. But early in life, he resisted French control. He was expelled from school after school because of his open opposition to the French administration; and consequently, he has had little formal education.

He obtained a job as a clerk in the Post Office at Conakry, and helped to organize a trade union in that bureau. This brought him once more in conflict with the ruling authority. He became well known as a union organizer, and the Communist-led World Federation of Trade Unions sent him to Prague and Bucharest for training courses.

In the late 1940's, Touré became a politician; before long, he emerged as his country's undisputed leader. He was elected mayor of Conakry, and also served as a representative to the French National Assembly in Paris. In 1961, he was elected President of Guinea by an overwhelming vote.

Touré is a leftist, but not a Communist; in his own words, he is an exponent of "African Marxism."

INDEPENDENT POLITICAL ACTION

Despite heavy going in the beginning, Guinea has prospered since independence. Under the leadership of dynamic Sékou Touré, Guinea has become one of the leading exponents in Africa of independence and of the policy of "total de-colonialization" of the continent. On any given question, Guinea's stand has appeared to be more to the left than that of any of its African neighbors.

ATTITUDE TOWARD SOVIET BLOC

When independence was proclaimed, the rebuffed French left the country. The Western nations, seeking not to offend France, offered little aid to Guinea. On the other hand, the Russian bloc set up trade agreements and sent technical advisers—help proffered in a time of great need.

Guinean statesmen admit that their voting record in the United Nations has been quite similar to that of the Soviet Bloc, but they say that this was so because the Soviet Union had been voting with the African states, and not because Guinea had gone along with the Russians. In contrast, they point out that the United States consistently voted with the colonial powers. They admit that this pattern changed with the crucial vote, by the United States, against Portugal, on the Angola question.

Guinea was a militant supporter of Lumumba. Guinea also lent its unqualified support to the Algerian F.L.N. Guinea is a founding member of the Casablanca group *(See Glossary)*.

Late in 1961, a Communist plot was discovered by the government of Guinea. The Soviet ambassador who was involved was expelled from

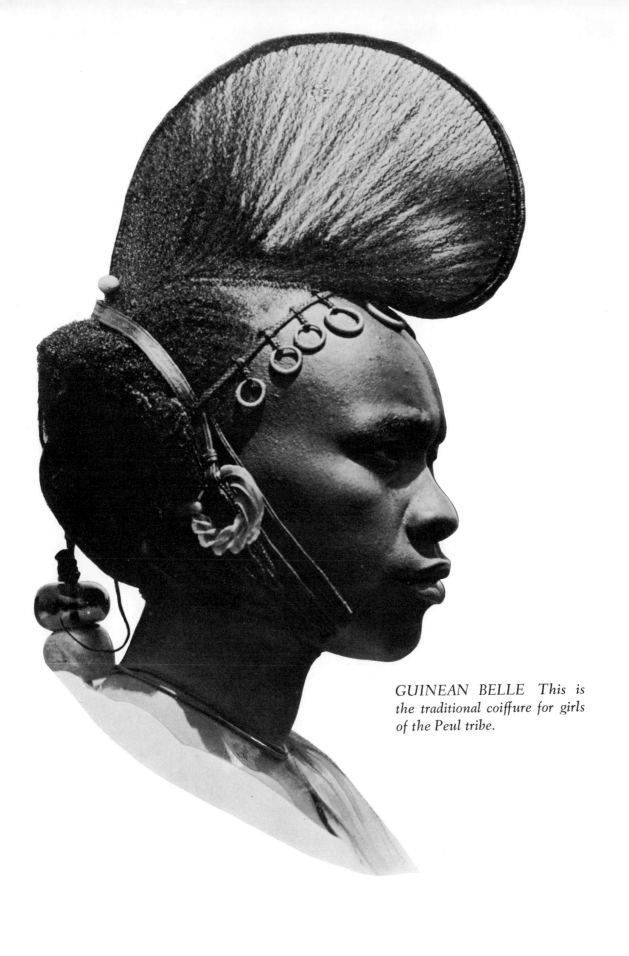

GUINEAN BELLE This is
the traditional coiffure for girls
of the Peul tribe.

ADULT EDUCATION IN LABÉ *Because of its dispersed population and lack of resources, the circle of Labé, on the north slope of Fouta-Djalon, has a very low school enrollment. Since 1949, the regional educational service has been trying to educate large groups of adults by using movies and posters. Prepared in Dakar, the posters are doubly useful: they give practice in reading, and they impart practical information. This poster shows the benefits that trees provide, particularly in preventing erosion. This hut at Poreko was built by the villagers themselves, for use by the traveling instructor.*

174

the country; and since then, Guinea's friendship with Russia has noticeably cooled, and friendly moves have been made toward the West.

There is evidence that Guinea has become disenchanted with the Soviet bloc. In the United Nations, Guinea did not support the Soviet campaign to replace the Secretary General with a three-man body (the Troika System); Guinea failed to back Russia in several votes on the Cuban situation; over tremendous objections from the Soviet Union, Guinea joined the World Bank and the International Monetary Fund; and Guinea requested the United States to send it more Peace Corpsmen.

In the fall of 1962, President Touré paid a state visit to the United States where he made a strong appeal for more American aid.

The Guineans point out that the situation in Guinea is quite unlike that which prevails in many of the other new nations of Africa, where the advisers of the government are nationals of the former colonial rulers. The Guineans claim that in such states foreign advisers still form policy.

Guinea, they maintain, has had its fill of foreign domination. Under no circumstances will they replace one form of domination—French, by another form—Russian. They will trade with and accept aid from anyone—East or West—if that helps Guinea. Their students attend college in France and in the United States as well as in Russia.

THE GHANA-GUINEA-MALI UNION

A major trend in the political development of Guinea is its drive toward the formation of a larger African political unit. To Guineans, their small country of three million persons is a mere geographical accident; its national boundaries arbitrarily set during the period of colonial rule do not coincide with either ethnic or natural geographic borders. Rather than remain a small, weak nation within these arbitrary boundaries, Guinea has sought to form some kind of a union with other African nations.

Ghana and Guinea actually signed an agreement that linked the two nations in a federal union; but no action was ever taken to put this agreement into effect. In mid-year, 1961, the governments of Ghana, Guinea, and Mali, formed a loose political union, with the explicit proviso that other African states would be accepted as full members. This Ghana-Guinea-Mali Union established a committee to study effective ways of merging the currencies, military commands, and cultural programs of the three states; and of coordinating their foreign policies.

Among the many problems that must be solved by the new federation is that of effective communication. The three nations do not share a common language. Guinea and Mali use French, while English is the official language of Ghana.

A UNIFIED SPIRIT

In contrast to many of Africa's newly independent nations, Guinea has achieved much of the social unification needed as the basis of an industrial society. A strong spirit of nationalism, centered upon Sékou Touré's party, as opposed to traditional tribal allegiance, has been aroused throughout the country. Much of this spirit was developed before independence, under Touré's leadership as a left-wing labor organizer.

There is only one party in the country, although there is no constitutional prohibition that bars other parties. In spite of this one-party rule, the country professes to be a democracy.

Today, Touré faces other problems: his nation seems relatively unified, but it is still poor, even by African standards. Guinea is independent—*very* independent, say the Guineans—but it is also cut off from the French aid that flows to nations of the French Community.

ECONOMIC ASPECTS

Private capital supports the aluminum works at the city of Fria. This enormous plant, with a current capacity of 480,000 tons of aluminum, is managed by a consortium, 48 percent of which is owned by the Olin Mathieson Chemical Corporation of the United States and the remainder held by British, French, Swiss, West German, and other foreign interests. It is the largest industrial operation in the nation.

Guinea's main resource is bauxite, the ore from which aluminum is made. Current estimates place Guinea's deposits at an estimated 100

CATHEDRAL AT CONAKRY   *The high bell tower is a landmark.*

million tons, the largest in the world. Five hundred thousand tons of bauxite a year are already being exported to Canada. The Fria plant is expected eventually to produce 1.2 million tons of aluminum, which would make it the world's largest single producer.

In addition to the great concentration of bauxite ore, Guinea also has appreciable deposits of iron ore, which, until the middle of 1961, were only slightly exploited. In 1961 a consortium, composed of groups from seven West European nations, was granted rights to mine more fully the nation's iron ore deposits. At the time, it was believed that the consortium would invest approximately $200 million in the project, a huge sum in Guinea's limited economy.

With the exception of bauxite and iron-ore mining, Guinea's industry is still severely limited. However, the government is doing much to encourage further industrial growth in the country, and headway is being made.

Agriculture in Guinea, as in the rest of Africa, can be divided into two parts: subsistence farming and the production of cash crops. Cassava is the major subsistence crop grown for domestic consumption. Coffee, bananas, tobacco, and rice are the major cash crops grown for export. In addition, some Guinean meat is exported to neighboring Sierra Leone and Liberia.

Efforts are being made by the government to increase the tourist trade. Tourists are attracted to Guinea by the big game in the interior, which includes elephant, hippopotamus, panther, monkey, crocodile, and antelope.

GROWTH OF EDUCATION

Following Guinea's independence, great strides were made in education. In 1955, only 11 percent of school-age children in the country were attending classes. Twenty-four percent was the comparative figure in neighboring Senegal. However, since 1955, Guinea has greatly increased her in-school percentage.

CONAKRY, THE CAPITAL CITY

The nation's major airport is at Conakry, the capital of the country, and a deep-water port. Conakry is a bustling seacoast town of about 75,000 people, with modern, up-to-date office buildings, beautiful coconut palms, café-bordered beaches, fine squares, and neat front lawns. The *Présidence,* built by the French as the residence of the colonial governor, now serves as the presidential palace. The Hotel de France, one of the finest examples of tropical architecture in West Africa, is built along the seashore, and its roof-top bar offers a delightful view.

By Western standards, Conakry is a small town; it can easily be traversed by foot. But this small town is immensely interesting, for in

GUINEAN DRUMMER   The tattered garments worn by the musician and by the boys are common enough. Most everyone is barefoot.

contrast to the African neighborhoods of the city, the newer sections epitomize the tremendous change-over in the way of life of many of the new nations of Africa.

IN BRIEF

AREA	About 95,000 square miles, the size of Oregon.
TERRAIN	Crescent-shaped country of four major regions: a low-lying coastal zone, or Lower Guinea; Middle Guinea, with sandy plateaus ranging from 1,500 to 5,000 feet, with waterfalls and deep valleys; Upper Guinea, with low plateaus reaching to the tall slopes of French Sudan, and stretches of rolling savanna; forest region of the Guinea Highlands with the country's highest point, Mount Minba (about 6,000 feet): The Niger River originates in the Highlands region.
CLIMATE	Lower Guinea has a rainy season July to October (average annual rainfall at Conakry is 168 inches), with little temperature variation. Middle Guinea has no marked dry season, but less rainfall and greater temperature changes. Upper Guinea has still less rainfall and an average daily temperature variation of 25°. Forest region has no clearly divisible seasons, constant high humidity, and averages 110 inches of rainfall annually.
CAPITAL	Conakry (population, 75,000).
POPULATION	3,000,000; about 10,000 non-African.
ETHNIC GROUPS	Foulahs, Peuls, Soussous, Mandingos, and Malinkes are the most numerous.
LANGUAGE	Official language is French. Many tribal languages and dialects are still spoken.
RELIGION	Mostly animist: there are some Mohammedans. Mohammedan practices often are combined with animist beliefs and ceremonies. Some Christians.
DATE OF INDEPENDENCE	October 2, 1958.

SÉKOU TOURÉ Touré, born in 1922, is a grandson of Almamy Samory, the legendary leader who fought the French so relentlessy during the colonizing period. In 1953, he led a general strike, which turned him into a hero. In 1955, he was elected Mayor of Conakry.

FORM OF GOVERNMENT
Republic with a National Assembly, popularly elected for five years; President is the head of state, and is directly elected for seven years. He appoints a Cabinet of Ministers, who are not members of the National Assembly. An independent judiciary. Member of the United Nations.

EDUCATION
11.5 percent of school-age children enrolled in 1958. By 1959, 79,373 students attended 485 primary schools, with 3,953 in secondary schools. No universities, but there is a technical college in Conakry.

HEALTH FACILITIES
Two hospitals, 26 medical centers, and 2 mission health centers existed in 1954.

CURRENCY
Guinea franc (247 francs = U. S. $1.00).

INDUSTRY
Aluminum plant at Fria is largest industrial unit; other industries are bricks, plastics, soap, mining explosives; processing of tobacco, rice, and pineapple.

CROPS: Coffee, bananas, and palm kernels are grown for export. Among the food crops are rice, cassava, potatoes, kola nuts, citrus fruits, corn, peanuts, tobacco, and taro.

STOCK: Cattle, sheep, and goats are raised in small numbers.

FISHING: Coastal waters provide fish for domestic consumption.

MINING: Bauxite ore, aluminum, and iron ore are major exports. Gold and diamonds are also mined.

TRADE

1958:	IMPORTS	$52,000,000
	EXPORTS	21,520,000
	DEFICIT	$30,480,000

MAJOR IMPORTS: Textiles, vehicles, iron and steel, machinery, fuel, and food. (Imports increased as needed with work on the beauxite deposits and the associated hydro-electric project.)

MAJOR EXPORTS: Iron ore, bauxite, diamonds, coffee, and bananas.

CANNERY IN CONAKRY   *Production line methods are used in canning pineapple juice.*

SHOPPING CENTER IN FRIA   *The stores are built without show windows, so the premises can be safely locked. Shorts are in vogue in this new mining town, which has just recently been hacked out of the bush. Fria boasts skyscrapers, restaurants, and modern places of amusement.*

TRANS-PORTATION	ROADS: 1,550 miles all-weather.
	VEHICLES: No figures available.
	WATERWAYS: Natural deep-water port at Conakry.
	RAILROADS: 410 miles of track (state railroad).
	AIR TRAFFIC: Two airports; eleven landing fields.
COMMUNI-CATION	One daily newspaper. In 1956, 69 telephone and telegraph offices, all government-owned, provided service. Submarine cables link communications to Dakar, Monrovia, and Freetown.

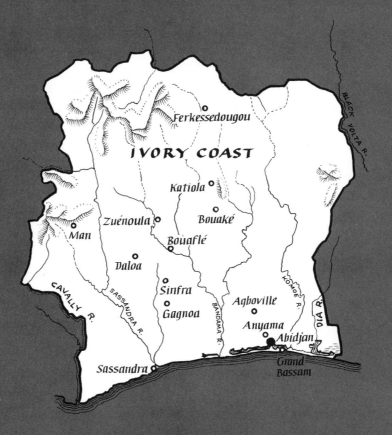

IVORY COAST

Self-Supporting Coffee-Rich Nation

Wealthiest of all the former French colonies in West Africa, the Ivory Coast is one of the most important emerging nations. By African standards it is a rich nation; by world standards, certainly a nation with great potential.

Ninety-five percent of the wealth of the country is derived from agriculture. Though the natives of the up-country grow cassava and yams for home consumption, Ivory Coast exports its major crops.

THE COFFEE CROP

The key crop is coffee. The Ivory Coast is the third largest coffee producer in the world, trailing only Brazil and Colombia. The coffee bean, of a neutral-taste variety called "robusta," is used primarily as a blending stock, and is also ideal for instant coffee. Major importers of Ivory Coast coffee are France and the United States.

Ivory Coast coffee, in contrast to that of most African export crops, is grown by native farmers—not on a plantation system controlled by Europeans. In fact, the plantation system produces only about 3 percent of the more than 113,000 tons of coffee exported (1956). This amount of coffee represents 47.3 percent of the dollar volume of annual exports. In 1959, a total of $64 million worth of unroasted coffee went abroad. Cocoa, at $42 million, or 31 percent of total export value, and wood— primarily mahogany and iroko—at 12 percent of total exports, are the second and third most vital items.

A STRONG TRADE POSITION

The structure of foreign trade is quite strong. In 1959, total imports were $114 million; total exports, $137 million.

The economic progress of the virile Ivory Coast from 1952 to 1956 may be compared with that of all the eight nations of former French West Africa (Ivory Coast, Dahomey, Guinea, Upper Volta, Mauritania,

185

Mali, Senegal, and Sudan). Ivory Coast, with only 7 percent of the total area and 17 percent of the total population of these eight former French colonies, produced 35 percent of the aggregate exports and absorbed 27 percent of the aggregate imports.

ABIDJAN—A MODERN CITY

Abidjan, the capital, is a growing city of 200,000, one of the handsomest cities on the continent. Green and white, with skyscrapers gleaming under the bright sun, Abidjan is a city of parks and squares and coconut palms. Here, in the Ifan Museum, one can see Ivory Coast carvings in ivory and wood, sculpture in gold and bronze. Shops, supermarkets, public buildings are modern and impressive.

The new harbor at Abidjan has played an important role in Ivory

TYPICAL FARM VILLAGE In the savanna regions of the agricultural North bordering on the Upper Volta Republic, houses are built like fortified stockades out of thick blocks of caked earth. The two towers on the left are purely decorative. The men are wearing long, Senegalese-type robes called boubous.

MUSICAL COMPETITION   Once a year, before graduation, The National School for Music and the Dance holds a musical competition. Awards are given to the best students.

Coast's economic development. This deep-water port, completed in 1950, after ten years' construction, includes the Vridi Canal, 1.7 miles long, 1,200 feet wide, and 50 feet deep. This canal, deep enough for the world's largest ships, has radically changed the port of Abidjan from a small lagoon to a modern harbor, by opening it directly to the sea. It is administered jointly by the governments of the Ivory Coast and Upper Volta. Upper Volta, a landlocked nation immediately to the north, depends on the port of Abidjan and the Abidjan-Nigeria Railroad for its major contacts with the outside world.

INDUSTRY, PRESENT AND FUTURE

The nation, however, is still limited industrially. Food-processing, with plants for producing instant coffee, leads the few small-scale industries, which include lumber, chemicals, textiles, metals, and construction. There appear to be some prospects for such minerals as

VIEW OF ABIDJAN   The Treichville quarter of this nation's growing capital of 200,000 is characterized by wide streets, low buildings and tropical vegetation. The beautiful church of Notre Dame is seen in the center.

colombo-tantalite, titanium, copper, chromite, asphalt, and bauxite; but findings are still tentative. Diamond and manganese production are increasing, manganese particularly showing promise as a large-volume export commodity. Gold is also mined, but in decreasing quantities.

Industrial development will be facilitated when the new hydro-electric dam on the Dia River near Arane moves into heavy production. This new plant currently produces 19,000 kilowatt hours, with 80,000,-000 kilowatt hours expected—which will be about two-and-a-half times the amount of power now produced in the Ivory Coast.

HOUPHOUËT-BOIGNY

The Ivory Coast is blessed with one of the ablest leaders in African politics. Félix Houphouët-Boigny, born in 1905, was graduated from medical school at Dakar in 1925, and practiced medicine for fifteen years before entering politics. He was one of the founders of the African Democratic Rally, a political party that has furnished the heads of state for seven of the new African nations. Originally strongly leftist, the party objectives became more moderate as the leaders drew away from Communist influence.

MASKED DANCERS   The eastern province of the Ivory Coast, the Region of Man, is famous for its beautiful forest landscapes and its gorgeously arrayed masked dancers. The high altitude (3,900 feet) makes stamina a necessity.

Before his nation became independent, Houphouët-Boigny served as a representative in the French Parliament, and then in several cabinets. He rose to the position of Minister of State in the de Gaulle government. To the disappointment of the more militant African nationalist leaders, he has retained close ties with France and the West. It was Houphouët-Boigny who, in 1960, initiated the formation of the so-called "Brazzaville Group," a group of twelve French-speaking nations loosely joined together for political action, who have also set up a joint economic secretariat. Although Houphouët-Boigny has always opposed the formal federation of independent African states, he has been in the forefront in encouraging economic and political coordination between the new nations of Africa.

The chief of state is a Catholic. Catholics form only 8 percent of the population of the Ivory Coast, but they are very influential and occupy the majority of seats in the National Assembly.

The 25,000 persons of European descent living in the Ivory Coast are considered an asset to the economy and are welcomed by the Houphouët-Boigny government. The majority of these Europeans are French, and parts of Abidjan are said to look more like a French city than an African one. By an electoral law passed in November, 1961, these French residents were granted the right to vote in elections for the National Assembly.

ONE DOMINANT PARTY

Although the Ivory Coast is firm in its ties to the Western world, its constitutional democracy is unlike any of its Western counterparts. As in many of the new African states, there is no free press and no real

COASTAL LAGOON   *The beautiful lagoons of Ivory Coast are one of the main tourist attractions. Within easy distance of the capital city of Abidjan, they run along the coast from Grand Bassam to Grand Lahou. Protected from the sea, the placid surface of this lovely lagoon makes a smooth base for narrow canoes. The natives throw fish nets into these waters with appreciable success.*

SURF FISHING   *Fishing is a community affair for the men of the coastal villages situated on the Atlantic Ocean's Gulf of Guinea. The harvest of the sea contributes heavily to the agricultural self-sufficiency of the nation.*

political freedom. For example, Houphouët-Boigny's chief political rival has been banished from the country and is currently living in exile in the Netherlands. What political freedom exists is channeled through the structure of the party in power, the Democratic Party, which holds all one hundred seats in the Parliament. In an Africa in ferment against political rule by outsiders, it is noteworthy that eighteen of these seats are held by persons of European descent. There is great political interest among the rank-and-file Ivory Coast citizens, but there is no real opposition party, and the people's will is expressed primarily through the one-party machinery.

President Houphouët-Boigny, a determined champion of free enterprise, wants his country to attract the capital which has become leery of "African Socialism." In 1962, on a state visit to Washington, he successfully negotiated for increased American aid.

THE GROWTH OF EDUCATION

More than 20 percent of the budget of Ivory Coast is earmarked for educational needs. In 1958, only 28 percent of school-age children attended school. Current construction plans for 1,040 new classrooms should enable 45 percent to attend in 1962. A serious problem involves education for the rural areas. More than 80 percent of the children attending school live in cities, the figures dropping sharply to about 10 percent in the upland and backland areas. By law, education is compulsory to age eleven, but this is difficult to enforce in the outlying regions. In 1958, although 145,000 pupils were in elementary schools, there were only 4,310 in secondary schools. The 1,131 college students had to attend foreign schools. In fact, the opening of the University of Abidjan in 1958 was a momentous event in the development of the educational system.

A novel library system has been established, using bookmobiles in the interior areas. The Ministry of Education also plans five regional educational centers equipped to teach reading by advanced audio-visual techniques,with a goal of 100,000 literate adults within two years.

IN BRIEF

AREA   124,503 square miles; larger than Arizona.

TERRAIN   Land rises gradually and evenly northward from the ocean. Rolling country is broken only by isolated mountains. Four major rivers run north to south: the Komoe, Bandama, Sassandra, and Cavally. None is navigable for more than 40 miles. Three major geographical regions: (1) Lagoons along the coast extend 185 miles; (rest of the coast is high and rocky). (2) Beyond the coast, tropical forest begins, gradually giving way to transitional area of wooded savanna. (3) In the north is the rolling savanna (grassy plains).

CLIMATE   Coastal climate is warm and humid; forest region has tremendous variation in temperature (57° to 103°); very heavy annual rainfall of 98 inches; northern region has both a rainy and a dry season.

CAPITAL   Abidjan (population, 200,000).

POPULATION   3,267,000; about 25,000 Europeans.

ETHNIC GROUPS   Major groups are Agnis-Ashantis-Baoulés in southwest (also Koua-Koua and Krounen). Mande clan in the northeast, Senoufo clan in the north, and Dans and Gouros in the center of the country.

ABIDJAN   A view of the skyline.

FÉLIX HOUPHOUËT-
BOIGNY *Born into a family
of Baoulé chiefs, the President is
the scion of a well-to-do planter.*

LANGUAGE	Official language is French, with over 60 African dialects also spoken.
RELIGION	Majority are animists; some Mohammedans.
DATE OF INDEPENDENCE	August 7, 1960.
FORM OF GOVERNMENT	Parliamentary democracy. The President and a 100-member National Assembly are elected for five-year terms. There is an independent judiciary and an Economic and Social Council. Member of Council of the Entente, the French Community, and the United Nations.
EDUCATION	28 percent of school-age children (about 145,000) attended 968 primary schools in 1958, but there were only 11 secondary schools. The University of Abidjan opened in 1958. Together with various institutes, it has 1,300 students.
HEALTH FACILITIES	62 hospitals and medical stations, plus 150 dispensaries, 58 maternity homes, and 6 leprosy centers.

CURRENCY   Unit is the French Community franc (247 francs = U.S. $1.00).

INDUSTRY   Food-processing plants (palm oil, flour, margarine, fruit, tuna fish, brewing, soft drinks, coffee, and cocoa); textiles, lumber, chemicals, machines, metals, and construction industries.

CROPS: Main food crops are yams, cassava, and rice; taro, corn, millet, and peanuts are also grown. Cash crops include coffee, cocoa, bananas, palm products, shea nuts, kola, cotton, pineapples and woods.

STOCK: Poultry raising is increasing rapidly; model farms encourage breeding.

FISHING: Sardines, tuna, and shellfish.

MINING: Diamonds; manganese. Some gold.

TRADE

1959:	EXPORTS	$136,842,000
	IMPORTS	114,372,000
	SURPLUS	$ 22,470,000

MAJOR EXPORTS: Agricultural (*see above*), and diamonds.

MAJOR IMPORTS: Sugar, wire, tobacco, cotton cloth, motor vehicles and parts, petroleum, machinery, and electrical appliances.

**TRANS-
PORTATION**   ROADS: 520 miles are surfaced. 6,200 miles are unsurfaced but all-weather.

VEHICLES: 15,000 passenger cars. 11,700 trucks (1959).

WATERWAYS: Abidjan is the only navigable port open to the sea. It is suitable for the largest ocean going vessels. The river ports are used locally by small boats.

RAILROADS: 375 miles of track.

AIR TRAFFIC: Large international airport at Abidjan can handle jets; 16 secondary airports.

**COMMUNI-
CATIONS**   Eight newspapers; only one daily, but many are published weekly, semimonthly or monthly. Nationwide radio station at Abidjan. Telephone lines run throughout the country.

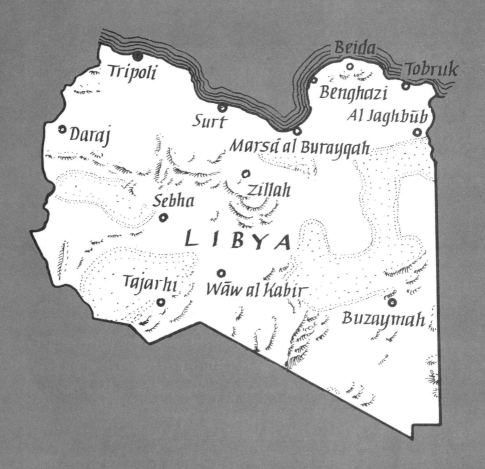

Tripoli

Beida

Tobruk

Benghazi

Daraj

Surt

Al Jaghbūb

Marsá al Burayqah

Zillah

Sebha

L I B Y A

Tajarhi

Wāw al Kabir

Buzaymah

LIBYA

Oil in the Desert

During the Second World War, Libya was the scene of Rommel's drive eastward to Egypt. At Benghazi and Tobruk, the twisted wreckage of tanks and trucks recall his motorized units. In the vastness of the Libyan desert, an 8-24 U.S. bomber was recently found in almost perfect working order, embalmed by the desert wind.

Side by side with these modern relics lie ancient ones, mostly Roman: ruins of buildings, cobbled roads with marks of chariot wheels, an occasional arch, a pillar.

Libya is a federated kingdom consisting of three autonomous provinces: Tripolitania, Cyrenaica, and Fezzan. On December 24, 1951, Libya became a sovereign state under U.N. auspices, and Amir Mohammed Idiris El Mahdi El Senussi was chosen as King.

WESTERN LIBYA: TRIPOLITANIA

Tripolitania, the most prosperous and well-developed of the three provinces, contains about two-thirds of the entire population of Libya.

Tripoli, the capital of this province, is also the political capital of the country, and the commercial nerve center of Libya.

Tripolitania, bordered on the west by Tunisia and Algeria, began its history as a series of Phoenician colonies on the Mediterranean coast. Named by the Greeks for its three cities (tripolis), the harbor of Tripoli waxed in importance until the Arabs, in their westward march, took the land, in 666 A.D. The ensuing see-saw struggle of the expanding Arab empire with Europe's medieval city-states, marked the end of Tripolitania's ancient culture. The vulnerability of its chief city of Tripoli to attack from Venice and Sicily initiated an era of changing masters.

When the Ottoman Empire was established, Tripoli had become a fearsome stronghold of Islamic pirates. The dreaded corsairs raided and controlled most of the Mediterranean. This was one of the factors

CATTLE MARKET   Here are typical Libyans transacting a deal.

that drove the Europeans to seek new trade routes to the Orient and thus discover the New World.

Tripoli continued its role as a pirate haven until the mid-nineteenth century. During centuries of shifting control by the Arabs and the Turks, Tripoli was in frequent conflict with Fezzan. Such interprovincial rivalry continued in Libya until its recent federation.

THE INTERIOR PROVINCE: FEZZAN

Fezzan, separated from Tripolitania by a 600-mile stretch of desert, began its known history as the southernmost outpost of the Roman legions. Originally called Phazania by Rome, it suffered less through the course of history than the coastal areas because it was not as hotly contested. Here, around the oases of the Kufra and the Homra—fertile spots stretching east-west across the desert—are found those dark tribes believed to be descendants of the original Libyan people. Roman ruins are occasionally uncovered by the drifting sands. Some of the few towns in this desert area appear to be constructed upon such ancient ruins.

Fezzan is much more African than Arabic in character. The two ethnological strains in the area are both Hamitic. It is thought that the Negroid tribes are descended from slaves brought into the region from Central Africa. The fair-skinned people are Tuareg.

There are no roads which run between Fezzan and either of the other two provinces.

To this day, the warlike Berber people remain practically unchanged. The very inaccessibility of this desert province has aided them in maintaining their tribal independence. Though suffering the overlordship, at various times, of the rulers of Tripoli and of the Turkish pashas, it was not until the invasion by Italy that some semblance of a national character was forged out of the union of the tribes of the south with the peoples of the other provinces.

EASTERN LIBYA: CYRENAICA

Cyrenaica, the easternmost province, separated from Tripolitania by the Syrte Desert, is, geologically speaking, a mass of limestone that drops sharply to the sea. The coast is marked by deep erosions. A series of oases stretch toward Egypt; they are known to have been formed by a prehistoric marine inlet or an ancient tributary of the Nile, long since silted up.

Drier than Tripolitania, hotter and less variable, most of Libya's several million sheep, goats, camels, and cattle are grazed in this province.

Barley and millet are grown in the fertile red soil of the higher areas that contain Libya's few forests.

The history of Cyrenaica is closely connected with the history of Alexandria and with that of the ancient Greeks. Separated from the other Libyan land masses by desert, Cyrenaica was mainly settled along the Mediterranean coast. From here, trade was carried on with inland Africa via the caravan routes across the Sahara Desert.

FARMERS' MARKET   *The date palms form an appropriate setting for this pastoral mart on the outskirts of Tripoli. Here farmers buy and sell sheep and other livestock.*

KING OF LIBYA   His Majesty Mohammed Idris El Mahdi El Senussi was born in 1890. The king also functions as head of the Senussi sect of Moslems.

When, in the seventh century, the Arabs conquered the area, they destroyed the remnants of the ancient cultures. In 1551, the Turks of the Ottoman Empire conquered the area; Cyrenaica ceased to be an important caravan terminus and lapsed into decline.

The central Turkish government permitted the local pashas to rule with great independence. In the absence of firm controls, the wild desert people, the warlike Tuaregs and the Berbers, gradually reduced the outlying towns to rubble. Cyrenaica remained a land of primitivism and anarchy until 1912, when after the Turco-Italian War, the Italians annexed the territory.

The whole of Cyrenaica contains but a handful of Italians and Berbers, the predominant stock being Arabs of the Senussi religious sect.

CARAVAN *Typical of native transport, this Berber caravan is passing a date grove near Zliten.*

The King of Libya is the leader of this sect, and Benghazi, the capital of Cyrenaica, is the seat of the royal court.

EMPIRE BUILDING AND SAVAGERY

Italy's desire for a sphere of influence in Africa was prompted by the examples of France and England. Aroused by dreams of a resurgent Roman Empire, an Italian expeditionary force landed in Libya in 1911. From then on, Italy displayed a brutality in Libya unparalleled except by the incredible acts of King Leopold's sadistic overseers in the Congo.

The Italian campaign, marked by savage cruelty, paradoxically showed the invaders' love for growing things. With tacit approval of the French, who said ". . . as long as they do not interfere with us in Tunisia, to which they haven't the least right, let them go in . . ." the Italian green thumb left its imprint everywhere on the Libyan coast. They left, too, a heritage of hatred.

RESISTANCE, WORLD WAR II, AND UNIFICATION

The semi-nomadic Arabs, the Senussi tribesmen, were the core of the Libyan resistance. So fanatic was their determination to remain independent, it took the Italians twenty years to subdue them. This war of attrition decimated the population but established the Senussi as leaders.

During World War II, these people formed the backbone of the Libyan Arab force. In recognition of their service, and to forestall any resurgent Italian interests in Libya, the British and French War Administrations—Great Britain in Cyrenaica and Tripolitania, and France in Fezzan—agreed to the choice of the present King, Amir Mohammed Idris El Senussi. This choice implemented the U.N. decisions of 1949 and 1950, leading to the establishment of a Libyan state.

GRAND HOTEL, TRIPOLI Under Italian rule, many fine modern buildings were constructed in both Tripoli and Bengazi. The Grand Hotel is a pleasant adaptation of Moorish architecture.

THE NEW NATION

Formally, the choice of king was made by a native assembly representing all the provincial factions. The assembly was mainly Arab, but included nominal representation of minority groups. The Libyan House of Representatives consists of 55 seats. Of these, 35 are allotted to Tripolitania, 15 to Cyrenaica, and 5 to Fezzan. Thus has democracy come to a feudal land.

One result of this sudden advent of a people's government was the guarantee of religious freedom to minorities, a condition not much in evidence among other Arab nations. This freedom has not, however, applied to Libya's Jews. Subjected to persecution, most of them immigrated to Israel.

On the other hand, the 45,000 Italians who remained in Libya have adapted themselves to the new political situation, and occupy leading positions in the country's economic life. Much of Libya's trade is with Italy.

THE RISE OF EDUCATION

Before World War II, illiteracy in Libya was the lot of the great majority of the inhabitants. After the war, the British and French administrations established a number of schools.

In 1956, a Libyan University was founded, with the faculties of Arts and Commerce located in Benghazi, and the faculties of Science and Geology located in Tripoli. A Teacher Training College has been set up in Tripoli, along with an arts and crafts school, an agricultural institute, and a technical college. This program has been reinforced by the building of 470 primary schools and 9 secondary schools. There is a continuous effort to bring in many European and Egyptian teachers.

THE LAND AND ITS PRODUCTS

Excluding the desert oases, the only arable land in Libya is a thin coastal strip, nowhere more than 75 miles deep. Here the Italians developed the richest citrus fruit groves of the North African coast. Orange

ROMAN FORUM   On the edge of the Mediterranean, 77 miles east of
Tripoli, stands Leptis Magna, once a flourishing city of ancient Rome. It was
founded around 600 B.C. by Phoenicians and flourished as an important port
under the Romans. The small town near this site is now known as Lebda. The
most extensive Roman ruins in all Africa are found here.

SIDEWALK HAT SOUK Fezes are made to order for summer wear. The open site and the seeming disorder do not prevent effective production. Parts are prepared in advance for final assembly.

and olive trees, grape vines and mulberry trees, were planted by the hundreds of thousands. Though fruit products are plentiful, these crops are not sufficiently valuable resources to bring in the revenue needed for industrial development: roads, irrigation projects, etc.

The staple item of diet is the date, which grows prolifically throughout the oases of the Fezzan. Water, surprisingly abundant in each oasis, is frequently found no more than four feet below the land surface.

The government is concentrating on the coastal area. A project of afforestation of the dunes to prevent sea erosion is being continued. This project will also increase the amount of arable land by providing a windbreak as well as a root system to maintain the level of moisture in the soil.

DISCOVERY OF OIL

Probably the most important thing that happened in the new nation of Libya is the discovery of oil in the Libyan Desert in 1958. About 150 wells have been drilled, and 50 percent of these have struck oil, a success story far better than the world average.

The government expects oil revenue of $10 million in 1962; and hopes that its income from this source will rise to $50 million per annum by 1967. Since Libya is much nearer to Europe than the Middle East is, the cost of the transportation of oil from Libya to Europe is approximately 70¢ less per barrel than it is for oil coming from the Persian Gulf. This gives Libya a great advantage in selling the European market.

Reserves of natural gas have also been discovered. Engineers believe that a pipeline placed along the sea bed of the Mediterranean can move this product from Libya to Europe without insuperable technical difficulties.

Perhaps the main drawback for improved agriculture in Libya—the lack of a reliable water supply in the dry areas—will,in time,be overcome. All that is needed to provide proper irrigation is sufficient capital to handle such projects. Income from oil, it is hoped, will be sufficient to transform the face of the land.

RAIN AND DESERT WIND

The 10-inch average rainfall at the coast decreases toward the desert interior where Tripolitania, an undulating plateau area, meets the abrupt, 2,000-feet-high massifs of the central Sahara.

The climate of Libya, as in most Mediterranean coastal regions, is variable. Further instability results from the occasional breath of the Sahara that alternates with the sea breezes. The dreaded *ghibli*, a violent dust storm,roars out of the desert and lays waste all in its path.

The climatic extremes in the desert areas are appalling. Temperatures range from 120° in the shade in summer to below freezing in winter. These frenetic climatic changes render oil prospecting particularly difficult. Violent dust storms, at times fearsomely persistent, clog up expensive, sensitive instruments, despite every precaution.

DIFFICULTIES OF TRANSPORTATION

Here then, is a truly primitive country facing a modern world. Nominally a unity, Libya is really three widely separated and distinct territories, where camel caravan is still a major means of transportation. Except for those who can afford the occasional air taxi from Tunis through Tripoli to Sebha, capital of Fezzan, the only other means of reaching Sebha is by motor bus across 625 miles of desert. It's that, or camel back.

There is only one railroad between two large cities in Libya, and that is the 100-mile long single track that runs between Tripoli and Benghazi. Across the entire length of the 1,000-mile shoreline, there is but one major automobile highway. The other roads are tracks in the desert. The government is now building a 500-mile highway to link Fezzan with the coast.

DEPENDENCE ON THE WEST

While other countries in the grip of nationalistic fervor were thrusting out their European overlords, Libya fell under the financial control of the Western powers. In 1960, the United States provided Libya with almost $4 million in aid, and Great Britain supplied approximately $9 million.

Libya is being used by the West as a strategically placed military depot. Wheelus Field, a major U.S. air base, is located here.

The major obstacle to this symbiotic relationship is Nasser's dream of an Arab hegemony, a dream which stirs up feelings in Libya of anti-Western color or of neutralism.

SILVERSMITHS IN TRIPOLI   *Silversmiths and brass workers carry on a skilled handcraft in a crowded combination of workroom and sales-shop.*

IN BRIEF

AREA	679,358 square miles. Larger than Spain, France, Italy and Germany combined.
TERRAIN	Libya consists of three provinces, separated by deserts. Tripolitania is a rolling plateau, bordered on the west by Tunisia and Algeria. Its fertile northern coast has great numbers of citrus fruit orchards. Cyrenaica is separated by the Syrte Desert from Tripolitania. It is bordered on the east by Egypt. It has a deeply fissured coast, and no beaches except around Benghazi and Tobruk. Fezzan is mostly desert, except for the oases of the Kufra and the Homra which run east to west. This province borders Algeria on the southwest and Chad on the south. The arable land of Libya runs as deep as 75 miles in from the coast. Between the arable land and the desert lie grazing areas for flocks and herds.

TRIPOLI   *A boulevard along the Meriterranean shore.*

CLIMATE   Variable in Tripolitania, subject to severe shift from sea mildness to desert heat. 10 inches rain on coast decreasing to interior. Temperature 51° in cold months ranging to 83° in warmest months. Sahara wind, the *ghibli,* raises temperature to 110°. Cyrenaica: less rain, strong winds, great temperature variation. In 1921, recorded change in one day from 38° to 113°. Fezzan: dry, extreme heat in day, cold nights, sometimes with frost.

CAPITAL   Tripoli, 186,000 (also capital of district of Tripolitania).

OTHER CITIES   Benghazi, 71,000 (capital of Cyrenaica and seat of king's court); Misurata, 57,000; Sebha, 7,500 (capital of Fezzan).

POPULATION   1,195,000; about 50,000 Europeans. Tripolitania, 815,000; Cyrenaica, 324,000; Fezzan, 56,000.

ETHNIC GROUPS   Arabs, Berbers, in north; Teda, Bornu in south; Tuareg mostly west. Small Greek, Italian, Jewish and Maltese groups.

LANGUAGE   Arabic; Berber dialects. Tongues of other small indigenous groups. Italian.

RELIGION   Predominantly Mohammedan. Also Christians and Jews.

DATE OF INDEPENDENCE   December 24, 1951.

FORM OF GOVERNMENT   Hereditary constitutional monarchy. Governors of provinces appointed by king. Two-chamber federation government: Senate 24 members, half chosen by king, half by each of 3 provincial councils, for 8-year terms; elections every 4 years. House of Representatives, one deputy for each 20,000 people. Each province has executive and legislative council with real executive power. President of the Council is chosen by king and governor. A federation Prime Minister. Member of U.N. and of the Arab League. Judiciary appointed by king.

EDUCATION   In 1960: Tripolitania, 68,923; Cyrenaica, 40,271; Fezzan, 7,077, in elementary and preparatory schools. Tripolitania, 4,205; Cyrenaica, 693; Fezzan, 25, in secondary schools. Also vocational schools. Libya University had 182 students in arts and teaching; 165 in commerce; 78 in sciences; and 279 students studying abroad.

HEALTH FACILITIES	No statistics available.
CURRENCY	Unit is Libyan pound. (£1 = $2.80 U.S.).
INDUSTRY	Light industries, such as sponges; local wool, imported cotton weaving and dyeing, oil wells started with imported pipelines, rigs etc., Home handicrafts. Tobacco processing plants, wool and hides, fishing, olive oil, wine.

CROPS: Date is staple crop; citrus fruits, olives, grapes, figs, mostly for export; barley and millet for domestic use; mulberry trees.

STOCK: Cattle, sheep, goats, camels, donkeys, horses.

FISHING AND HUNTING: Domestic fishing.

MINING: Oil wells are being developed.

TRADE

1959: IMPORTS $113,638,000
      EXPORTS $12,040,000
      DEFICIT $101,598,000
        (Deficit offset by U.S. and Great Britain.)

MAJOR IMPORTS: Manufactured products, cotton.

MAJOR EXPORTS: Hides, cattle, sponges, wine, olive oil, citrus fruits, petroleum, oil.

TRANS-PORTATION

ROADS: A 1,000-mile coastal road; desert roads.

RAILWAYS: One single track, 123 miles long.

WATERWAYS: Harbors at Tripoli and Benghazi. Motor busses run east-west.

AIR TRAFFIC: Tripoli to London, Cairo. Interior, small line to Fezzan.

COMMUNICATIONS: Telegraph; Tripoli to Malta; phone to Tunis; overseas wireless to Europe from Tripoli, Benghazi. In 1958, 8,500 phones; 15,000 wireless sets. Newspapers and magazines in Arabic, Italian and English.

BENGHAZI ARCH   This is the entrance to the old Arab town. The inscription on the arch, evidently inscribed before Libya obtained its independence from Italy, reads:"To the Committee: Our objective is complete independence and a Sunusied Arabian Kingdom."

Diego Suarez

Ambilobe

Vohémar

Ambanja

Sambava

Analalava

Antalaha

Majunga

Moroantsetra

Soala

MALAGASY

Besalampi

REPUBLIC

Maintirano

Tamatave

Miandrivazo

Tananarive

Belo

Morondava

Mahanoro

Antsirabe

Manja

Mananjary

Morombe

Fianarantsoa

Beroroha

Manakara

Tuléar

Farafangana

Bekily

Ampanihy

Fort Dauphin

MALAGASY REPUBLIC

Island with an Asian Past

Malagasy Republic, known as Madagascar before it became independent of France in 1960, lies about 200 miles southeast of Africa. But, paradoxically, in wildlife and historical development, the island seems more closely related to Asia. Many of its problems, however, are like those of the other new African nations.

Even from the standpoint of geology, Malagasy Republic is not a part of the African mainland. In common with nearby islands in the Indian Ocean, it is thought to be part of a large body of submerged land, stretching out toward the Indian subcontinent. Fourth largest island in the world, Malagasy Republic might be described as an immense block of crystalline rocks, rising sharply from the sea along its eastern coast, and tapering gradually down, along the western coast, in a series of plateaus to the sea. Madagascar is almost 1,000 miles long.

After much study, anthropologists are of the opinion that the first settlers were probably far-ranging voyagers from southeast Asia who reached Malagasy's shores before the Christian era. During the course of centuries, many other immigrants came from Africa, the Arab countries, Asia, and Oceana. They ultimately intermingled and created the Malagasy people. The Malagasy language, spoken throughout the island, is an Indonesian dialect.

THE MERINA TRIBE

Also known as the Hova, the Merina tribe is one of several tribes which settled in the fertile central plateau. There they became the largest tribe on the island, and politically, the most important. The island has an ancient tradition of rule by powerful Merina kings.

Though Madagascar became a French protectorate in 1885, the Merina tribe was not completely subjugated until 1904. Under French

PHILIBERT TSIRINANA
The son of a peasant family of the Tsimihety tribe, Tsirinana was born in 1912 and spent a good deal of his youth herding cattle. He won a scholarship to the Ecole Normale, at Montpellier, in France and attained a teaching license there. After teaching in the Tananarive Technical School, he entered politics in 1946. He was elected President of the Republic in 1959. He is a Catholic and has a family of eight children.

rule, the Merina continued to play the role of the leading tribe, providing the island with its best intellectuals and its shrewdest politicians. Later, it was the Merinas who took the lead in the movement for independence.

A GREAT COLONIAL GOVERNOR

During the colonial period of Africa's history, men of varying ability and vision were sent by the European powers to rule the new domains. Some of these men cared little for the countries to which they had been assigned. Others sympathized with the needs of the subjugated African nations, but saw no point in opposing Colonial Office policies. Colonialism was almost invariably oriented toward commercial interests and empire building, rather than toward the peoples' needs. Although some of the colonial administrations were actively cruel and malevolent, a fair number were truly concerned with the interests of the native people.

Between 1896 and 1905, Malagasy Republic was fortunate in having as a governor, General Gallieni, one of the greatest and most far-sighted of colonial administrators. His work stands as a prototype of humane contribution by a colonial power.

Gallieni initiated a program that was to be the basis for a modern

Madagascar voluntarily allied with France. He demanded, and got, French Treasury funds to open the first government-supported schools for Malagasy children and to begin a free medical service for the people. Instead of attempting to supplant the Malagasy language with French, he actively encouraged studies in the native tongue. With paternal care, he selected native administrators to participate in the colonial government. He created the Malagasy Academy, to encourage the study of the island's cultural and natural history. He was ahead of his time in undertaking economic developments. Through his efforts, a railroad was built, rural agricultural stations were set up, and new crops were introduced.

THE DRIVE FOR INDEPENDENCE

After World War I, no colonial policy, however enlightened, could stave off Africa's emerging nationalism and the drive for independence.

After the Second World War, Malagasy Republic experienced the same unrest, borne on the tide of nationalism, that was sweeping through Africa. French calculations about the situation in Malagasy Republic underestimated the swiftness of the movement toward independence and the strength of the underlying passions.

Though Malagasy Republic received a measure of self-government in 1945, France had no intention of granting her the status of an autonomous nation. Malagasy Republic was to remain an overseas territory. Instead of heeding the rising clamor of nationalism, the French intrigued against the people, creating a puppet political party. For a while, the colonial administrators set tribe against tribe, applying the ancient theory of divide and rule.

This policy failed. An explosive revolt, led by the leaders of the Merina tribe, broke out in 1946. The rebellion was cruelly suppressed. The nationalist leaders reported 80,000 Malagasy killed. The French admitted to 11,505 known dead.

Inevitably, new independence parties were formed. Continued relentless pressure finally brought Malagasy Republic freedom on June 26, 1960.

CORN HARVEST *The women participate in harvesting and processing the large crop, a staple of the island.*

THE POLITICAL SITUATION

The most important political force is the Social Democratic Party which holds 75 of the 105 seats in the National Assembly.

Philibert Tsiranana, President and Prime Minister, was a peasant by origin. Educated at the École Normale in Montpelier, France, he became a teacher in the Tananarive Technical School. He entered politics in 1946. In 1956, he founded what is today the dominant political party. It was he who coined the term "French Community." Tsiranana is a Catholic. He is strongly allied to French culture, and is regarded as a staunch liberal.

EDUCATION AND THE FRENCH INFLUENCE

The cultural influence of the French has strongly penetrated the island. Malagasy politicians and intellectuals—many educated in France

—express themselves in perfect French. A few write poetry which finds publication in Parisian literary journals.

However, most of the inhabitants are illiterate; and the large majority are pagan. Only 20 percent are Catholics, and only 14 percent Protestant. Of the 5,000,000 Malagasy, only 70,000 are of French origin. The population includes some Chinese and Indians who, in proportion to their numbers, have an enormous influence in commerce.

But, by and large, the Malagasy are a pastoral people who, as yet, have not been heavily touched by education. The government seeks to remedy this situation. In 1960, a university was founded in the capital city of Tananarive.

THE PROBLEM OF POPULATION GROWTH

Although Malagasy Republic is underpopulated, the nation's birth rate of 3.5 percent is one of the highest in the world. Moreover, 40 percent of the present population is under fifteen years of age, which places a tremendous burden on the educational system and on the various social services.

Obviously, the immediate solution for Malagasy Republic is to expand its economy. To do so, the country must first solve some difficult and serious trade problems.

EXPORTS AND THE BALANCE OF TRADE

Raw coffee is the leading export crop. More than 40,000 tons of coffee were shipped out of Malagasy Republic in 1960—about 40 percent of the country's total overseas sales. France deliberately pays pegged high prices for Malagasy products in order to sustain the Malagasy economy.

Sugar and vanilla are also important exports. There has been an increase, too, in the export of processed products, such as peanuts and tobacco; but larger quantities than ever of these products are being sold in the domestic market. As the standard of living rises, consumer goods are increasingly in demand.

An anomalous situation has developed. As the standard of living goes up, a greater trade deficit results. Exports do not keep pace with

FARM LABORER   In the northernmost regions of the country, large quantities of vanilla and coffee beans are grown. This field hand in Diego Suarez carries his own firewood, two baskets of food, and his cooking utensils.

imports although agricultural output has been rising about 4 percent a year, since 1951. The nation, trying to build an industrial economy, imports capital goods, fuels, and raw materials, but holds consumer goods to one-half of total imports. This is meant to permit a larger proportion of the country's revenue to be devoted to national development.

Malagasy Republic is the world's largest producer of graphite, and France's main source of radioactive minerals.

PHYSICAL CHARACTERISTICS

The rugged terrain, principally mountainous and cleft by deep valleys, retards agriculture. The climate is equally baleful, with extreme variations from cool to torrid. There are serious problems of soil erosion.

220

MANANJARY ROAD SUSPENSION BRIDGE This beautiful
steel and concrete bridge has replaced the rickety, wooden, single-file
foot-bridge which used to be the means of getting across the river at
this point near Mananjary.

THE ZOMA *This famed market in Tananarive is a mart for food, clothes, and many other kinds of merchandise. The pavillion on the lower right sells tobacco. To the left of it, there is a creamery. Merchants, in the open, offer peanuts, pistachios, potatoes, and fruits. The pointed, tiled roofs of the pavillions are characteristic of Madagascan architecture. Some houses, built in the same manner, can be seen in the residential quarter on the hillside. Zoma means Friday in the Malagasy language, and this market was originally held on Fridays. Some of the signs are in English. This is a recent development which has come about since the large influx of English tourists after independence of the Malagasy Republic. The tower on the top of the hill is the Catholic Église St. Joseph.*

Roads and railroads have been difficult to build, and difficult to maintain.

These geographical characteristics have not only impeded agriculture and transportation, but have hampered the development of major harbors. The topography made it advisable to develop a large number of small ports, each serving a limited area, rather than to develop a few large ports. Today, however, the lack of large ports seriously hinders efficient distribution of goods.

PLANS FOR THE FUTURE

The government plans to improve the dockside and harbor facilities of Tamatave, the country's largest port. Two other ports of medium size, Majunga and Diego Suarez, will also be modernized; and these three ports will be the principal centers for international trade.

During the next decade, the government plans heavy emphasis on road construction and the development of light industries that can use local raw materials. Malagasy Republic is attacking its problems with great energy. This became evident on June 26, 1961, the first anniversary of independence, when the government announced a reduction of $7 million in its trade deficit. Unfortunately, the value of exports had remained stationary, since the deficit reduction was achieved solely by cutting down imports. Belt tightening is still necessary.

Attempting to solve Malagasy's serious trade problem by cutting imports is like treating a symptom rather than curing a disease. Only a substantial increase in productivity and in exports will provide a genuine solution to the unfavorable balance of trade.

IN BRIEF

AREA	227,800 square miles; fourth largest island in the world; about the size of Texas.
TERRAIN	Geologically, the island appears to be a large block of crystalline rocks, rising abruptly from the sea along the eastern coast, tapering gradually down a series of plateaus to the sea along the western coast. Mount Mazomokotzo, highest point on the island (9,450 feet), cuts off the northern region from the rest of the island. Narrow strip of the east coast has few anchorages; there is a line of lagoons behind the coral beaches. A canal is under construction to link these lagoons.

MALAGASY TYPES *The Malagasy are not African in origin, being basically of Malayo-Polynesian and Melanesian stock. In appearance, customs, and language, they resemble the people of the Indian and Pacific archipelagos.*

ANTAKARANA

BÉTSILÉO

SAKALAVA

HOVA

SAKALAVA

SAKALAVA

BETSIMISARAKA

CLIMATE   The east coast is hot and wet; west coast is hot and dry. The southwest is semi-desert; higher points in the north have moderate temperatures.

CAPITAL   Tananarive (population: 248,000).

POPULATION   5,298,000; about 70,000 Europeans.

ETHNIC GROUPS   Fifteen to twenty different tribes. Major groups are the Merina (or Hova), the largest tribe; others are Betsimisaraka, Bétsiléo, Sakalava, Antaisaka, Antandroy, Bara, and Tanala.

LANGUAGE   Official languages are French and Malagasy.

RELIGION   Mainly Asiatic in origin, involving belief in the soul's immortality, a supreme being, and lesser divinities. Ancestor worship is universally practiced. There are about 1,000,000 Catholics and 1,000,000 Protestants.

DATE OF INDEPENDENCE June 26, 1960.

FORM OF GOVERNMENT Parliamentary democracy with a President and a Parliament of two houses. The National Assembly is popularly elected; two-thirds of the Senate are elected by provinces and local territorial units, the remaining third is appointed by the government. High Council of Institutions is responsible for the constitutionality of laws. Member of French Community and the United Nations.

EDUCATION   47.8 percent of all school-age children attended primary school in 1958. In 1959, 371,197 children were enrolled in 2,470 primary schools, and 18,083 in 196 secondary schools. University of Tananarive is being organized with schools of law, science, and liberal arts already open.

HEALTH FACILITIES Two large hospitals in Tananarive, plus five smaller hospitals in the provincial capitals; 150 medical centers; 238 infirmaries, one sanatorium in Fensarive, one psychiatric hospital, one physical therapy center for polio victims, and one children's hospital.

CURRENCY   Unit is the French Community franc (247 francs = U. S. $1.00).

INDUSTRY

Only light industry for processing agricultural products.

CROPS: Rice, the largest crop, is exported, and is also the staple food of the people. Cassava is the other main food crop. Also grown for home consumption are sweet potatoes, corn, beans, potatoes, peanuts, mangoes, papaya, lichees, pineapple, guava, apples, apricots, plums, and peaches. Main cash crop is coffee; others are vanilla (producing two-thirds of world supply), tobacco, cloves, sisal, and sugar.

STOCK: Cattle (native breed is the zebu), hogs, sheep, and goats.

FISHING: Sardine, tuna, fresh-water fish for domestic consumption; these and other dried fish for export.

MINING: Graphite, mica, quartz are the important exports. Industrial beryls, columbite, phosphates, and precious stones are also mined.

TRADE

1958:	IMPORTS	$107,543,000
	EXPORTS	81,796,000
	DEFICIT	$ 25,747,000

MAJOR IMPORTS: Foodstuffs, tobacco, textiles, fuel, raw materials, semifinished goods, and capital goods.

MAJOR EXPORTS: Dried vegetables and agricultural products (*see* Crops).

TRANS-PORTATION

ROADS: 1,100 miles surfaced. 4,000 miles unsurfaced all-weather.

VEHICLES: 15,553 passenger cars. 17,288 commercial vehicles.

WATERWAYS: Two major ports, many other smaller ones; inland water traffic along 400 miles of the Pangalanes Canal; 1,550 miles of navigable rivers, mainly in the northwest.

RAILROADS: Four lines, 532 miles of track.

AIR TRAFFIC: One international airport; three major fields and 100 other airfields.

COMMUNI-CATIONS

Seven radio stations (four short wave) and 50,000 radios. Major cities have postal services, telephone, and telegraph.

Newspapers and magazines in French and local languages.

Taoudenni

Tessalit

Mabrouk

Etelia

M A L I

Goundam

NIGER R.

Gao

Noiro

Nara

Mopti

Ségou

Bamako

MALI

Laboratory for African Irrigation

Mali is a country of close to one-half million square miles—considerably larger than Texas and Oklahoma combined.

Its population of over 4,000,000 is mostly illiterate: less than one person out of twenty knows how to read and write. In 1958, only 8 percent of the children of school age were enrolled in schools. There were only 277 primary schools in the entire country, and only 10 institutions even roughly comparable to an American high school. There is no college in Mali.

The greater part of the population are Moslems, though there are a substantial number of animists, and a sprinkling of Christians.

THE CITY OF BAMAKO

Despite the backwardness of the hinterland, in Bamako, the capital city, one can find all the appurtenances of a Western city. Located on the banks of the Niger River, Bamako has a population that is over 100,000.

The streets are charming and the living comfortable. With its gracious tree-lined avenues, fine public buildings, and lush gardens, this city, built in the heart of the desert, is somewhat startling, and stands as a monument to man's indominatable will.

The Ifan Museum contains a rather full exhibit of artifacts and art objects which tell of the long cultural history of this fascinating region. The city is graced with a well-designed zoo. The Ophthalmology Institute carries on research for eye disease; the Marchoux Institute of Leprosy does valiant work.

Bamako is noted for its tailoring. Scores of shops, each open to rain, sun, and air, each with its sewing machine, cater to anyone who wants a suit or a dress to be cut from the many materials on sale in the markets.

GOING TO MARKET Natives carry fruits and wares in baskets made of a golden grass to the market at Mopti. They are passing the **ancient** mosque built of beaten earth reinforced by wooden spikes. There are three mosques of this type in Tumbuktu. From the tall gates facing east, the Imam calls the faithful to prayer several times a day.

SOURAI GIRL She wears the wide metal bracelet and the headdress characteristic of her tribe. Her necklace, made of little pearls, sets her apart as a person of means.

NEUTRALISM AND MARXIST LEADERS

The country is considered to be one of the most left-oriented in Africa; its leaders have always been somewhat radical; and today, its neutralist, and perhaps pro-Communist position, is well recognized.

Modibo Keita was graduated from the Normal School of Dakar in 1936. In 1952, he was elected as a deputy to the French National Assembly in Paris. In 1958, he was appointed as an assistant minister in the Gaillard cabinet. On September 22, 1960, the day that Mali became independent, Keita was chosen President.

As early as March, 1961, Keita signed an economic and technical aid pact with the U.S.S.R.

In September, 1961, at the Belgrade Conference of Non-Committed Nations, Keita emerged as a leading spokesman for the neutralist posi-

MARKET IN TIMBUKTU   While waiting for customers, one vendor is spinning wool thread. The large, chipped vessel contains peanuts.

tion. Later that month, he headed a mission to Communist China.

In February, 1962, France approved a technical aid pact with Mali; but in May, Keita, speaking in Moscow, reiterated that Mali, unconditionally choosing socialism, would continue to follow a policy of nonalignment. By September, 1962, the U.S.S.R. Communist Party had established such close ties with the dominant Sudanese Union Party, that two Soviet delegates attended the party congress in Mali.

Keita's similarity to other leaders of the new African states is not confined to his endorsement of neutralism. He has been described as a man "whose agreeable manner sometimes conceals his driving ambition and his authoritarian leaning." Authoritarianism is characteristic of many of the new African leaders. Despite his Marxist orientation, Keita claims to scorn Communism. The Marxist orientation of African leaders is, at least in part, rooted in the pressing economic problems that face these underdeveloped nations. The absence of adequate private capital makes it impossible to achieve the necessary economic growth without extensive government participation in industrial expansion.

To many of the leaders and people of the new nations in Africa, the Marxist idea of government ownership of all capital enterprises seems to offer a simple and organized solution to the complex problem of setting up a money economy. These people are not deterred by fear that such a solution may lead to dictatorship. They have lived for centuries under authoritarian rule and are used to being told what to do. The authoritarianism of the past kept them in poverty. They hope that

WASHING These women of Bamako are washing clothes on the banks of the Niger, near the city's modern bridge which was completed in 1960.

TUAREG TRIBESMAN For ages past, the Tuaregs, known as "people of the veil," have been nomads roaming the sandy plains of the Niger Bend. Now many are settling in cities such as Gao and Timbuktu. This rider wears the loose robes of the desert and the white veil of the vassal class.

their own self-imposed authoritarianism, which at least promises a better life, will bring some amelioration of their lot.

THE NEW NATION'S PROBLEMS

The northern and central parts of Mali are largely desert. Since ancient times, these areas have been inhabited by Arab peoples. The southern part of Mali is inhabited by Negroid tribes. The cultural chasm between these two groups has led to great animosity.

GRINDING CORN   *Sourai women use wooden mortars to grind cereals.*

Most of the population is engaged in agriculture and livestock raising, both predominantly on a bare subsistence level.

Mali's exports amount to only $11 million annually, of which peanuts and peanut products account for 90 percent. The country is, however, largely self-sufficient in foodstuffs, with millet and rice being the most important food grains for domestic use. Mali lacks important mineral wealth. There may be some large manganese deposits, but these are as yet undeveloped.

WELL NEAR BAMAKO Malinke women gather near a well to wash children, clothes, and utensils. Their houses are made of uncooked bricks covered with earth. Rain and wind gradually wash away the surface mud, exposing the bricks.

THE OFFICE DU NIGER DEVELOPMENT

In view of the country's relative poverty, it is significant that a large development project called *Office du Niger* was launched. This hydro-electric and irrigation plan for the Niger River is Africa's potential TVA.

The plan was conceived as far back as 1920. In 1932, a part of the over-all plan was begun, which involved the irrigation of 4,000 square miles of rice and cotton land, to be tended by nearly one million people. However, the plan did not swing into large-scale operation until 1948,

when the Sansanding Dam on the Niger River was completed. By 1958, about $100 million had been expended on the project, but only 35,000 people had settled on the irrigated land, and only 100,000 acres had been put under cultivation. The prospects, however, are very bright.

The land involved in this project is located in the rich central delta of the Niger, extending from Ségou downstream almost to Timbuktu. Most of the area can be well irrigated by the gravity flow of the impounded waters. The agricultural outlook is greatly improved; and ultimately, the project may benefit an area as large as 30,000 square miles.

Africans who wish to settle in the project area receive a rent-free house, livestock and tools, seed and fertilizer, a supply of food to tide them over until the first harvest, and ten acres or more of irrigated land. The standard *Office du Niger* contract provides for a ten-year period of adaptation. At the end of that time, a successful farmer is granted a "lease of permanent establishment." In other words, he has proved his homestead; and the land becomes his, just as in the days of the American frontier.

In recent years, the total value of crops grown by the settlers has averaged $250 per person. Some households have had a gross income of over $2,000, and profits of $750, annually.

The *Office du Niger* project has hit a number of snags in the past few years, and has not yet attained its full potential. Nevertheless, it is important not only for the economy of Mali and the welfare of its people,

MODIBO KEITA   *Born in 1915 into a leading Mohammedan family, this son of the Bambara tribe studied in Dakar, and then became a teacher in his own country. At one time, he was a member of a French Cabinet. He was elected President when the country became independent in 1960.*

TUAREG WARRIOR His black veil sets him apart as a noble. The charms which hang from the bracelet of braided leather made by the Tuareg women usually hold a script of Koranic text. The women wear similar bracelets embellished with pearls, but do not wear veils.

BLIND DRUMMER This man of the animist Dogon tribe performs at religious dances.

but because it is one of the finest examples in Africa of the harnessing of rivers to improve agriculture. Projects similar to the *Office du Niger* are likely to develop throughout Africa in the near future.

IN BRIEF

AREA	464,874 square miles, about the size of Texas, New Mexico, and Oklahoma combined.
TERRAIN	Mostly flat or undulating low plateau, broken occasionally by rocky hills, particularly around Bandiagara near the southeastern border. Much of the Niger River lies in Mali, and the river valley is heavily populated. Northward, the land becomes progressively drier; roughly one-third of the country lies within the Sahara Desert.
CLIMATE	Southern part gets about 40 inches of rainfall annually, mostly from June through September; it is adequate for agriculture. In the northern areas, there is a virtual absence of rain.
CAPITAL	Bamako (population, 100,000).
POPULATION	4,100,000; about 8,000 non-African.
ETHNIC GROUPS	Among the sedentary cultivators are the Bambara (1,000,-000); next largest tribes are the Sarakole (about 250,000); the Songhai (about 250,000); and the Malinke (about 225,-000), a people closely related to the Bambara. Among the nomadic pastoralists (Saharan regions) are the non-Negro, warlike Tuareg and the Peul or Fulani.
LANGUAGE	French is official language. Many ethnic languages.
RELIGION	Most of the population is Moslem or heavily influenced by Islamic religion and culture, except for the predominantly animist Bambara, who have long resisted Islamic influences.
DATE OF INDEPENDENCE	September 22, 1960.
FORM OF GOVERNMENT	Republic, with popularly elected Assembly and Prime Minister. One party, Union Soudanaise, holds all seats in Assem-

bly, and also controls press, labor unions, youth organizations, and most other aspects of public life. United Nations member.

EDUCATION

In 1958, 8 percent of school-age children were enrolled: 42,052 in 277 primary schools and 1,790 in 10 secondary schools. No universities.

HEALTH FACILITIES

In 1958, a 400-bed hospital was opened in Bamako. There are 700 dispensaries in the country.

CURRENCY

French Community franc (247 francs = U.S. $1.00).

INDUSTRY

Limited to a few small industrial plants, mostly in Bamako.

CROPS: Peanuts, millet, cotton, sisal, tobacco, rice, corn.

STOCK: Cattle, sheep, goats and camels.

FISHING: Large-scale on Niger River.

MINING: No important mineral wealth. Though manganese deposits have been found, there are no plans now for production.

TRADE

1960: EXPORTS $11,000,000
IMPORTS   Figures not available

MAJOR EXPORTS: Peanuts. Peanut products account for 90 percent volume. Considerable dried fish.

MAJOR IMPORTS: Sugar, salt, canned goods, flour, electrical appliances, hardware, textile, and industrial equipment.

TRANS-PORTATION

ROADS: 1,761 miles federal highways.

VEHICLES: 1,570 passenger cars; 3,600 commercial vehicles (1956).

WATERWAYS: Sections of Niger River are navigable for small barges part of year.

RAILROADS: Branch spur of Dakar Railroad runs from border of Senegal to Bamako.

AIR TRAFFIC: Airports at Bamako, Mopti, Ségou, Keta, and Timbuktu.

COMMUNI-CATIONS

Seven publications appear in Bamako; various Moslem periodicals are issued throughout the country.

Fort Gouraud

Port Etienne

Atar

Akjoujt

MAURITANIA

Nouakchott

Tichitt

Rosso

Kiffa

Néma

SENEGAL R.

Kaédi

MAURITANIA

Mining Projects in a Primitive Country

Mauritania reflects the movement of Islamic peoples from the Middle East across the northern coast of Africa, and thence down through the Sahara into tropical West Africa. The Moors are the main ethnic group in Mauritania, accounting for about 75 percent of the country's 655,000 population. About 99 percent of the population is Mohammedan. For centuries, Mauritania has been known as a center of Koranic scholarship. The Islamic Institute at Boutilimit is famed throughout the Moslem world.

Before the arrival of the Europeans in the fifteenth century, the history of Mauritania was dominated by Arab and Berber invasions. Negro Africans, living in the path of the invaders, were pushed south. These Moslem invasions imposed the Islamic religion on those peoples of tropical Africa whose borders were close to, or within, the Sahara Desert. Today, Islam is the state religion of Mauritania, but freedom of worship is constitutionally guaranteed and protected.

A POOR COUNTRY

Much of Mauritania is desert, and its nomadic Arab and Berber tribesmen are largely engaged in animal husbandry. Tribal movements north and south are determined by the growth of grass after rains in the various areas. The nomads camp in tents amid their flocks, and live on a simple diet of milk, millet, and dates. They are a handsome and hardy people who have learned through centuries of experience to survive under the rigorous conditions imposed by the desert.

Here are a few facts about the country:

• There are no paved roads and no railroads. Most of the roads are simply desert paths.

• There was until recently no radio station; administrative contact for government activities was maintained through radio-telephone.

• In 1955, only two towns, Rosso and Port Étienne, had electricity.

• In 1957, there were no hospitals in Mauritania. In 1954, there were exactly seven European doctors in the country — six in the Public Health Service and one with a private company. There were no African doctors, and no dentists or pharmacists, either European or African.

• In 1957, there was only one secondary school in Mauritania.

• Until very recently, there were no libraries, no museums, no newspapers, no magazines.

EGGEEW PLAYING TIDINEET   This professional entertainer's instrument, played by men only, is a leather-covered gourd called a tidineet. Probably from Timbadgha, his musical talents will make him welcome in every section of the nation. He wears the national garb; the turban is traditionally Mauritanian. A male musician, an eggeew, is usually accompanied by a woman who plays the ardeen.

PLAYING THE ARDEEN   The single-stringed ardeen, made of leather stretched over a gourd or over carved wood, is played only by women. The musician may pluck the string or use a bow. In both styles of play, the woman at the same time beats out a rhythm on the instrument. Generally, the ardeen player works with a male musician who plays a tidineet.

CAMEL HERDSMAN   Nomads are the chief camel raisers, particularly in the extreme north and extreme south. Camels are a vital aspect of Mauritania's economy. Hundreds of thousands are sold to neighboring nations. Camel hair is woven into soft material for fine wearing apparel, and also woven into coarse cloth for the nomads' tents. Ropes are also produced from camel hair. To the nomads, the camel is more than a beast of burden. It provides milk, butter, cheese, meat, and leather.

• There is only a handful of Mauritanians who have had a college education.

Mauritania, in short, has been one of the poorest and least developed countries of Africa. It has no potential water power. The country is dry; there are no rivers which can supply hydro-electric power or irrigation. The Senegal River, at the southern boundary of the country, is not suitable for either of these needs.

246

ENERGETIC LEADERSHIP

Despite these problems, the leaders of Mauritania, recognizing the potential of the country's abundant mineral wealth, are enthusiastic and energetic.

President Moktar Ould Daddah, a young man of 38, who is married to a French Catholic, was educated in Dakar and Paris. An ardent Moslem, his ambition is to make Mauritania a link between Arab Africa and Negro Africa.

NOMAD MOORS IN PORT ÉTIENNE   They have purchased supplies at the market and wait for the train to return home. The MIFERMA Railway runs over 419 miles of track between Port Étienne and Fort-Gouraud.

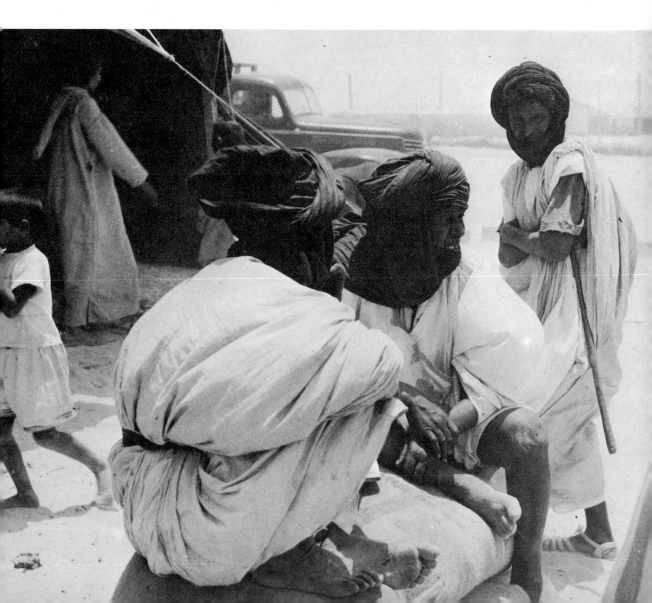

The Mauritanians have built an entirely new capital city. In colonial times, for reasons of local administrative convenience, the capital of Mauritania was Saint Louis in Senegal. The new city, Nouakchott, along the coast, near the country's agricultural and mining regions, is about half completed. It already has a busy college, a radio station, and an airport.

The coast of Mauritania offers few potential port facilities. Port Étienne is located at the one spot along the coast at which ocean-going vessels can lie close to shore.

IRON AND COPPER

Port Étienne is located 125 miles from Akoujit where great copper deposits have been discovered. The city is about 250 miles distant from the Kaedi d'Idjill Mountains, literally "mountains of iron," known to contain 11 million exploitable tons of high-grade iron. Extensive reserves are unestimated. These great iron deposits near Fort Gouraud are of the same quality as high-grade Swedish ores, yielding the remarkable average of 63 percent iron.

CLINIC   *In the new scheme of things, patients, many of whom have never in their lives seen or visited a doctor, are given modern medical treatment.*

CONSTRUCTION AT NOUAKCHOTT   *In the new capital, large
building projects, to accommodate the rapidly increasing population, are
speeded with day and night shifts. In 1957, Nouakchott's population was
300; today 8,000 people reside in the town. Cement is imported, but the
cement blocks are made in Mauritania. Much of the construction will
house public officials and civil servants. In addition to its governmental
functions, the city is a potential seaport.*

NOMAD CAMP   *Here a camp of black tents is pitched outside of
Nouakchott. A few years ago, there was only a collection of mud huts
here. These Moors live mainly on milk, millet, and dates; and go with
their flocks to any area where there may be a sudden growth of grass
after rains.*

In 1960, when its prospecting activities uncovered the richness of the ore deposits, a corporation called MIFERMA (*Societé des Mines de Fer de Mauritanie*) secured a loan of $66 million from the International Bank for exploitation of the mines. A mining town is rising at Fort Gouraud; and a railroad, to connect that town with the seaport of Port Etienne, is being built. When the railway is completed, there will be 2 million tons of iron ore ready to be transported. By 1966, MIFERMA expects to be exporting some 4 million tons annually.

A corporation called MICUMA (*Societé des Mines de Cuivre de Mauritanie*) plans to exploit the copper mines; but the work is proceeding slowly. Copper reserves are estimated as high as 500,000 tons, but the true figure may be less than half this estimate. Copper is very important to France, whose balance of trade has been adversely affected because of her need to import copper from areas outside the French Community.

Other good news may be in the offing. It seems likely that there is petroleum in the sedimentary basin of the Senegal River. Three companies are busy exploring. Within a few years, Mauritania will know the answer.

MOKTAR OULD DADDAH   The President of Mauritania was born in 1924. He studied at the Sorbonne, qualified as a lawyer, and also obtained a diploma from the School of Oriental Languages. Definitely a progressive, he is trying hard to overcome the strongly-embedded conservative traditions of his country. Though he is a devout Moslem, he is married to a French Catholic.

BOUTILIMIT   One of the older towns in Mauritania, Boutilimit
has produced many of that country's prominent men, including the President, Moktar Ould Daddah. These are government buildings at the edge
of town.

NATURAL RESOURCES POLICY

During the era of African colonialism, it was customary for European firms to enter African colonies, exploit the agricultural and mineral
resources, and keep the profits. Colonial governments served to enforce
the rights of such commercial interests. The era of exploitation for the
exclusive benefit of private companies has passed, but most of the new
nations of Africa do not yet possess the capital or the technical know-how
to exploit these resources by themselves.

Mauritania's arrangements with MIFERMA and MICUMA for
developing the iron and copper deposits are a fairly good solution to this
problem. These companies are supplying the administrative organization, the technicians, and the capital—supplemented by loans from
such agencies as the International Bank. They also agree to undertake
certain improvements, such as the development of railroads and electrical
power, to get the mines in operation. In exchange, the government of
Mauritania has granted them a license to conduct the mining activities.
All profits of the operation are shared equally between the companies and
the government. Arrangements similar to this are being worked out by a
number of the African nations that have important mineral resources
they wish to develop.

With this remarkable mineral wealth, Mauritania will soon have at its disposal the means to rise swiftly from its poverty. The wise use of the substantial funds that the government will receive from the mining operations will be one of the major challenges facing Mauritania in the next few years.

POLITICAL ORIENTATION

Mauritania became a French colony in 1904, and became an independent state in 1960. But neighboring Morocco has refused to accept the independence of Mauritania, claiming that the country is really a part of Morocco. Morocco makes no secret of the fact that its wish to annex Mauritania is motivated by the newly discovered mineral wealth of its southern neighbor.

Mauritania maintains a customs union with neighboring Senegal.

Mauritania is the recipient of considerable financial and technical aid from France, and is a member of the French Community. France maintains military bases in Mauritania, and the French Army exercises considerable influence in the country.

Mauritania cannot, at present, meet its budget. The deficit is supplied by France.

IN BRIEF

AREA   419,230 square miles, about the size of Texas and California combined.

TERRAIN   Almost all low-lying desert. Valley along the Senegal River, with cultivated farmland, marks the southern boundary.

MOORISH VILLAGE   This group of shanties, outside of Nouakchott, is a typical Moorish settlement. The Moors often shave the heads of their children, leaving only a clump of hair in the front of the head. Some of these people will leave two clumps on the shaved head—one on the front of the scalp, and one on the back.

Higher plateau regions form a crescent dividing the flat eastern and western sections of the desert. Coastline has only one navigable harbor, Port Étienne.

CLIMATE Hot, dry desert climate; along the Senegal River and coastline only slight temperature variations occur from night to day. Southern section has greater rainfall.

CAPITAL Nouakchott (population, 8,000; city still under construction).

POPULATION 656,000; about 2,000 Europeans.

ETHNIC GROUPS Mainly Moors. Toutcouleurs, Peuls, and Bambara are Negroes.

LANGUAGE French is official language, but Arabic is widely spoken.

RELIGION 99 percent profess Islam, the state religion.

DATE OF INDEPENDENCE November 28, 1960.

FORM OF GOVERNMENT Parliamentary democracy patterned on France. National Assembly composed of 40 directly elected members. Premier, elected by National Assembly, has executive power, and chooses his Council of Ministers. An independent judiciary. Member of French Community. U.N. membership vetoed by U.S.S.R., 1960.

EDUCATION Nomadic life results in irregular schooling. In 1957 about 7 percent of school-age children were enrolled: 6,493 in primary schools and 291 in secondary schools; of this number only 5 to 8 percent were girls. Government now experimenting with nomad schools traveling with the tribes.

HEALTH FACILITIES 3 hospitals, 7 maternity centers, 13 medical centers, 30 dispensaries, and numerous mobile health units and teams.

CURRENCY French Community franc (247 francs = U.S. $1.00).

INDUSTRY No heavy industry; fish-processing and ore-washing plants.

CROPS: Gum arabic is exported; corn, millet, dates, beans, peanuts, and sweet potatoes are grown for domestic consumption.

STOCK: Cattle, sheep, goats, and camels are raised for food and/or export.

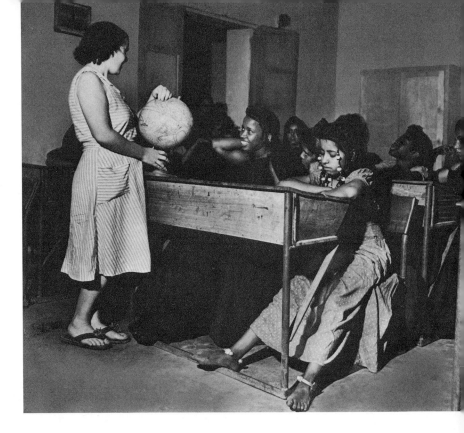

NEW STYLE SCHOOLROOM This desert school for children of nomadic tribes measures the advance in education since Mauritania became independent. Better school buildings have been constructed in the desert; more teachers are being trained.

FISHING: Coast has one of the largest concentrations of fish in the world.

MINING: Iron and copper ore plentiful.

TRADE Most imports are brought in overland by small traders.

TRANS-PORTATION

ROADS: No surfaced roads. Trans-Mauritania Highway, 850 miles of all-weather road; all others desert trails.

VEHICLES: 992 registered vehicles, of which 85 are privately owned (1957); 17 service stations.

RAILROADS: 419 miles

AIR TRAFFIC: 17 airfields, with most traffic at Atar and Port Étienne.

WATERWAYS: Senegal River is only navigable waterway.

COMMUNI-CATIONS No radio station except a local station in the new capital (Nouakchott); 25 post offices, 15 with telephone service.

Tangier

Rabat
Casablanca

Fez
Meknès

MOROCCO

Marrakech

Agadir

IFNI

MOROCCO

Ancient Kingdom of Berbers and Arabs

Persons familiar with Africa often speak of "Africa, South of the Sahara", and distinguish the area from "Africa, North of the Sahara." This reflects the fact that the two areas are profoundly different. Morocco illustrates many of the features that differentiate the nations of North Africa from their neighbors in the tropical zone.

CENTURIES OF EUROPEAN CONTACTS

To begin with, the northern coast of Africa has been in touch with European civilization since antiquity, and the cities of North Africa have suffered successive invasions that brought with them elements of European and Middle Eastern culture. Morocco was invaded by the Phoenicians in the eighth century B.C.; and later, by the Romans, the Vandals, the Byzantine Greeks, and the Arabs. Existing records testify to some of these invasions. By contrast, "Africa, South of the Sahara," has had little contact with European civilization. Particularly, very little is known of the pre-colonial history of large areas of tropical Africa, because few historical records exist.

Africa, north of the Sahara, has had a very long experience with dynastic government, and with governmental adminstration on the pattern of Europe and the Middle East. By contrast, in tropical Africa, the tribe long remained the principal political unit. As early as the eighth century A.D., an empire was established in Morocco. During the Middle Ages, some of the sovereigns who ruled Morocco were of sufficiently high culture to become patrons of the arts. The effective continuity of rule may be judged from the fact that King Hassan II who ascended the Moroccan throne in 1961, upon the death of King Mohammed V, claims direct descent from the founder of the Alaouite dynasty which began its rule in 1649.

Because of the long, ingrained tradition of unquestioned allegiance to the throne, the present King is able to rule with an absolutism somewhat out of keeping with this century. At the close of 1962, Hassan II granted the nation a new constitution, which provided for a Legislative Assembly. The joker is that the King can veto any law.

POLICY OF NEUTRALISM

As a result of its long history of foreign invasion, Morocco has developed a relatively high level of sophistication, as well as an attitude of suspicion and hostility toward outside forces. These effects have contributed toward Morocco's leadership in the North African policy of neutralism in the Cold War.

After the Second World War, the colonial administrators of North Africa, though often enlightened, failed to keep pace with rising nationalistic aspirations. This lack of vision on the part of the European overlords is responsible, in great part, for the emergence of Africa's present-day neutralism.

COLONIAL RULE

France invaded and occupied northern Morocco in 1860. Spain was also involved in the colonization of the area, and the two countries divided Morocco. Spain received a zone of influence along the Mediterranean coast north of the French Protectorate, along with control of a small southern enclave called Ifni. In 1923, the region around Tangier, just across the Straits of Gibraltar, was established as an international zone for the trading convenience of European nations. None of this foreign activity and intervention was acceptable to the Moroccans. Combined French and Spanish forces were obliged to fight for almost five years during the 1920's to win the Rif War. Temporarily, Morocco's bid for independence, under the Rif leader, Abd-el-Krim, was halted.

Despite this history of opposition to invaders, when United States forces landed on the Moroccan coast in November, 1942, large detachments of Moroccan troops promptly joined the Allied cause. At the end of World War II, the nationalists of Morocco called for immediate independence, citing, among other things, Morocco's wholehearted commitment to the Allies.

DRIVE FOR INDEPENDENCE

The independence movement and the Independence Party were supported by the Sultan (later King Mohammed V). The French resisted the drive for independence; and, in 1953, the French exiled the Sultan to Madagascar (now Malagasy Republic).

However, the Sultan was a strong personality and his subjects were very much attached to him. They refused to accept a French-

STREET IN CHAOUEN   *This holy city, at the foot of Mount Mezjal, is famous for its gushing springs. Vendor and buyer at the outdoor stalls wear the flowing garments that accord so well with the age-old cobblestone streets.*

COTTON RESEARCH STATION *Irrigation has opened many areas to cotton growing on the Bani Amir plain. Researchers at Tadla study cotton genetics, seek to improve the soil, and to find weapons against the enemies of cotton.*

backed puppet, and demanded that the Sultan be returned.

Riots, terrorist bombings, and assassinations followed. France accepted the inevitable. The Sultan was returned to Morocco; and on March 2, 1956, Morocco was granted independence. Except for the cities of Ceuta and Melilla, and some small islands administered directly by Spain, all of Spanish Morocco along the northern coast of the Mediterranean, and what was then the international zone of Tangier, were incorporated into the new nation.

UNITED STATES RELATIONS WITH MOROCCO

In 1950, the United States and France signed an agreement that called for the United States to build and operate four air bases in Morocco as part of the defenses of the North Atlantic Treaty Organization. These bases at once became an important factor in the economy of

Morocco. Their construction brought in over $100 million to the country. Annual maintenance expenditures amounted to about $20 million. United States military and civilian personnel spent an additional $20 million annually. Nevertheless, the bases served as a focus of Moroccan hostility toward the Western Bloc, since their presence involuntarily aligned Morocco with the West in the Cold War.

When Morocco became independent, the government was under great pressure to get the Americans out. In 1959, President Eisenhower and King Mohammed issued a joint communiqué announcing that the bases would be evacuated by the end of 1963. The United States simultaneously undertook to close the "Voice of America" radio relay station in Tangier.

Throughout the 1950's, the United States grants of aid to Morocco amounted to about one-half the total of all American aid to Africa. For the fiscal year ending June 30, 1960, United States aid to Morocco

MODERN HORTICULTURAL SCHOOL   Training in agriculture is part of the curriculum in secondary schools. Six regional schools—like this one at Meknes—offer instruction to prospective farmers.

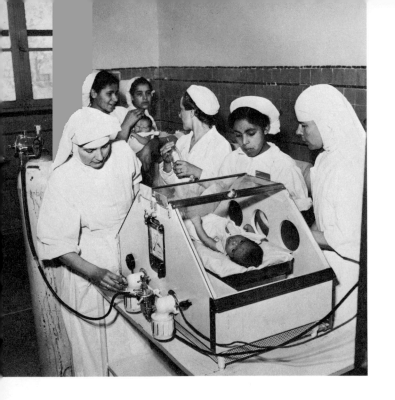

NURSERY TRAINING
French nuns in Fez—the traditional nurses in French African colonies—instruct young Moroccan trainees in the hygienic care of the newborn, including use of a modern electric incubator.

CLASS IN MECHANICS
Local cooperatives furnish individual farmers with agricultural supplies and equipment in a drive to multiply food production. This project is called "Operation Plough." Young men at Agadir eagerly learn the make-up of a modern farm machine.

amounted to $73 million. This included military aid, technical assistance, capital investment in large-scale irrigation, and the development of hydro-electric power in the eastern part of the country.

Though economic aid was welcomed, military aid was accepted with mixed feelings and provoked bitterness in left-wing quarters. Leaders of the National Popular Forces, the party in opposition to the leading Istiglal Party (Independence Party), openly expressed apprehension that there might be political strings attached to military aid from the United States. They feared that the acceptance of such aid would endanger Morocco's policy of neutralism.

THE ECONOMIC SITUATION

Despite the huge grants by the United States, the Moroccan economy has faltered and the country is burdened by financial problems.

In 1956, the per capita income was about $320. Though this is well above the level of many of the new nations of Africa, this low per capita income is insufficient to make Morocco economically independent.

There have been several causes of economic instability. In 1956, when Morocco became independent, strained relations with the former colonial ruler resulted in the wholesale exodus of French capital and French technicians. In 1960, a severe drought drastically reduced the export of wheat. To repair the resulting deficit in the balance of trade, Morocco was forced to suspend imports of all oil products from the French Community. In addition, the Moroccan economy is vulnerable to shifts in world market conditions.

Morocco, in common with most African nations, really has two economies—a traditional economy that depends heavily on subsistence farming and barter, and a modern economy based more directly on money. The contrast between the two is interesting. The "money economy"—including modern agriculture, fishing, mining, manufacturing, industry, and related service industries—accounts for more than two-thirds of the domestic products, although it employs only about 30 percent of the working population. Seventy percent of the workers, therefore, account for only one-third of the gross yield. A rapid growth of this money economy is essential to Moroccan development.

More than 80 percent of the people derive their living, directly or indirectly, from the soil. Principal crops include grains, citrus fruits, and wine grapes.

Phosphates are profitably exported. Significant quantities of cobalt, manganese, iron, lead, and zinc are also found in the country. Studies are now being made of potential petroleum deposits.

THE EUROPEAN AND JEWISH MINORITIES

Many European settlers left Morocco after independence was proclaimed. As for those who remained, there has been no strong heritage of bitterness to mar their relations with the Moroccans. The government, well aware that the country has a great need of technicians, has striven

GIRLS' SCHOOL AT SALE   Embroidery is taught in a high-ceilinged room whose tiled walls and tiled arches testify to the enduring Moslem tradition that forbids representation of living beings. The embroidery designs are geometrical for the same reason.

CASABLANCA   The Avenue of the Royal Armed Forces, the main artery of the city, is flanked by soaring blocks of buildings built in the latest architectural styles. Casablanca, as large as Paris in area, with a fine location on the banks of the Mediterranean, has almost a million inhabitants.

MOSAIC WORKER IN TETUAN   At the School of Popular Arts,
a craftsman patiently labors on a mosaic, a traditional craft of Moslem
Moroccans.

to curb anti-foreign agitation and the consequent Jewish flight.

Jews have been in Morocco for centuries; before independence, that community numbered upwards of 250,000. The Jews were far more Westernized than the Moslem population. They had been discriminated against by the old regime; but Sultan Mohammed acted as their benevolent despot and refused, under strong Nazi pressure and even under the pressure of the Vichy government, to pass anti-Jewish legislation. Nevertheless, after independence, the atmosphere became precarious, and vast numbers of Jews left for Israel, despite the fact that such organized emigration was prohibited by law.

Many Jews are skilled artisans and experienced traders; many have acquired a technical education. The government, quite aware that the Jews constitute a desirable and needed economic element, is endeavoring to induce them to remain.

But Morocco's membership in the Arab League and its ties to openly anti-Semitic Cairo have left the Jewish population with grave misgivings. With a strong residue of religious hatred still existent, and with hostility towards an economically more secure minority as a dynamic force, the Jews are jittery. If they organize formally for self-protection, they lay themselves open to the charge of separatism and of being labeled "Zionists," a hate-charged term of great opprobrium in this part of the world. If they remain passive, they stand in dire fear that any foul wind, whether in economics or politics, will cause them to be chosen as a scapegoat. Refugees have reported police attacks on the Jewish community in Casablanca. These sources say that only the hand of the Sultan has stayed bloody pogroms.

THE POLITICAL SITUATION

On March 4, 1962, the left-wing Popular Forces National Front demanded that Hassan II arrange for a constitutional monarchy. In rejecting the demand, the King declared that the nation's immediate needs were economic and social; political democracy would have to come later. While his absolute rule is bitterly opposed by the progressives and by organized labor, the King remains a highly popular figure.

INTERNATIONAL ATTITUDES

Morocco continues to be one of the great exponents of neutralism. At the Belgrade Conference of neutralist countries in 1961, King Hassan II was a principal spokesman.

The Soviet Union has been quick to see the potentialities of the situation. It offered military assistance to Morocco, including a squadron of MIG-17 jet fighters and several bombers. The Moroccan government, pleased to demonstrate its neutralism by taking arms from both sides, promptly accepted the offer. Although the planes were to be flown by Moroccan pilots, military observers felt that the presence of the Soviet aircraft in Morocco neutralized to some extent the NATO bases.

Although Morocco has followed a neutralist path in the United Nations, a survey of the Moroccan voting record shows that its representatives have sided with the Soviet Union in most major controversies. It is doubtful that this record reflects active sympathy with all the causes espoused by the U.S.S.R. For the Moroccans, it may demonstrate an independence of action on the international scene, and may reflect lingering resentment of its former colonial ruler.

AGITATION AGAINST COLONIALISM

The Moroccan government has long been urging the liberation of the enclave of Ifni, as well as certain parts of northern Morocco which are still held by Spain. It has also agitated for the annexation of Mauritania and parts of Algeria. In the chaotic conditions which followed Algeria's independence, Morocco seized a number of Algerian border outposts, claiming them as Moroccan.

Morocco was rebuffed when, in the U.N., it sought recognition of its claim to Mauritania. However, such claims are likely to be presented at a later date. These claims are powerfully rooted in the fact that arbitrary boundaries, established during the colonial era, split tribal and ethnic groups among separate political territories. Moreover, the strong surge of nationalist feeling in most of the new nations of Africa promotes the desire for national aggrandizement.

BAB EL MANSOUR   *This monumental gate of the ramparts of Meknes is decorated with green ceramics. Built during the 17th century, it was within these walls that the Sultan stored supplies for his troops, and maintained stables for his steeds.*

269

IN BRIEF

AREA	171,583 square miles, about the size of Utah and Wyoming combined.
TERRAIN	Land of great scenic beauty. Fertile coastal plain runs along Mediterranean and the Atlantic Ocean. Farther inland, Atlas Mountains run through the country in three parallel ranges. To the south and east lies the Sahara Desert.
CLIMATE	Temperatures are moderate in the region of the Atlantic Ocean and the Atlas Mountains. Mean temperature is 61.5° to 72.3° on the west coast, and 50° to 80.6° in the interior. Light rainy seasons are October to November and April to May. Maximum annual rainfall (30 to 40 inches) occurs in the northwest.
CAPITAL	Rabat (population, 225,000).
OTHER CITIES	Casablanca, 965,000; Marrakesh, 243,000; Fez, 216,000; Meknes, 177,000; Tangier, 142,000; Ouja, 129,000; Tetuan, 101,000.
POPULATION	11,600,000; about 400,000 foreigners.
ETHNIC GROUPS	Largest is the Berber peoples, in many areas closely intermingled with various Arab groups. Smaller groups are the African Negroes, and some 160,000 native Jews.

KING HASSAN II   He received private instruction in Arabic and in modern studies, and then graduated with honors from law school. Appointed Commander-in-Chief of the Moroccan Army, he became responsible for its reorganization. He is accounted to be a rigid conservative, and has been under criticism by progressive groups. Nevertheless, he maintains the strong support of the Army and the rural population.

FIELD HAND *Wearing pantaloons and a typical Moroccan hand-knitted cap, this worker cuts and binds grain.*

LANGUAGE

Classical Arabic is the official language. Almost half the population speaks Berber. Many speak Arabic-Berber dialect. Also French and Spanish.

RELIGION

Mohammedanism is the state religion and widely practiced. Christians are accorded full religious freedom. Jews are under severe pressure.

DATE OF INDEPENDENCE

March 2, 1956.

FORM OF GOVERNMENT

Absolute monarchy. The country has a national consultative Assembly appointed by the King. Member of the United Nations.

EDUCATION

In 1957, 615,838 pupils were enrolled in primary schools and 33,091 in secondary schools. Six institutions of higher learning with 1,978 students enrolled; Kairaween University at Fez was founded in A.D. 859.

HEALTH FACILITIES

1,667 doctors, and 16,873 hospital beds. One psychiatric hospital of 1,850 patients is devoted mainly to treatment of hashish addicts.

CURRENCY

Unit is a dirham (5.06 dirhams = U.S. $1.00).

INDUSTRY

Small industries include chemicals, leather, flour, stone, beverages, textiles, carpet weaving.

CROPS: Grains, citrus fruits, grapes, corn, olives, dates, hemp.

STOCK: Sheep, cattle, donkeys, camels, horses, and pigs.

FISHING: Sardines, tuna, anchovies, and shrimp.

MINING: Phosphates, cobalt, manganese, iron, lead, and zinc.

TRADE

1960:	IMPORTS	$413,000,000
	EXPORTS	354,000,000
	DEFICIT	$ 59,000,000

MAJOR IMPORTS: Sugar, petroleum products, cloth, vehicles and parts, machinery and parts, tea, iron and steel.

MAJOR EXPORTS: Phosphates, agricultural products (*see* Crops), canned fish, lead ore, and iron ore.

TRANS-PORTATION

ROADS: 8,072 miles are surfaced. 10,956 miles all-weather.

VEHICLES: 117,100 passenger cars. 44,300 commercial vehicles (1959).

WATERWAYS: Eight ports on Atlantic coast.

RAILROADS: 1,175 miles of track.

AIR TRAFFIC: Extensive network of airports. Casablanca is main international airport serving most major airlines. The most common mode of transport is by commercial bus line.

COMMUNI-CATIONS

National radio, with 12 stations. Two television stations; about 5,000 TV sets. Postal, telephone, and telegraph services are government-supervised. Newspapers and magazines in Arabic and European languages.

COVERED ALLEY IN FEZ   A canopy made of cane stalks, held together by wood supports, protects the buying and browsing public from the hot sun in this market place of the old city. The men wear a robe with an attached hood. The typical Moroccan cap—the tarbouche—is very common.

NIGER

Survival in an Arid Land

A good part of Niger is arid, and like all African nations that border on the Sahara, or include part of the Sahara, Niger's citizens find that they must bend their individual lives and their national fortunes to the will of the desert.

The Niger River, which gives its name to this country, flows through the southern tip of the land for only 185 miles. Here, the waterway provides greenery and tropical wildlife, and here most of the semi-nomadic people of this land live. The dry northern desert is too hostile to sustain human life.

FAMINE AND RAINFALL

The rainfall in Niger's capital, Niamey, is 30 inches a year. Situated in the west on the Niger River, Niamey has 36,000 inhabitants and is the only major city in a country that is larger than Texas and California combined. Roughly one-half the land receives less than 4 inches of rain annually. A quarter of the land gets between 4 and 14 inches; while the remaining quarter of the country averages no more than 17 inches. By contrast, the normal annual rainfall in New York City is 42 inches, and in Arizona it is 7.12 inches. In northern Niger the heat is sometimes so great that rain evaporates while falling.

In a country so dominated by the desert, economic problems tend to be transformed from issues of development to issues of basic survival. Ninety-four percent of the people of Niger derive their income from agriculture and stock raising, yet only 2 percent of the land can be cultivated. When the rains fail, the already arid country faces famine—and in Niger, famine claims many victims. Crops are raised for the most part in the extreme southern area of the country; but even here, a regular food supply cannot be depended upon.

An important first step to prevent famine during the dry years is to save a portion of the crops that are grown in the good years. Farmers' associations have been formed and communal granaries have been organized for this purpose.

PEANUTS AND MILLET

The closeness of the desert has simplified the agricultural pattern. For a long time, the farmers of Niger have been raising millet to eat and peanuts to export.

The peanut crop accounts for more than 80 percent of the country's exports. One might expect, then, that Niger is another country struggling futilely with an adverse balance of trade; in actuality, Niger's import-export balance is very favorable. In 1958, the country enjoyed a credit balance of over $7 million.

Niger is thinly populated. Consumer demands are light, and this helps to keep the trade balance favorable.

Through the tremendous energy of the farmers, peanut acreage has risen from 482,000 acres in 1954, to 803,000 acres in 1958. The value of the crop is tremendously dependent on the amount of rain that falls in that particular year. However, as the productive acreage is increased, the country's ability to withstand all but the worst moods of the Sahara becomes greater.

For home consumption, Niger's farmers grow millet, a small cereal grain similar to wheat. Slowly, other crops are being introduced; but the proximity of the desert makes it wise to devote most acreage to especially hardy crops.

Everywhere in Niger the desert calls the turn. Every step forward is tentative, at best. So far, emphasis has been laid on soil conservation rather than on improved farming methods. Above all, the most important objective is to save precious water. The planners of Niger feel that agricultural diversification can come only after soil conservation and irrigation have made possible a more reliable annual yield.

LIVESTOCK RAISING

While farming dominates in the south, it gives way to stock breeding, as one moves in toward the edge of the Sahara. Stock raising in the

DOSSO CAVALRY *About 75 miles from Niamey, Niger's capital, Dosso horsemen assemble for a parade. Traditionally, these men were daring warriors and the trappings of their glorious past is still in evidence. The tom-tom player squats near his instrument. Like the U.S. cavalry bugler, the tom-tom player summons the warriors to assemble, and keeps beating his drum while they are assembling. Men and horses wear the cloth decorative coverings which once were used to conceal metal armor. The horsemen are armed with sabers and shields. Hat feathers vary with each tribe. This group sports ostrich plumes.*

STREET IN ZINDER
This beautiful house in Arab-Sudanese style, the home of a merchant, depicts traditional artistry of the Zinder region. Houses in this area are built in a similar manner, more or less elaborate, depending upon the wealth of the owner. Note utility pole in foreground.

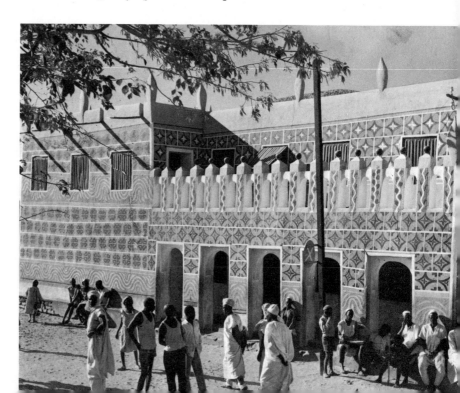

ENROUTE TO MARKET *Among the cattle - raising tribes, oxen provide transportation for women—the men ride camels. The long bundles are millet stalks; the grain has been stripped off to use for flour. The pouches contain water and milk for the women; the sacks tied beneath the millet stalks contain miscellaneous products to be sold at the market.*

Niger Valley is the country's second most important economic activity. The government estimates that there are 3.5 million cattle, 6.8 million sheep and goats, and 350,000 camels.

POPULATION MAKE-UP

Three-quarters of the population are Negro farmers or fishermen. The remaining 25 percent are Caucasian Hamites who live principally in the central and northern areas. Among these are the Tuareg warriors, an immensely proud, courageous, and warlike people, who long balked French efforts to convert Niger into a colony. The Tuaregs are mostly nomadic herdsmen and cattle breeders.

Though the desert permits herds to exist, it exacts a grim toll by diminishing the quality of the stock. In the continual search for forage and watering, the animals become lean and haggard. The problem is made even more acute by the fact that the herds are often owned by tribes who regard cattle as conferring status and who, therefore, refuse to kill or sell their animals.

In 1955, the government began a program to create a meat-processing industry. Refrigerated slaughterhouses, cold-storage depots, refrigerated transport were features of the plan. It was hoped that there would be an eventual replacement of nomadic stock-raising by modern ranching. Because of the overpowering desert and the strong tribal traditions, this plan has been making slow headway.

EDUCATION IN THE DESERT

The sparseness of the population and the nomadic life of the herdsmen render progress in education extremely difficult. In 1945, only 1 percent of the children attended school. By 1960, 6 percent were enrolled—a very small number indeed, but a figure that nevertheless bespeaks a genuine effort.

CHILDREN PLAYING MARELLA   *Marella is like tic-tac-toe. The object is to keep your opponent from getting three men in a row.*

POLITICAL LIFE

In the nation's political life, the desert, too, is a silent and powerful force.

The profound differences between the Semitic and the Hamitic people of the north, and the Negroes of the south, have been a source of tension for centuries. This touchy situation is responsible for one interesting feature in Niger's political life: the continuing, regular election of many tribal chiefs. It is this factor that has preserved tribal and religious authority within the framework of Niger's democracy. Since the great majority of the population is Moslem, religion has served as a link between the two ethnic groups of the country.

President Hamani Diori, a Moslem, is a teacher. He studied education in Paris before World War II, and returned to Paris after the war as a deputy of the French National Assembly. He is regarded as a conservative and pro-French.

ALLIANCES FOR ECONOMIC BENEFIT

The economic development of Niger will be a long and arduous task. One step that the government has taken is to enter into a "Council of the Entente" with Ivory Coast, Upper Volta, and Dahomey. These four countries are coordinating their plans and policies in the fields of taxation, public administration, labor legislation, public works, transportation, and communication. The four members of the Entente have entered into a customs agreement with Senegal, Mali, and Mauritania.

Niger, largest in size of the Entente states, has been the poorest in natural resources; but in 1961, extensive deposits of iron ore were discovered.

BUILDING A BARGE   In Gaya of southwestern Niger, men of the Dandi tribe, a Moslem group, are building a pirogue. Trees in the area are not large, and several must be joined together to build a craft such as this. Perforations are made in the wood with a steel bar, which has been heated so it can burn through to the required depth. The mud huts are used for storing corn, rice, and other such products. The several storage floors, within the hut, are marked by the pegs which protrude from the walls. These pegs are part of the supports for each floor.

INDEPENDENCE DAY *In front of many huts, the national flag was displayed on this historic day.*

SONGHAI GIRL *Carrying a jug, this girl is on her way to the river to fetch water.*

BERI BERI GIRL *The plaited coiffure takes a few hours to do. Her nose is pierced for a jewel; her face bears the markings of her tribe. The gold earrings, the shape of a fish, are a symbol of good luck to Moslems.*

DJERMA GIRLS *These young ladies, dressed up for a festival, wear bands of silver coins, bracelets of silver, and earrings of gold. Before marrige, the head is shaved to leave two criss-crossed bands of hair on the scalp.*

IN BRIEF

AREA 458,995 square miles, larger than Texas and California combined.

TERRAIN Except for a strip of productive land in the south, all the northern portion of this landlocked nation forms part of the Sahara Desert. A few mountainous peaks in central Niger. Niger River flows through country for 185 miles. This is the most fertile land.

CLIMATE Hot and dry with very little rain in the northern desert area. In the south, rainfall varies from 8.7 inches to 30.1. Rainy season from June through September.

CAPITAL Niamey (population, 36,000).

POPULATION 2,800,000; about 3,000 Europeans.

ETHNIC GROUPS About three-quarters of the population are Negro farmers or fishermen (Haoussas, Djermas, and Songhais). Northern nomads are indigenous Caucasians: the Peuls and the Tuaregs.

LANGUAGE French is official language, but tribal languages are prevalent in each ethnic group.

RELIGION 80 percent Mohammedan; some Negroes hold animistic beliefs.

DATE OF INDEPENDENCE August 3, 1960.

FORM OF GOVERNMENT Parliamentary democracy with a Legislative Assembly of 60 members elected for 5 years. Assembly invests a President of the Council after each general election; he holds executive

HAMANI DIORI President of Niger, Hamani Diori was born in 1916, and was educated in Senegal. He became a teacher in Niger, and then taught the Hausa language in Paris.

power. An independent judiciary and an Economic Council. Member of Council of the Entente, French Community, and United Nations.

EDUCATION

In 1960, 6 percent of all school-age children were enrolled; 192 primary schools had 21,054 students and 8 secondary schools had 1,040 students. No universities.

HEALTH FACILITIES

2 hospitals, 21 medical centers, 35 dispensaries 1 tuberculosis sanitarium, and 6 private institutions.

CURRENCY

Unit is French Community franc (247 francs = U.S. $1.00).

INDUSTRY

A little light industry (mostly food-processing plants).

CROPS: Primarily, millet for local use, peanuts for exports. Other food crops are sorghum, cassava, beans, rice, corn, and onions. Some cotton.

STOCK: Cattle, sheep, goats, horses, and camels.

FISHING: For home consumption, from the Niger River and Lake Chad.

MINING: Very little; some salt, natron, tin, and tungsten.

TRADE

1958:	EXPORTS	$18,095,000
	IMPORTS	$10,952,000
	SURPLUS	$ 7,143,000

MAJOR IMPORTS: Foodstuffs, tobacco, textiles, fuels and lubricants, raw materials, and semifinished goods.

MAJOR EXPORTS: Peanuts, livestock, hides, and skins.

TRANS-PORTATION

ROADS: 1,117 miles all-weather roads.

VEHICLES: 4,113 (1959).

WATERWAYS: Niger River is partially navigable, from October to March.

RAILROADS: None.

AIR TRAFFIC: International airport at Niamey, about 11 other minor airfields.

COMMUNI-CATIONS

35 post offices, 30 telephone-telegraph bureaus. Radio Niger, in Niamey, reaches 500 miles.

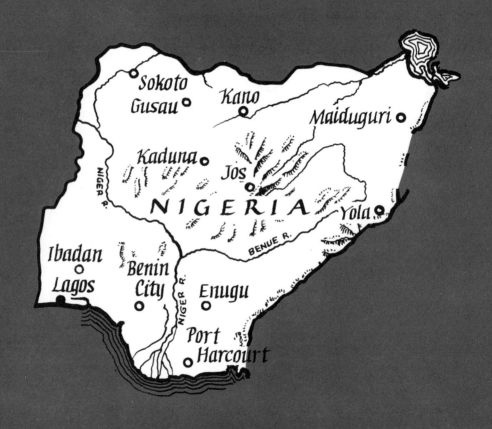

NIGERIA

Federation of Diverse Regions

Nigeria is considered by many to be the most fascinating country in Africa. Dynamic and picturesque, it is of absorbing interest to the student of art and the student of archaeology. Moreover, serious and qualified observers believe Nigeria is destined to be the political leader of the new nations of Africa.

A HUGE POPULATION

Nigeria is the twelfth most populous nation in the world, with an estimated 36 million people, 10 million more than the next largest country in Africa. One of every seven people now living on the continent of Africa is a Nigerian.

Nigeria is the most densely populated large nation of Africa. Roughly 42 percent of this population is under the age of fifteen. Most of the breadwinners are petty farmers, unskilled workers, or clerks. The average annual income is less than $90. Housing is unsanitary, and life expectancy is low.

AN AGRICULTURAL ECONOMY

Farming employs 80 percent of the population, provides 50 percent of the gross national product, and accounts for 85 percent of exports.

The major crops for local consumption are yams, cassava, sorghum, millet, corn, rice, and beans. Nigeria's agricultural productivity has just about reached a point where it can satisfy the enormous population of the country.

GROWTH OF THE ECONOMY

Nigeria is seeking to industrialize rapidly and to lessen its economic dependence on agriculture. Only 2 percent of the gross national product is currently derived from industrial sources. With 36 million people,

Nigeria has a built-in home market for many of its factory products, and need not rely on foreign markets to absorb its output.

Natural resources represent Nigeria's great potential. During 1960, the production of tin ore reached 1.5 million tons. Recent explorations have revealed substantial oil reserves; and the construction of an oil refinery is being planned.

Nigeria has the only coal deposits in West Africa, enough coal to export more than 100,000 tons yearly to Ghana. Nigeria is one of the world's largest suppliers of columbite. The country contains large areas of timber.

INAUGURATION OF GOVERNOR-GENERAL Dr. Nnamdi Azikiwe, formerly Prime Minister of the Eastern Region, is Governor-General of the Federation of Nigeria. The governor-general is the official head of state, equivalent to a president. The actual head of government is the prime minister. Dr. Azikiwe, in the black skull cap, stands between Mrs. Azikiwe and Prime Minister, Sir Abubakar Tafawa Balewa.

THE PARADOX OF NIGERIA'S STABILITY

Nigeria is a federation of three autonomous regions—Western Nigeria, Eastern Nigeria, and Northern Nigeria. The Eastern and Western Regions differ from each other about as much as Germany differs from Ireland; and Northern Nigeria differs from its other two partners even more dramatically—as much as Europe differs from China.

More than 250 languages are spoken in this country of vivid contrasts; and Mohammedanism, Christianity, and animism are contending religious forces in the land.

Each of the three regions of Nigeria enjoys autonomous government, and each region has its own legislature. But each of these three regions is jealous of the other two; and the three are in constant competition for aid from the federal government.

Despite this clear lack of homogeneity, despite the huge differences in culture, and despite the regional competition, the federal government of Nigeria is perhaps the most politically stable of all the new African nations. This political stability allows Nigeria to concentrate on urgent tasks, and provides a favorable climate for foreign aid and foreign investment.

How did Nigeria develop a secure and respected government?

The British took over in Nigeria in the early nineteenth century; shortly after, slavery was abolished. In 1960, after about a century of British rule, Nigeria gained complete independence. During Britain's tenure, the colonial administration developed thousands of capable African officials. It was this experience in political life, administration of bureaus, and limited self-government, that prepared Nigeria for its role as an independent self-governing nation.

EN ROUTE TO MARKET   The Benue River is navigable only during two half months of the rainy season, during which trading canoes carry livestock.

FULANI DANCERS   *Slender, tall people, men and women alike wear necklaces and dresses, decorated with colorful wool balls. The faces of the dancers are painted for a performance.*

Nigeria had never been heavily exploited by the British. The long history of Nigeria's struggle for self-government was not a bitter one. It was under British control that the regions of Nigeria were united into a federation.

NORTHERN NIGERIA

Northern Nigeria is the federation giant, covering more than half the area of the entire country, and containing more than half the entire population of the country. Practically the entire population of this region —about 20 million people—are Moslems. Despite its size and great numbers, Northern Nigeria is the least developed region of the country. But by all accounts, it is the most picturesque and the most interesting.

It was not until 1903 that Northern Nigeria was occupied by the British; and it was not until 1958—just a scant year and a half before the

FULANI HERDSMAN Among these people, it is traditional that the youngest son tends the cattle. At night, the herdsman fences in his charges with a thicket of thorns, and sets his dogs at watch here. He, himself, seeks protection from prowling hyenas by making and crawling into a low bower of branches and leaves, in which he sleeps for the night.

FULANI GIRLS These young ladies are on their way to market with calabashes containing milk, sour milk, butter, and cheese. The diet of the Fulani consists almost entirely of dairy products. The girls are all dressed up, as the market is something of a social gathering as well as a place to transact business.

TUAREG GIRL   Among the Tuareg, it is the women who are the owners of livestock and movable property. Moreover, it is the women—not the men—who can read and write the Tuareg script derived from a Libyan alphabet of the fourth century B.C.

SONGHI WOMAN   Women of this race are distinguishable at once by their distinctive manner of dressing the hair over a raised pad. A plaited lock hangs down on either side. This woman of means wears gold coins as head ornaments.

FULANI ELDER   The Fulani are also known as Fellani, Fellata, Filani, Foulah, Ful, Fulbe, Peul and Pulla. A pastoral people, this man tills the soil while his youngest son herds his cattle.

HAUSA MAN   The markings on the face of this man indicate that he is a member of the Pabir tribe. Among these people, clothing, ornaments, and facial scars differentiate the tribal groups.

nation obtained independence—that this region attained full self-government.

The Sardauna of Sokoto, Sir Ahamadu Bello, leader of Northern Nigeria's strongest political faction, the Northern People's Congress Party, is the Premier of Northern Nigeria. A moderate who enjoys great prestige, he is accounted as a man of vigorous intellect.

The Moslem North has been traditionally conservative, and agreed to join the Federation of Nigeria only after it obtained assurances that its institutions and traditions would be maintained and respected. Among the terms of agreement was the stipulation that the women of the Northern Region would not be given the right to vote.

The Northern Region has had less contact with Europeans than either of the other two regions. The literacy rate in Roman script is only

COVERED-IN DUG-OUT CANOES   The rivers and creeks of Nigeria provide means of transport to places that are inaccessible by road or rail. Approximately 4,000 miles of these waterways are navigable by rivercraft. The journey by water may last for quite a while, and this type of boat offers protection from the elements.

2 percent; while in Eastern Nigeria and Western Nigeria, the rate is approximately 17 percent. Consequently, the government of Northern Nigeria still relies heavily on Europeans to handle administrative jobs.

Although it has had limited contact with Europe and Western civilization, Northern Nigeria has had a long history, and has had active contact with many countries in Africa. Its traditions are rich and proud; its culture, complex. For many, many centuries, Northern Nigeria has conducted trade with the Sudan, and with all countries bordering the Sahara. Caravans from as far away as Tripoli used to make their way here after a journey of many, many months across the hot desert sands. For Northern Nigeria was—and continues to be—one of the great trading centers of North Africa. But today, the airplane has, to a large extent, replaced the camel.

THE HAUSA AND THE FULANI

The two main ethnic groups of this region are the Hausa and the Fulani. The Hausa, at one time in control of the country, are a powerfully built race, peaceful, and industrious.

The Fulani, a mixture of Berber and Negro stock, invaded the land in 1810, and then intermarried, to a large extent, with the Hausa population. The Fulani, distinguished by intelligence, today number 3,000,000. The language of the region is still predominantly Hausa.

A MOSLEM COUNTRY

On the whole, Northern Nigeria has been isolated from Christianity. Since the late fourteenth century, the region has been under the influence of Islam. Although there is still a good deal of animism, and Christianity is practiced by some, Northern Nigeria is overwhelmingly a Moslem country.

Until fairly recently, Northern Nigeria has had little contact with modern education and modern commerce. The region was controlled by hereditary Emirs, who were able to maintain traditional institutions and who discouraged social change.

ALHAJI THE RT. HON. SIR ABU-BAKAR TAFAWA BALEWA, P.C., K.B.E., M.P., LL.D., O.B.E., C.B.E. The Prime Minister of the Federation of Nigeria is a man of many titles. Alhaji indicates that he has been on a pilgrimage to Mecca. Tafawa Balewa is the name of the village where he was born.

KANO, NIGERIA'S PICTURE CITY

One of the most interesting cities in all Africa is Kano, chief city of the Northern Region. This is an ancient city, and the stories of its kings are recorded in annals that go back to 900 A.D.

Built on an open plain, Kano lies 518 air miles northeast of the federal capital of Lagos. Kano is surrounded by an ancient wall, 11 miles long, with ramparts that are as high as 50 feet, and as thick as 40 feet at the base. A deep moat surrounds this wall; and in the middle of the moat, there is yet a smaller wall.

The ancient houses of Kano are built of clay, have flat roofs, and are impervious to fire. The palaces of the Emir, the showplaces of the city, cover 33 acres.

Side by side with this ancient civilization, stands a modern city, with a golf course, race track, and an up-to-date, enormously busy airport.

Kano, with a population of 130,000, is one of the greatest commercial cities in Central Africa. The market for camels, horses, oxen, asses, and goats is most colorful; and the city is also noted for its hand-dyed cloth and its leather goods.

EASTERN NIGERIA

Because missionaries were active in this region, there is a high literacy rate in Eastern Nigeria. There are 4,000 Europeans in the area.

The Ibos, the main ethnic group, constitute two-thirds of the population. They are a village people, and are composed of hundreds of small tribes.

The Ibos are the traders of Nigeria. They bear a reputation for industry and business acumen. Ibo country is densely populated; and economic pressures have led the Ibos to migrate into other regions, particularly to Northern Nigeria, where Ibo clerks and artisans form an important factor in the economy. In most cities of Nigeria, Ibo saleswomen are found behind the shop counters.

There are no big cities in Eastern Nigeria. The capital city, Enugu, has only 63,000 people.

GOLD MINE   *A shallow, alluvial deposit in Ilesha.*

The leader of the region, Nnamdi Azikiwe, is known throughout the length and breadth of Nigeria as "Zik." The political party he founded, the National Council of Nigeria and the Cameroons, spearheaded the movement for national independence. Azikiwe, a Protestant by religion, and a member of the Ibo tribe, spent nine years in the United States, studying at Lincoln University and the University of Pennsylvania. When he returned home in 1937, he founded a bank, several newspapers, and various commercial enterprises. Later, he became active in politics.

ANCIENT KANO   Built by the Hausa about one thousand years ago, the walled city of Kano, northern Nigeria's largest city, numbers 130,000 inhabitants today. Through the narrow alleys between its mud-walled houses, wander sheep, goats, and donkeys. From hundreds of miles around, merchants come to sell their produce in Kano's crowded, noisy market.

Among the books he has written are *Renascent Africa* (1937), and *Political Blueprint of Nigeria* (1943). He has been an editor of African newspapers for many years.

WESTERN NIGERIA

The two main groups in Western Nigeria are the Yoruba and the Edo. The Yoruba are counted as among the most advanced of any of the African peoples.

Back in the twelfth century, long before the Europeans arrived in Africa, the Yorubas lived in large, well-organized communities. Today, the Yoruba people comprise two-thirds of the entire population of Western Nigeria. Their religion is pantheistic, and their spiritual head is termed the Oni of Ife.

Fifty percent of Yorubas are townspeople. They are easily distinguished by the blue clothing they wear.

EKPAKHA DANCER   *In Big Qua Town in Eastern Nigeria, there still flourishes the Ekpo, a secret society. On important occasions, such as the death of a chief, or at a festival, the Ekpo ceremonial carving is taken from its private shrine to the market place, to be viewed by the public. It is carried on the head of the daughter of a chief, who is accompanied by an umbrella carrier and another attendant. The carving, made of wood, has symbolic significance. There are four heads on the top of it; and from each face, there protrudes a pipe. These heads rest on a tray, separated from the base, by gaily-painted rims. The pipe motif is repeated on the four corners of the base in the form of birds. Such a sculpture has a socio-religious significance, and at times, consists of comical carvings and caricatures. The bearer will stoop to permit children and adults to touch the mystic images. She wears gold jewelry, encrusted with costly stones. The scarves caught in the handles of the sculpture are fine examples of the Yoruba batik.*

CHIEF AWOLOWO

Obafemi Awolowo, who heads the dominant party of Western Nigeria, the Action Party, is a deeply religious Protestant of the Yoruba tribe. Raised in direct destitution, Awolowo somehow managed to get an education at a British mission school in Ibadan. By dint of enormous effort, he made his way to England and studied law in London, where he became a barrister.

A cultivated man of the highest intelligence, he is the author of many books, among which *Path to Nigerian Freedom* achieved substantial status. He has also written on the artistic and cultural history of his country—particularly about the famous bronzes of Benin.

WESTERN NIGERIA'S CAPITAL CITY

Ibadan, with a population of 660,000, is the largest Negro city in the world, and has more people than any city lying between Cairo and Johannesburg. Until recently, it was a drab town of tiny tin-covered houses; and around its perimeter, there stood great mud walls. Today, in sharp contrast to these tin dwellings, there are the new Parliament building, the Western Nigerian ministries, and the Teaching Hospital, an ultra-modern institution which can accommodate 500 patients.

Ibadan is a city of skyscrapers. The city is the seat of University College, which has an enrollment of 1,200 students. It is affiliated with the University of London, and degrees are conferred by that institution. University College is fast becoming the most important and largest university on the African continent.

THE ART TREASURES OF NIGERIA

From Western Nigeria come, perhaps, the best works of African sculpture. Particularly renowned are the bronzes of Benin.

Benin was discovered by Portuguese traders in the fifteenth century. The kingdom of Benin was then in an advanced state of culture; and the Portuguese were so impressed that they invited the king of the country to visit Portugal, which he did. Relations were most cordial and

THE JEMAA HEAD This was the first arch-
aeological find of the Jos area and still the most
impressive sculpture unearthed.

MODERN SCULPTURE   In this
ebony door post, the artist has attempted to portray the dignity of
motherhood. A painter and wood
carver, Bamgboye is one of the most
highly respected artists in art-con-
scious Nigeria.

IFE BRONZE This naturalistic casting,
probably produced during the fifteenth century, bears comparison with first-rate works of
Western sculpture.Made of dark green bronze,
the Buddha-like features, high-rounded cheeks,
slanted eyes, slightly flaring nostrils, lend an
impassive and enigmatic expression to this
work of art.

TERRA-COTTA HEAD *Found at Ita-Yemoo in 1957, this work has become famous throughout the art world.*

CENTRAL MOSQUE *In front of this famous mosque, a microphone relays the Friday prayer to people who have come here from as far as 100 miles away. The bicycle is the principal means of transportation to this well-known mosque in Kano.*

satisfactory, so much so,that Portugal and Benin exchanged ambassadors.

In 1897, the British discovered the art treasures of Benin—great wall plaques, and bronze busts of a superb quality. Many of these pieces grace the halls of museums throughout the world; others can be seen in the Lagos Museum in the capital city of Nigeria—marvelous carvings in wood and ivory, and castings in bronze and brass, which have been acclaimed as masterpieces by Western art critics.

ARCHAEOLOGICAL FINDS

In the 1930's, at a little village called Nok, near the town of Jos, excavations revealed one of the most important finds in modern archaeology, artifacts that experts say place the early Nok civilization somewhere around 2,000 B.C., and mark this region as the situs of the earliest Iron Age in West Africa. Relics of the Stone Age had been upturned in this region much earlier.

THE FEDERAL TERRITORY OF NIGERIA

The three autonomous regions of Nigeria, Northern Nigeria, Western Nigeria, and Eastern Nigeria, operate under a federation, with the federal authority having its seat in the city of Lagos.

Lagos, the national capital, with a population of 364,000, is situated in Western Nigeria, and is the commercial center of the country, handling 50 percent of the nation's cargo. Built on an island in a large lagoon, Lagos is connected to the mainland by bridge. The city grew haphazardly, without careful planning, and became one of the most squalid cities on the continent. It was once an important slave trading center, and the area around Lagos was once known as the Slave Coast. Only in recent years has this shabby collection of shanties been transformed into a city. Today, there is new construction everywhere; and almost overnight, modern office buildings of considerable height have sprung up. There is a new luxury hotel, charmingly situated overlooking a lagoon. With national pride riding high, the Nigerians are building a capital city they can be proud of.

The public market in Lagos is especially colorful and fascinating. As in many such marts in Africa, an enormous variety of merchandise is on sale. In the market of Lagos, practically every commodity under the sun is offered for sale: marmalade, music boxes, magic accessories such as dried rats and human skulls. In contrast, the city also has some up-to-date department stores which handle fine merchandise.

Lagos is a city of gay informality, replete with all the amusements of the Western world, such as night clubs, yacht clubs, cinemas, and dance halls.

BARCLAYS BANK BUILDING   Situated on Marina Street, in the center of the city of Lagos, stands this new structure, typical of the building activity now going on in this capital of 364,000 people.

SIR ABUBAKAR TAFAWA BALEWA

The man who heads the federal government, the first Prime Minister, is a conservative from Northern Nigeria. Sir Abubakar Tafawa Balewa received a traditional schooling in Nigeria, followed by higher studies in Education at the University of London. He was a teacher, entered politics comparatively late in life, and became one of the founders of the Northern People's Congress Party. He is highly respected by all factions.

NIGERIAN POLITICS

There are three main political parties, each party deriving its main strength from one of the three regions of the country. The predominant party of Western Nigeria is the Action Group. The predominant party of Eastern Nigeria is the National Council of Nigeria and the Cameroons. The predominant party of Northern Nigeria is the Northern People's Congress.

306

In 1959, the general election resulted in the N.P.C. winning 140 seats, the N.C.N.C. winning 89 seats, and the Action Group winning 75 seats. The coalition government elected Sir Abubakar Tafawa Balewa as Prime Minister.

Keen competition exists among the three regions of the country, each wishing to attract new industries and each wishing to extend its welfare services. Invidious comparisons are constantly being made by rival politicians, who draw comparisons among the achievements of each of the three autonomous governments. Despite the federal structure and growing national pride, tribal loyalties are the most important factor in voting. Nigerians, in sickness and in misfortune, tend to turn to the family and tribe. Clans, organized as cooperatives, provide scholarships for higher education and collect funds to build local schools. The national government does not as yet have well-organized welfare services, and Nigerians have, by habit, depended upon tribal help, and continue to do so. The result, of course, emphasizes and perpetuates parochialism.

CHEMISTRY LABORATORY   *The Yaba Technical Institute at Lagos serves 600 students.*

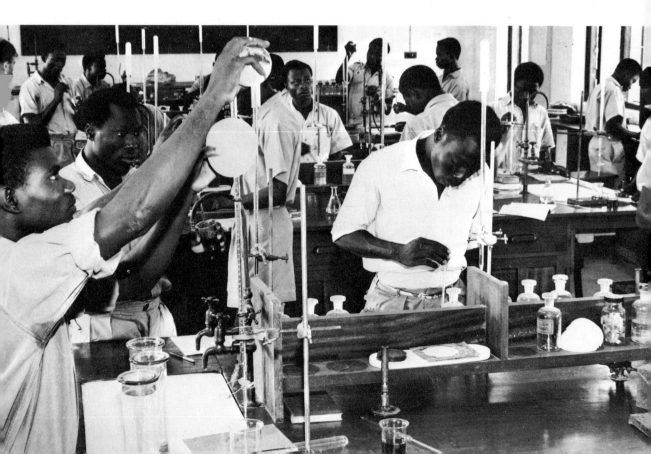

Nevertheless, modern communication, especially the radio, is forcing Nigerians to look beyond the local scene; and at least a few of the leaders think in terms of Nigeria, the nation, rather than of their local polities.

DISEASE AND POVERTY

Nigeria is not a wealthy country; the per capita income is well under $100 a year, less than half that of Ghana. The climate of West Africa, generally, is unhealthy, and Nigerians are exposed to many debilitating diseases. Smallpox, yellow fever, leprosy, and sleeping sickness are now under partial control; but malaria, pulmonary tuberculosis, cerebro-spinal meningitis, yaws, trachoma, Guinea worm, and bilharzasis are far from conquered.

In many areas of the African bush, a man is considered well off if he suffers from only one serious disease. Good health is rare. Many Africans, not actually victims of a specific disease, would still be classified as unwell by Western standards.

In Nigeria, health problems are handled by the regional governments. A determined effort is being made to provide more hospitals, mobile dispensaries, maternity homes, and clinics.

Many diseases in Nigeria can be directly attributed to inadequate diet, a result of substandard living. However, other unhealthful conditions can be abolished only by overcoming the resistance offered by primitive religious beliefs.

DEVELOPMENT OF TRANSPORTATION

In less than fifteen years, railroad mileage has increased 50 percent. Inland waterways, along the Niger and the Benue rivers are being developed. Airways are being expanded to connect Nigeria with the major cities of Europe and the United States.

An unfortunate consequence of the improved transportation facilities is that diseases, once confined to a small area, now become widespread throughout the continent. As Africans gain quick access to other regions, they often carry disease from one country to another.

CHIEF OBAFEMI AWOLOWO   The son of a poor Yoruba farmer, Awolowo was born in 1909. He studied law in London, and set up practice in Ibadan in 1947. A Protestant, he is Premier of the Western Region of Nigeria.

SENSE OF DESTINY

Nigerians believe that their country is on the move. The leaders look to the day of a new Africa, economically sound, physically sound, and culturally creative. In one of his famous speeches, Azikiwe epitomized the hopes of his country when he said, "Let us bind the nation's wounds, and let us heal the breaches of the past, so that in forging our nation, there shall emerge on this continent a hate-free, fear-free, and greed-free people, who shall be in the vanguard of a world task-force whose assignment is not only to revive the stature of man in Africa, but to restore the dignity of man in the world."

IN BRIEF

AREA
339,169 square miles, larger than Texas and Oklahoma combined.

TERRAIN
Belt of mangrove swamp forest runs along coastline and extends inland from 10 to 60 miles. Further inland is the zone of tropical rain forest. In the east, land rises to an enormous plateau region, with elevations running from 2,000 to 6,000 feet. In the extreme northeast is the approach to the southern Sahara Desert. The Niger River enters Nigeria from the northwest and empties into the Gulf of Guinea through a many-channeled delta.

CLIMATE   Wet and dry seasons are well defined; rains last from April to October. Annual rainfall varies from 70 inches in the southwest coastal area to almost 200 inches in the southeast. The north near the Sahara Desert is quite dry. Temperatures along the coast seldom rise above 90°, but humidity is high. Farther north, temperature changes are extreme, ranging between 50° and 110°.

CAPITAL   Lagos (population, 364,000 in 1953).

REGIONAL CAPITALS   NORTHERN NIGERIA: Kaduna, 51,000.
EASTERN NIGERIA: Enugu, 63,000.
WESTERN NIGERIA: Ibadan, 660,000.

OTHER CITIES   Kano, 130,000.
Ogbomosho, 140,000.

POPULATION   35,752,000; about 27,000 non-Africans.

ETHNIC GROUP   Principal tribes are Yoruba (about 5 million) in the west, Ibo (about 5.5 million) in the east, Hausa (about 5.5 million) in the north; also 3,000,000 Fulani.

LANGUAGE   Official language is English. There are nearly 250 native tongues. Most widely used is Hausa, spoken by about 40 per-

TYING REEDS   Nigeria has a great reserve of fish in Lake Chad. At the lake's edge, there are swamps and papyrus islands. Native fishermen make rafts from papyrus stems, tied together with grass rope. They use these rafts for fishing. The catch is plentiful.

SAINT PAUL'S PRIMARY SCHOOL On Breadfruit Street in Lagos, stand these modern school buildings. There are nearly 20,000 primary schools in Nigeria. A school like this can accommodate up to 600 children.

cent of the inhabitants of the northern region.

RELIGION In the north, two-thirds of the people are Mohammedans. In the west, Mohammedans, Christians, and animists are about equally divided. In the east, there are Christians and animists.

DATE OF INDEPENDENCE October 1, 1960.

FORM OF GOVERNMENT Constitutional democracy, with a popularly elected House of Representatives and a Senate chosen indirectly by the regional governments. The Prime Minister, who is majority leader of the House of Representatives, forms his own Cabinet. Member of the British Commonwealth of Nations and the United Nations.

EDUCATION In 1958 about 2.5 million children attended primary schools, and 85,000 attended secondary schools. The Nigerian College of Arts, Science, and Technology, with three branches, had over 800 students in the 1958-1959 session. The University College at Ibadan, organized in 1948, has over 1,200 students.

311

THE RT. HON. DR. NNAMDI AZIKIWE
Born in 1904, the son of a civil servant, Azikiwe began his career as a teacher. He has become one of the most noted journalists in Africa, and now holds the position of Governor-General of Nigeria.

HEALTH FACILITIES	In 1957 Nigeria had 819 doctors and 188 hospitals, providing 13,000 beds. There were 479 maternity centers, 6 rural health centers, and over 1,000 dispensaries. The hospital associated with the University College at Ibadan will eventually graduate 50 doctors a year.
CURRENCY	Unit is the Nigerian pound. (Official exchange rate: £1 = U.S. $2.80).
INDUSTRY	Most industrial activity is on a small scale. Several factories of substantial size include a sawmill and a plywood plant in the west, a weaving and spinning mill in the north, and a cement factory in the east. Industries using and processing local raw materials include palm-oil mills, cotton gins, rice mills, soap factories, fruit and fruit-juice canning, and boat-building concerns.

ALHAJI SIR AHMADU BELLO
Born in 1909, in Northern Nigeria, and educated in local schools, the Premier of Northern Nigeria is tall, broad-shouldered, and dignified. He is generally referred to as the Sardauna, an ancient title indicating that he is Commander-in-Chief of the Army.

CROPS: Corn, millet, rice, maize, and cassava are grown for local consumption; peanuts, cocoa, and mahogany are principal export crops.

STOCK: Substantial numbers of cattle, sheep, and goats are raised. Pigs are raised only for domestic consumption.

FISHING: 150 varieties of fish exist in Nigeria's rivers; trawling is extensive in the rivers and along the coast.

MINING: Tin and columbite are principal minerals exported, also gold, lead, silver, and tungsten, although at present minerals contribute less than 2 percent of national income. Only country in equatorial West Africa that produces coal; some oil deposits, extent not known.

TRADE

1960: IMPORTS $603,000,000
      EXPORTS $462,000,000
      DEFICIT $141,000,000

MAJOR IMPORTS: Textiles, machinery, and transport equipment, mineral fuels, tobacco, salt, sugar, beverages, and canned foods.

MAJOR EXPORTS: Palm-oil products, peanuts and peanut products, cocoa, cotton, tin, timber, bananas, canned and dried fish. Major source of world's supply of columbite.

TRANS-PORTATION

ROADS: 4,000 miles are surfaced. 37,000 miles all-weather.
VEHICLES: 24,150 passenger cars; 17,900 commercial vehicles (1958).

WATERWAYS: Niger and Benue Rivers are navigable. Coastal shipping exists at ten ports. Shipping was nationalized in 1959.

RAILROADS: 1,770 miles of track.

AIR TRAFFIC: Two international airfields, one at Kano and one at Lagos, plus many smaller airfields. A ten-year expansion program, now underway, will ultimately connect Lagos directly with major European and United States cities.

COMMUNI-CATIONS

Newspapers (1957): 12 daily, 3 semi-weekly, and 12 weekly. There are a number of radio stations; several television stations currently operate in Western and Eastern Nigeria.

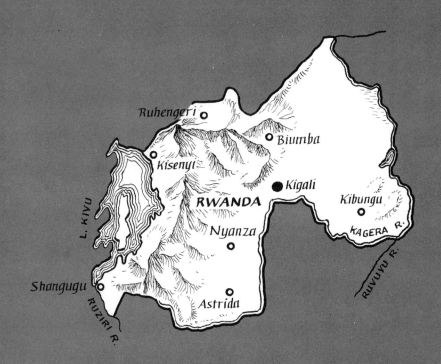

RWANDA

Tribal Rivalry in an Overpopulated Land

Eighty miles or so southwest of Lake Victoria lies the tiny former trust territory of Rwanda-Urundi, of which the new state of Rwanda forms the northern half. Separated from its neighbors—Uganda to the north, and Tanganyika to the east—by giant, almost impassable swamps and lakes, the area was virtually impenetrable to explorers for many years. Although the colonization of Africa by European powers was well under way in the nineteenth century, it was not until 1892 that the first European entered the country.

Situated on a high plateau, averaging 3,000 to 6,000 feet in height, the land is subject to an agreeable,temperate climate. Daily temperature varies from 55 to 75 degrees all the year round, and rainfall averages only 44 inches a year, slightly more than in New York City.

The colonial exploiters of Africa long ignored this poor land because of the formidable geographical obstacles. Left largely to its own devices by German and Belgian colonizers, the country long retained its feudal social system. The Watusi, the famous giant warriors, have reigned as overlords of the Bahutu, the tribe that comprises 83 percent of the population. A third people, the Twa, lives in the equatorial forests and has played little part in Rwanda politics. They are pygmies whose chief wish is to be left alone.

A FEUDAL HISTORY

The Tusi people, or Watusi tribe as they are better known, are believed to have entered this territory about 400 years ago. A Hamitic people, they are related to the Ethiopians, and more distantly to the ancient Egyptians. Anthropologists believe that they emigrated thousands of years ago, from their original home in the Nile River basin, moving gradually into the Sudan and Ethiopia; and ultimately, to the area of Rwanda-Urundi.

Although outnumbered eight to one by the Hutu people, or Bahutu

315

THE MWAMI OF RWANDA
Charles Mutara Lugalugwa, tall even for a Watusi, was king, (mwami), until his death in 1959.

WATUSI PRINCESS Sister of the former Mwami, Charles Mutara Lugalugwa, she is typical of the Watusi aristocracy. She wears the icyanganga, a band across the forehead, insignia of the wife of a chieftain. Heads of female children are bound, to produce the long oval shape, considered a mark of beauty and distinction. The bead necklace is of ivory and the hide of water buffalo.

tribe as they are generally called, the superior might of the Watusi, as well as a number of unique socio-economic circumstances, brought about the subjugation of the Bahutu.

The Bahutu is one of the numerous Bantu peoples. The tribe has subscribed to the tradition, common to many African tribes, that cattle are a symbol of prestige. The land has been primarily used for grazing livestock. Arable areas have been utilized for subsistence agriculture.

The Watusi, once established as rulers, bought the services of their subjects by offering cattle in payment. In the peculiar Bahutu social system, the most flea-bitten, sickly animal was considered so valuable that these people were, in effect, willing to become servants of the Watusi to get possession of cattle. By exploiting this preoccupation, the Watusi were able to maintain their feudal aristocracy throughout the period of European colonization.

THE EUROPEANS ENTER

Rwanda-Urundi was neglected during the squabbles between England and Germany over Tanganyika, but was ultimately made part of German East Africa. After the First World War, it became a Belgian mandate under the League of Nations.

Belgium, concerned primarily with the exploitation of the Congo, paid as little attention to Rwanda-Urundi as had the Germans. The country remained relatively unknown, governed from Europe, and administered distantly from the Congo. The prevailing political and social system was left practically untouched by the Belgians and Germans alike. A mwami, or king, ruled in the north; another in the south. Kings, chiefs, and sub-chiefs, were, almost without exception, Watusi.

Commercial interests were limited to the development of coffee plantations; and to this day, coffee remains the country's major resource. The Bahutu were frequently forced into the coffee groves at gun-point by their Belgian overseers. Local government was left to the Watusi.

But in the fervor of nationalism that swept Africa after the Second World War, the tide turned against both the Belgians and the Watusi. In 1946, the area became a U.N. Trust Territory, administered by Belgium. Time was running out for all colonizers in Africa; and even in a territory of as little interest as Rwanda-Burundi, the effect of nationalism became evident. The Bahutu rose against the Watusi. There were armed clashes, massacre, pillage.

Little experience in self-government had been developed before the territory came under U.N. trusteeship. When Rwanda-Urundi came under the control of the U.N., Belgium attempted to reorganize the country's political system along more democratic lines. Greater freedom was allowed for political expression, and native political parties developed.

But it was not until the legislative elections of September, 1961, that the Africans were given a voice in their government. Setting aside their conflicts, both the Bahutu and the Watusi insisted on self-government.

RWANDESE DANCERS   Very tall and slender, the natural grace of the young Watusi is manifested in the elaborate dance at a ceremony in the village of Kagbayi. Their skills were prominently shown in the adventure movie, "King Solomon's Mines."

SEWING CLASS *This is a tailoring workshop of the Léon Classe Institute in Kigali. This institution, founded in 1945, gives a four-year course which trains young craftsmen.*

POLITICAL UNREST AND STARVATION

In the elections of September, 1961, under U.N. supervision, Parmehutu, a party of the Bahutu, won 35 of 44 seats in the legislature. At the same time, a referendum established that the majority wished to abolish the monarchy. At one stroke, the ancient suzerainty of the Watusi was overturned. The Mwami, Kigeri V, fled to Uganda.

Subsequent disorders have left thousands of Watusi homeless. Raids by groups of these giant warriors have been churning the land into a vast unrest. Care of the meager crops has been seriously impaired. Starvation threatens.

LIMITED RESOURCES AND SUBSISTENCE FARMING

Rwanda is a very poor country. The 2,600,000 people live in an area the size of Vermont. They raise just enough crops to meet their own needs. Coffee, of good quality, is the major export.

At present, Rwanda receives aid from various relief agencies, particularly American organizations; but the undernourished cattle provide little milk for processing into dairy products. The Bahutu people are still loath to part with their cherished symbols of social prestige.

319

THE NTORE *This elite corps de ballet is composed of the sons of chiefs and notables. Like all Watusi, the height of this group ranges from six to seven feet. The members of this company receive education in politics, law, military science, good manners, refined speech, and choreography. They are paid and maintained in keeping with the high station in which their special art is regarded. Clothed in short skirts of real leopard skins, the dancers wear on their heads a fringe of white colobus monkey fur, attached to a beaded headband. Small bells gird their ankles, and the tinkling sounds punctuate the staccato of their dances. In action, the dancers brandish a stick, decorated with a long tail of raffia. The exact type of stick is determined by the theme of the dances. This particular group has been dubbed "The Unsurpassables." In the past, the dances were warlike and bore such names as "The Lance," "The Shield," "The Bow." Today, the dances bear such names as "The Female Provoker," "The Crested Crane," and "That Puts an End to All Discussion."*

The President of the new state, Gregoire Kayibanda, a member of the Parmehutu Party, is faced with almost insuperable problems. As other young nations of Africa have not discovered, independence has conferred self-support.

The Rwanda government has asked Belgium to leave troops in the country to quell expected uprisings. The ability of the administration to prevent bloodshed will be some indication of the competence of the persons in power.

IN BRIEF

AREA	10,169 square miles; slightly larger than Vermont.
TERRAIN	Most of the country is an undulating plateau, 3,000 to 6,000 feet high. Near the western border runs a chain of mountains, 6,000 to 10,000 feet high. The country is landlocked over 600 miles from the nearest coast.

BAHUTU VILLAGE   Comprising 85 percent of the population, the Bahutu inhabited Rwanda before the Watusi conquest. Similar small villages of the Bahutu are found throughout Rwanda and neighboring Burundi.

CLIMATE	Pleasant, temperate climate, due to its elevation, despite proximity of the equator. The mean temperature is 66°F. and varies little throughout the year. In a usual day, temperature range is 55 to 75. Annual rainfall is 44 inches (slightly more than New York City); but there is a three-month dry season (June through August) with almost no rain.
CAPITAL	Kigali (Population: 2,000).
POPULATION	About 2,600,000.
ETHNIC GROUPS	The Bahutu and Bantu make up about 83% of the population. The Watusi total about 16%. There are 50,000 Twa, a pygmy group. Very few outsiders in the country.
LANGUAGE	The Bahutu language is spoken by most of the population.
DATE OF INDEPENDENCE	July 1, 1962.
FORM OF GOVERNMENT	Democracy. The legislature was elected in September, 1961, in elections supervised by the United Nations. President, Premier, and 44-member Assembly elected by universal suffrage.
EDUCATION	About half the children of school age are currently enrolled in primary schools. In 1960, less than 3,000 pupils were receiving secondary school or technical training. No university.
CURRENCY	Unit is the Congolese franc. (50 francs = U.S. $1.00 official rate of exchange.)
INDUSTRY	Almost none except for some minor dairy processing.
	CROPS: Mostly subsistence farming. Cassava meal is important. Coffee is major export crop; some palm oil, tobacco.
	STOCK: Large numbers of undernourished cattle of poor quality. Also sheep and goats.
	MINING: Small quantities of tin, gold, tungsten, tantalum, mined. No important mineral deposits discovered as yet.
TRANSPORTATION	ROADS: The basic road system is one of the densest in Africa. 6,080 surfaced roads in former Ruanda-Urundi.
COMMUNICATIONS	1,814 telephones known to exist in former Ruanda-Urundi (1960).

SENEGAL R.

St. Louis

Matam

Tivaouane

SENEGAL

Bakel

Dakar   Thies

Diourbel

M'Bour

Kaolack

GAMBIA

Ziguinchor

SENEGAL

The Moderate Path in Africa

"Personally, I have never felt more fraternal toward the Europeans, particularly toward the French," said President Léopold Sedar Senghor of Senegal recently.

At a time when, in many African countries, the deprecation of former colonial masters is a political necessity, this was an unusual statement for an African leader to make..

The leaders of Senegal sincerely seek close ties with the French. Senegal, independent since August 20, 1960, maintains some 1,500 French specialists and administrators in government posts, some with substantial power. In 1961, for example, a Frenchman served as Minister of Finance.

Economically, Senegal is quite dependent on France. In addition to providing technical and economic assistance, teachers' salaries are paid in part by France. The French give financial support to the French-commanded Senegalese army. Senegal's entire peanut crop—85 percent of the country's exports—is purchased by France, at prices which are well above the market price.

CENTURIES OF WESTERNIZATION

In the seventeenth century, the French established trading settlements in Saint Louis, which was near the present site of Dakar. In the eighteenth century, the British moved into Senegal. They held control of the country until 1815. Then the French took over again.

Senegal has many survivals of the half-century of British overlordship. Many a Senegalese has retained the family name given to his ancestors by the British. Alfred Dodds, for example, is a Senegalese who rose to be a general in the French army and who took a prominent part in the French conquests of Dahomey and Indochina.

When, in 1848, all African slaves were emancipated by France, the Senegalese gained French citizenship for the first time. This occurred roughly one hundred years before Africans in other French territories were granted citizenship rights under the new French constitution of 1946. Dakar, the capital of Senegal, was, during colonial days, the capital of French West Africa. With their city an international metropolis for so long, the people are accustomed to associating with Europeans.

The warrior tribes of Senegal provided excellent recruits for the French Army. In World War I, French Premier Georges Clemenceau, paid many tributes to the valor of these troops; and Senegalese performed with distinction in World War II.

The extensive cultural ties between France and Senegal are symbolized by President Senghor, who was a famous French poet long before he became a political leader. Senghor, born in 1906, a member of the Serer tribe, received a good part of his education in France. He taught French literature in a high school in Tours, and later became a professor of philosophy in a French Lycée. He is considered to be one of the foremost intellectuals of Africa, and is undoubtedly one of the best-educated men on the continent. Senghor is a Catholic, and is married to a French-woman.

At the outbreak of World War II, he enlisted in the French Army; and during the war, was taken prisoner by the Germans. He later served as minister, in 1955, in two French cabinets. He helped to frame the post-war Constitution of the French Union; and it is said that he corrected the grammatical errors perpetrated by the French members of the drafting commission.

Another Senegalese who has successfully combined African and European culture is Alioune Diop, an internationally known intellectual who is President of the Society for African Culture. Diop was also editor of an important Paris magazine, *Présence Africaine*.

Senegal maintains one of the finest universities in Africa; the University of Dakar is reputed to have a very high standard of instruction.

CHANGING IMPORTANCE OF DAKAR

Despite the close relationship between Senegal and France, there are elements of instability that might operate to loosen Senegal's ties to

VIEW OF DAKAR   *The new section of this capital is a glittering oases of white, many-windowed buildings, and broad, tree-lined avenues.*

WOLOF WOMAN   *There are over 700,000 people of this race in Senegal. The Wolofs are distinguishable by their beautiful, silken-smooth, dark skin and high-domed foreheads. They are tall, well-built, and generously proportioned. The headdress is a peruke made of lamb's wool fibers that have been braided. The head has been shaved to accommodate the wig. A scarf is customarily worn over the hair and fancifully arranged to suit the wearer.*

LÉOPOLD SENGHOR   *Accounted as the outstanding intellectual of Africa, the President of Senegal enjoys an international reputation. His poetry finds inclusion in many anthologies, and his philosophical works have influenced European thought.*

to its cultural godmother, France, and to the other nations of the West.

When Dakar was the capital of French West Africa, it served as both a political and trading center for a vast area. Now it is the capital only of Senegal, a country about the size of South Dakota, with a weak, single-crop economy and scant mineral wealth. Since independence, Dakar's functions have become more limited; its status as an international cultural center and a crossroads of Africa will inevitably become

UNIVERSITY OF DAKAR   *This institution was founded in 1948. Today, it contains departments in medicine, pharmacy, law, science, and liberal arts. The present campus, inaugurated in 1957, is beautifully laid out, with fine athletic fields. In 1958, the University had an enrollment of 1,315 students.*

affected. Dakar is suffering from a recent shift in trade routes. Dakar was a coaling stop for European ships bound for Latin America. Later, Dakar became a half-way station for planes going from Africa or Europe to South America. But the coming of the jets has made direct flight to these destinations possible, and so Dakar has lost a good deal of its commercial importance.

STUDENTS *Two typical undergraduates converse on the campus of the University of Dakar.*

SHIFT FROM FRENCH DOMINATION

During the colonial period, some of the older generation of Senegalese, including President Senghor and Premier Mamadou Dia, received great honors from France. These men have deep emotional ties to the former mother country. In contrast, some of Senegal's younger generation — intellectuals, students, and trade union members — although French-educated, grew up in an atmosphere dominated by the move toward freedom. The emphasis shifted to solving African problems and enhancing African culture. For these men of the new day, the culture of France, the politics of France, the ideas of France, are not the

HOTEL DE N'GOR   *A striking landmark is the splendid curve of Dakar's show-place. Tennis courts, terraced lawns, and a private, white-sand beach enhance its popularity.*

central influence of their lives. These men think primarily in terms of Senegal and Senegalese culture. They would adopt a far more independent attitude toward France; and as they move into positions of power and influence, their voices will be increasingly heard.

Changes in the world price of peanut oil may also become a crucial factor in affecting the relationship between France and Senegal. For years, France has been paying Senegal an artificially inflated price for peanut oil. However, prices on this product have steadily risen; and in 1961, the market price nearly reached the subsidy price paid by France. It is likely that the price rise will continue. When Senegal can dispose of its peanut crop anywhere in the world at a price that is comparable to that paid by France, then the Senegalese may take a more independent attitude toward France. Even those officials most friendly to France may consider it wise to break the ties of complete economic dependence. Most certainly, there will be increased pressure on the old guard leaders to do just that.

STRENGTHENING THE ECONOMY

The younger officials complain about the rate of economic progress. They protest that the leadership has not initiated a program strong enough to insure dynamic change. Pressures for a bold approach toward bettering the economic and social condition of the Senegalese masses continue to mount. Many observers feel that leaders such as President Senghor would have no trouble maintaining close friendship with France, if at the same time they undertook some radical and far-reaching reforms.

In April, 1961, Premier Dia announced an ambitious four-year plan for economic and social advancement. This called for an investment of $400 million, based on aid of $117 million from foreign countries. The plan projects a 3.5 percent annual rise in the standard of living, predicated on an 8 percent annual increase in production. It is supposed to provide 10,000 new jobs in light industry. It simultaneously hopes to raise the literacy rate to 50 percent.

This plan has French support. Other Western nations are currently

STORY TIME   As in every country in the world, these children identify strongly with their favorite radio character. Here, three girls are listening to the story of Thiaba, the little African school girl, a popular program for youngsters. Notice the pin-ups on the wall.

studying it. Aid from the United Nations, the United States, and other countries, seems likely.

WESTERN TIES MAINTAINED

When he announced this four-year plan, President Senghor delivered a strong tribute to President de Gaulle of France for having granted full independence, within the course of two years, to fifteen former colonies. He also praised de Gaulle for his efforts to solve the Algerian crisis. In this matter, Senegal's stand was more pro-French than that of most other African countries. Senghor openly rejected the policy that he called "the radical neutralism" of such countries as Morocco, Guinea, and the United Arab Republic. However, even Senghor, the outspoken Francophile, believes that Africans should not slavishly imitate the West. Senghor, who created the term "New Negro," states that Africa and the West must learn from each other. His political philosophy, vis-a-vis the West, is epitomized in his slogan:"To assimilate —not be assimilated!"

As colonialism becomes a thing of the past, other African nations may adopt the more moderate approach to the West that Senegal follows.

POLITICAL PRESSURE OF NEW GENERATION

There are strong pressures within Senegal for a swing to the left. In December, 1961, the students of Dakar University went on strike after the government banned a conference of the General Union of West African Students. Several student leaders were arrested; others, expelled. In March, 1962, the Minister of Information announced he had uncovered a spy network and that a coup d'état had been planned. These simmerings of discontent auger a move away from conservatism.

The future course of African politics remains obscure. All that can be said is that today Senegal stands as a strong outpost of pro-Western feeling despite the fact that in most parts of Africa, powerful nationalist orientation has rendered European ties somewhat unfashionable.

IN BRIEF

AREA 77,401 square miles, about the size of South Dakota.

TERRAIN Mostly lowlands (altitude less than 650 feet) drained by four major rivers, Senegal, Saloum, Gambia, and Casamance. In the southwest, plateaus rise to 1,640 feet, forming foothills of the Fouta-Djalon mountains in Guinea.

CLIMATE Wet and dry seasons are well defined, with dry season from November to July. Temperature during rainy season is in low 80's.

CAPITAL Dakar (population, 300,000 in 1960).

POPULATION 3,140,000; about 52,000 Europeans.

OTHER CITIES Kaolack 50,000; St. Louis 40,000.

ETHNIC GROUPS Wolofs, numbering 700,000, are the largest. Others include Serer, Lebu, Toutcouleur, and Fulani. All are of tropical African stock.

LANGUAGE Official language is French, but Wolof language is widely spoken.

RELIGION About three-quarters of the people are Mohammedans; about 100,000 are Christians; most of the rest are animists.

DATE OF INDEPENDENCE August 20, 1960.

FORM OF GOVERNMENT Constitutional democracy. President, elected every seven years, appoints President of the Council of Ministers. The Council wields delegated executive power. National Assembly of 80 members is elected every five years by direct universal suffrage. Member of United Nations.

EDUCATION In 1958, 28 percent of school-age children attended school. In 1959, 91,900 students were enrolled in over 400 primary schools, with 7,000 students in 25 secondary schools. University of Dakar had an enrollment of 1,315 in the 1958.

| **HEALTH FACILITIES** | 5 main hospitals, 2 secondary hospitals, 25 health centers, 137 dispensaries, 39 specialized medical units (including maternity hospitals), mobile health and prophylaxis units for the rural population. |

HEALTH FACILITIES

5 main hospitals, 2 secondary hospitals, 25 health centers, 137 dispensaries, 39 specialized medical units (including maternity hospitals), mobile health and prophylaxis units for the rural population.

CURRENCY

Unit is French Community franc (247 francs = U.S. $1.00).

INDUSTRY

Highly industrialized, with soap factories and oil mills that process a large part of the peanut crop. Dakar has a sugar refinery, several other food-processing plants, three textile mills, and several chemical manufacturing plants.

CROPS: Rice and cassava are grown for domestic consumption; peanuts are main export crop.

STOCK: Livestock raised for local consumption.

FISHING: Only small-scale.

MINING: Mineral resources not fully explored. Some phosphates now being mined.

TRADE

1959:	IMPORTS	$147,730,000
	EXPORTS	99,405,000
	DEFICIT	$ 48,325,000

MAJOR IMPORTS: Foodstuffs, textiles, fuel, raw materials, capital goods, and semifinished goods.

MAJOR EXPORTS: Peanuts, palm oils, gum arabic, leather and hides, and mineral products.

TRANSPORTATION

ROADS: 450 miles surfaced roads; 2,000 miles all-weather roads.

VEHICLES: 13,870 passenger cars; 10,772 commercial vehicles (1958).

WATERWAYS: Several ports and four navigable rivers.

RAILROADS: 730 miles of track.

AIR TRAFFIC: Fifteen airports.

COMMUNICATIONS

In 1956, five major newspapers had a total circulation of about 40,000. Dakar has two radio stations, one international; also telecommunications and a postal system.

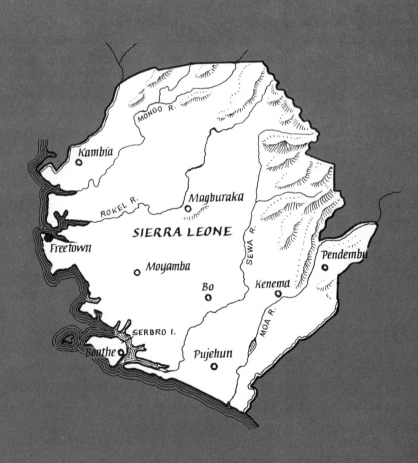

MONGO R.

Kambia

ROKEL R.

Magburaka

SIERRA LEONE

Freetown

Moyamba

Bo

SEWA R.

Kenema

Pendembu

MOA R.

SERBRO I.

Bonthe

Pujehun

SIERRA LEONE

A Great University and a Great Harbor

On the heights of Mount Aureol, overlooking the quiet, late-Victorian city of Freetown, stands a small collection of buildings that ranks as one of the proudest outposts of learning in the entire world. It is the University College of Sierra Leone, formerly called Fourah Bay.

FOURAH BAY COLLEGE

Founded in 1827, Fourah Bay was for a full hundred years the only institution of higher learning in West Africa. It became affiliated with Durham University in England in 1876, and has functioned ever since as if it were one of Durham University's colleges. Its academic program, examinations, and degrees are all under the supervision of Durham and its standards are equivalent to those of the English university.

Many leaders of the new nations of West Africa, including Sierra Leone's first Prime Minister, Sir Milton Margai, are graduates of Fourah Bay. In preparing the men of Sierra Leone and its neighboring countries for positions of leadership in their newly independent nations, the college has made an immeasurable contribution to the future of Africa.

Fourah Bay has carried on its great mission with pitifully meager accomodations. As the college expanded, classes were held in makeshift wooden buildings. But when Sierra Leone became independent in 1961, concerted efforts were made to house the entire university in modern buildings. From its commanding position, high above the city, the university overlooks a harbor that similarly presents a sharp contrast between its current development and its potential.

FREETOWN—A NATURAL HARBOR

Freetown's harbor is the finest on the west coast of Africa, and one of the greatest in the world. Theoretically, it should be able to accom-

modate 240 ocean-going vessels, but until the present time it has not had
the necessary piers and docks. Large vessels must be unloaded by lighters.
The first quay was recently completed, but it can accommodate only
three ocean-going vessels.

Freetown, itself, is one of the most squalid capitals in Africa. Most
of the city is a collection of unbelievably ghastly shacks. The British
made no attempt to build much of lasting value. The new independent
government is taking steps to cure this shameful condition.

THE EFFECT OF THE CLIMATE

One of the reasons for Sierra Leone's slow rate of development is
its climate. Freetown receives about 150 inches of rain annually, almost
all of it during the wet season, which lasts from April through November. July and August are the wettest months. In each, the average rainfall is 35 inches. Although this is by no means the highest rate of rainfall in Africa, its effect on every facet of life in the city and the entire
country is inevitably profound. To paraphrase the statement of Roy
Lewis, who has written so much about the country, the rain and accom-
panying humidity are what keep Freetown small and the port facilities
inadequate; maintain idlers humming on street corners to the counter-
point of throbbing tribal drums in the interior; preserve the lush greenery
of the mountains; abet the failure of well-planned schemes; and account
for the conservative wisdom and patience of the country's government.

Lethargy is one of the by-products of a hot, humid, uncomfortable
climate. European businessmen and technicians who could contribute to
the development of the country, tend to shun such a climate. In Sierra's
population of 2.5 million, there are only 2,000 Europeans.

The extremely heavy rainfall seriously interferes with construction work. Projects literally get stuck in the mud. Delays in a project mean that the ever-present jungle and forest close in on it rapidly,
and constant efforts must be made to keep clearings open. Both in the
cities and in the interior, the climate has produced a slow-tempoed life
which lacks the vigor needed for the development of a new country.

Sierra Leone lies in the Equatorial Monsoon Region. The major
climatic characteristic which distinguishes this area is that it has one dry

season of three to four months. This has a significant effect on the vegetation. There is less jungle, therefore more dry forest; fewer evergreens, and more deciduous types of flora.

Freetown has a mean daily temperature of 81 degrees; throughout the year, the average varies only 3 degrees. The city is pelted with 150 inches of rain each year. The heat reaches its peak just before the onset of the coming rainy season. The sky is clear from December through March, but the heat continues, nevertheless.

STREET SCENE   *Throughout Sierra Leone open-air shops are common. The hanging garments are khaftans, the native gown that is usually worn with a colorful or black overgarment, but sometimes by itself. Behind the passers-by, a man is making European-style shirts. Calabashes, seen stacked, and one on a pedestrian's head, are hollowed-out gourds used as baskets.*

JUSTICES OF THE SUPREME COURT   *The three Justices of the Supreme Court of Sierra Leone are, left to right: Chief Justice Sir Salako Benka-Coker; Justice S. B. Jones, Puisne Judge; Justice J. B. Marcus Jones, Puisne Judge. The wigs and gowns are in the British tradition.*

During certain days of the dry season, Freetown experiences the harmattan, a very dry wind that sweeps down from the Sahara. Despite the dust it brings, the harmattan is often welcome, even on hot days, for its slight relief. Here, as in most of Africa, the winds are little better than light breezes. They usually die away at sundown, adding to the discomfort of the tropical nights.

HISTORY AND POLITICS

The history of Sierra Leone can be traced back to 1460, when Pedro da Cintra, a Portuguese adventurer, visited the coast. Apparently he thought he heard lions roaring in the mountains, for he called it Sierra Leone—the land of the lion mountains. Actually, no lion has ever been seen in the country.

Progressive social change began in 1787 when the territory was established by England as a home for liberated slaves. In 1799, the area received a royal charter, and Freetown was incorporated, with a mayor and aldermen. This makes it the oldest incorporated settlement in West Africa.

During the nineteenth century, there was a great influx of people into Sierra Leone, not only eager freedmen from England and the British West Indies, but also colonial administrators and missionaries. So many Europeans were killed off in the ensuing years by the prevalent diseases, that the land became known as "the white man's grave." In recent times, however, medicine has made vigorous inroads on these diseases.

The descendants of the liberated slaves called themselves Creoles. They now number about 100,000. For a long time, they held leadership status in Sierra Leone. This was quite similar to the situation in Liberia, where returned slaves from the United States assumed leadership, and still maintain it.

SIR MILTON MARGAI

As Christians, the Creoles looked down upon the animist tribes of the interior. However, with encouragement by the British, the backward tribes began to compete with the Creoles for leadership. Sir Milton Margai, Prime Minister of the country, comes from one of these tribes.

Margai was educated at a Protestant mission school, and then at Fourah Bay College. He completed his medical studies at the University of Durham. As a practicing doctor, he became interested in social welfare schemes, and this brought him into politics in his middle years.

SCHOOLS AND THE CIVIL SERVICE

In addition to Fourah Bay College, primary and secondary school facilities were established many years ago by the colonial government and by the missionaries. Educated Africans were taken into the civil service at an early date, and from 1951 on (beginning with the year the new constitution was adopted), the functions of government were rapidly turned over to Africans. Sierra Leone, with so many capable leaders, moved smoothly into independence on April 27, 1961.

UNDERGROUND WEALTH

Sierra Leone is fortunate in having important sources of mineral wealth to supplement its basic agricultural economy. The country is

DIAMOND MINING　Queen Elizabeth and Prince Philip observe the production-line operation in Hangha, at the second largest diamond-producing field in the British Commonwealth. This is an alluvial deposit, and the mining proceeds from the surface to a relatively shallow depth. The panning operation of the man at the right is reminiscent of the gold-panning practiced by old-time American prospectors.

rich in diamonds and in iron ore; deposits of chrome ore and rutile have also been discovered and are now being developed.

The existence of alluvial diamond deposits has given Sierra Leone a unique problem: diamond smuggling is one of the most serious difficulties facing the nation's economy. Unlicensed diggers find it easy to pan out diamonds surreptitiously, and Sierra Leone loses untold millions of dollars that it would ordinarily receive as its share of the revenue from legal mining operations. In the immediate future, the problem of developing a favorable trade balance may well depend on whether or not the government can control this smuggling. A number of steps have been taken, with some success. Among other things, the government recently expelled 20,000 Liberian and Guinean diggers who had infiltrated into the southeastern provinces. According to the government, not only did their smuggling adversely affect the balance of trade, but their presence in the country accentuated existing food scarcities and inflated living costs.

ECONOMIC OUTLOOK

The discovery of diamonds in Sierra Leone illustrates once more the problem many such new nations face when substantial underground wealth is discovered. In most instances the economies of these countries depend heavily on subsistence agriculture. When mineral wealth is discovered, many people leave the farms and go to the cities or the mines. This means fewer agricultural workers, and, if the population movement is rapid, the pattern of the economy can be substantially upset.

In Sierra Leone, prior to 1956, the colony had been self-sufficient in rice, the basic food crop. As the diamond-mining activity grew and the resultant wealth increased purchasing power, Sierra Leone found it necessary to import rice for the first time in her history, purchasing 31,000 long tons in 1957 at a cost of nearly $4 million. Despite this food problem, her diamond mining continued to provide important trade benefits. In 1957, the value of minerals shipped abroad, including diamonds, exceeded agricultural imports for the first time, by over $19 million. Even today, with diamond smuggling not yet under control, Sierra Leone's trade deficit is quite small—less than $2 million.

Besides her mineral resources, the country produces a diversity of flourishing cash crops, the most important of which are palm kernels and palm oil. Cocoa and coffee are also being successfully grown, and the acreage devoted to these crops is rapidly being expanded.

With this diversity of agricultural and mineral wealth, with the slowly developing harbor of Freetown, and despite the heavy tropical rain, Sierra Leone looks forward to a steadily expanding economy during the coming decade.

ENTERTAINERS AT KENEMA   A barri, or shelter hut, is erected for all festival occasions. The stilt dancer and the musicians are waiting to perform for Queen Elizabeth II and Prince Philip on their 1961 visit to Sierra Leone.

PRIME MINISTER *Sir Milton Augustus Strieby Margai chose modern history as his special subject while taking his Bachelor of Arts at the University College of Sierra Leone. Born in 1895, the son of a merchant, Sir Milton had been respected for many years as a skilled surgeon, before he achieved political fame. He has played an important role in the political, medical, and cultural development of his country.*

IN BRIEF

AREA   28,000 square miles, about the size of South Carolina.

TERRAIN   Three main regions: coastal belt of mangrove swamps; stretches of wooded hill country; upland plateau.

CLIMATE   Wet and dry seasons are well defined, with dry season from November to May. Rain, heaviest on the coast, falls mainly from July through September. Mean temperature is about 80°; temperature range and relative humidity are more varied inland than on the coast.

CAPITAL   Freetown (population, 88,000).

OTHER CITIES Bo, 20, 000.

POPULATION   2,500,000 (1961); 2,000 Europeans.

ETHNIC GROUPS Mende and Temne peoples make up about 60 percent of the African population. About 27,000 Creoles (descendents of the freed slaves) in Freetown area.

LANGUAGE   English is the official language, with many tribal languages also spoken.

345

RELIGION	Mohammedans are about 28 percent of population. Christianity, long established, has many adherents; but pagan beliefs of the Mende people, who worship Ngewo, and the Temne people, whose supreme being is Kurumasaba, remain powerful.
DATE OF INDEPENDENCE	April 27, 1961.
FORM OF GOVERNMENT	Constitutional democracy; popularly elected House of Representatives, which elects its own speaker. Leader of majority party becomes Prime Minister, and chooses his cabinet. Member of British Commonwealth of Nations and of the United Nations.
EDUCATION	In 1958, 69,276 students attended 522 primary schools; there were 5,904 students in 26 secondary schools. University College of Sierra Leone, formerly Fourah Bay College, is the oldest institution of higher learning in western tropical Africa. Current enrollment about 300 students.
HEALTH FACILITIES	26 government-aided hospitals; plus 2 hospitals and 4 dispensaries owned by the mining companies. Also, 25 health centers, 15 mission dispensaries, and 35 treatment centers.
CURRENCY	Unit is West African pound, equal to £1 British (£1 = U.S. $2.80).
INDUSTRY	Mostly light industry, including processing of fish, timber, and rice.

CROPS: Rice is main food crop; cassava, sweet potatoes, maize, millet are also grown for domestic consumption. Export crops include palm kernels, kola nuts, piasava (used in making brooms), ginger, coffee, and cocoa.

STOCK: Some cattle.

FISHING: 5,000 tons are caught annually; most smoked or dried.

MINING: Iron ore, chrome ore, and substantial diamonds.

TRADE	1960:	IMPORTS	$73,640,000
		EXPORTS	71,960,000
		DEFICIT	$ 1,680,000

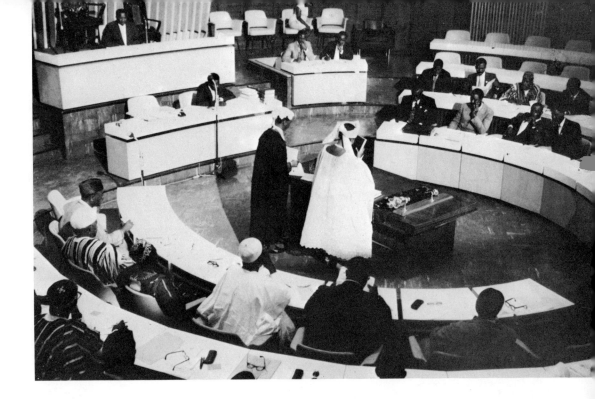

HOUSE OF REPRESENTATIVES—*The only woman member of Parliament, Paramount Chief Madam Ella Koblo Gulama, minister without portfolio, takes the oath on the official opening day, July 10, 1962, in the new House of Representatives.*

MAJOR IMPORTS: Fabrics, clothing, machinery, iron and steel, manufactured goods, food, building materials, and petroleum products.

MAJOR EXPORTS: Diamonds, iron ore, and agricultural products (*see* Crops).

TRANS-PORTATION

ROADS: 2,900 miles all-weather.

VEHICLES: 515 passenger cars; 2,216 commercial vehicles (1958).

WATERWAYS: 493 miles of inland waterways; several are navigable only three months of year.

RAILROADS: 311 miles of government track; 57 miles of private track for carrying ore.

AIR TRAFFIC: One international airport at Freetown and four smaller airfields.

COMMUNI-CATIONS

National broadcasting service began in 1955. Ten newspapers published, two daily.

Dante

Berbera DARRAR R. Hɵrdio

Hargeisa

Bender
Beila

Eil

S O M A L I A

Iddan

Lugh
Ferrandi SCEBELI R. Harardera

Itala

GIUBA R.

Brava

Chambione

SOMALIA

A Desert People with a Banana Crop

On July 1, 1960, the Republic of Somalia, formed from the territories until then known as Italian Somaliland and British Somaliland, was declared an independent nation. Four days of joyous celebration followed; cannons roared, crowds danced in the streets of Mogadishu, the capital city.

But when the shouting was over, Somalia faced the same serious problems—problems that had not been automatically solved with the attainment of independence.

BASIC PROBLEMS

Somalia does not have an adequate foundation for a self-sustaining national economy. The chief export crop—bananas—accounting for 55 percent of the country's exports, is not commercially successful. Italy purchases the entire crop and subsidizes its production, in order to create a favorable balance of trade for Somalia.

More subtle are the problems involved in fusing into a homogenous nation territories dominated for centuries by disparate tribal allegiances, and in overcoming the clannish conservatism of a nomadic people, resistant to social change.

Social standing is, for the most part, based on lineage; and strife is common.

There are large blocs of Somali people in neighboring states. Inevitably, tensions will grow as Somalia brings pressure to bear on its neighbors for the annexation of territory. Somalia and Ethiopia have had a long-standing boundary dispute that is difficult to resolve.

SOMALI CULTURE

The Somalis are an ancient, proud Hamitic people. Stemming from the Middle East many centuries ago, they invaded Somali country; and intermingling with another Hamitic group, the Galla, and with the

FERRY AT JUBA RIVER   *Somalis are crossing the river on free ferry service at Lugh Ferrandi.*

Bantu tribes, they evolved a culture.

The Somalis are Mohammedans. They have their own language, with an oral body of poetry, but have been unable, among themselves, to agree on a written script. Two Somali scripts have been proposed, one based on Arabic characters, the other on Roman characters; but political and religious questions have so far prevented a settlement.

THE TWO SOMALILANDS

Italian Somaliland, extending south along the Indian Ocean, was claimed by Italy as a protectorate, in 1899. A decade later, the British established themselves in British Somaliland. Together, the two countries formed a rough figure 7, with British Somaliland lying at the top—athwart the Italian protectorate.

After the Second World War, the leaders in both colonies began to clamor for independence. Italian Somaliland, the larger of the two, became a United Nations Trust Territory, which made it easier for it to find a ready ear, in the U.N., for its demands for independence.

The trusteeship arrangement worked out well for Italian Somaliland. In November, 1949, with the approval of Italy, the General Assembly of the U.N. resolved that Somalia would receive its independence by December 2, 1960. The date was later advanced to July, 1960. Italy was designated the administering authority during the ten-year period of trusteeship; and the trustee rapidly moved to transfer governing powers to the Somali people. The Italian government continued to provide financial and administrative assistance, as Somalia prepared for independence.

In May, 1956, the first all-Somali government was established. Somalia's international relations and defense remained under Italy's control.

During the ten years of trusteeship, the Italian government granted Somalia about $100,000,000 in economic and technical assistance. Between 1954 and 1960, the United States provided $5,000,000 in economic aid. With this help, Italian Somaliland was able to make a start on a few of her difficult problems.

WATTLE VILLAGE These huts are constructed of wattle—interwoven rods, reeds, and branches. This wood interlacing forms the foundation on which mud or straw is spread to make a wall or roof. A man may own many huts, depending on the amount of his wealth. Each hut houses a wife, and the huts are interconnected. The partially whitewashed structure belongs to the chief.

VILLAGERS *Only women draw water and haul water gourds—work considered beneath the dignity of a man. The boy is biting off the bark at the end of a stick. Such sticks are carried by natives in imitation of the white man's badge of authority, the riding crop.*

Meanwhile, British Somaliland remained a British protectorate. However, in 1960, the British agreed to grant British Somaliland its complete independence, so that it could unite with Italian Somaliland to form the new nation of Somalia.

THE ROLE OF THE DESERT

The Somalis are a nomadic, pastoral people. The current of recent political changes has barely affected them. The greatest difficulty is in furthering education. It is all but impossible to establish regular schools in a land where the population is thinly spread over wide, semi-arid areas, and is constantly on the move. Outside of Mogadishu, there are few schools. Ninety percent, or more, of the Somalis are illiterate.

The introduction of scientific animal husbandry is also extremely slow and difficult. To the nomads, cattle have for centuries been regarded as an important type of personal wealth; and this attitude militates against the cooperation needed for successful commercial development of the herds. In fact, many African herders will not sell any of their cattle, even when they have many more than the land will feed, more than they can possibly use for food or for trading purposes. Little effort is made to improve breeding strains. As a result, the animals frequently have but poor market value.

Finally, the nomadic life seems to create close tribal loyalties and fierce inter-tribal jealousies, making it difficult to form a united people out of so many disparate, individualistic groups.

The population density of Somalia of 7.7 persons per square mile is just about what it is for most of the other desert countries of Africa. The country has no railroads, and most vehicular roads are impassable during the rainy season.

OUTDOOR COUNCIL MEETING   Members of a local Council at Chisimaio hold a meeting outdoors to discuss civic affairs, during the U.N. Trusteeship Administration.

BUILDING THE ECONOMY

The wealth of the country consists of camels, sheep, goats, and cattle. Somalia exports close to $3 million in livestock and hides.

The country's limited commercial crops are grown mainly near the Shebeli and Juba Rivers. The basic cash crops are bananas and sugar. Only about 17 percent of the land in Somalia can be tilled; 44 percent is useful only for grazing; and the remainder is barren.

After studying Somalia's economic problems, the International Bank for Reconstruction and Development reported that financial assistance at the approximate rate of $5,000,000 a year, would be necessary for twenty years. Italy, the United States, and Great Britain have offered to underwrite the trade deficit that Somalia will incur in the near future; and it is likely that the United Nations will also contribute financial and technical aid.

BOUNDARIES AND STATESMANSHIP

Another difficulty stems from the drawing of capricious boundary lines during the colonial period. There are 30,000 Somalis in French Somaliland, and 50,000 Somalis in the Ogaden Province of Ethiopia. There are also considerable numbers of Somalis in the northern part of Kenya, which is a dry desert-like steppe, not unlike most of Somalia. Although the government of Somalia has advocated a conservative approach to the creation of "Greater Somalia," faster action is constantly being urged by the pro-Arab Greater Somalia League, which supports the program of the United Arab Republic.

In September, 1961, Emperor Haile Selassie of Ethiopia and President Osman of Somalia met, quietly and informally, to discuss their border problems. In spite of the inflammatory feelings fanned by the Greater Somalia League, they agreed to exchange good-will missions to repair the strained relations. In the turbulent events of today's Africa, such seemingly inconsequential acts are frequently overlooked; yet they are of genuine significance. Even when dealing with the most emotionally charged issues, a higher level of statesmanship has begun to characterize relations between African states.

MOSQUE OF THE FOUR CORNERS   *In the heart of Mogadishu, at the junction of First of July Avenue and Somali Avenue, there stands this Arab mosque which dates back to the fifteenth century.*

TIME OUT   *A camel driver in Villagio Abruzi rests his charges.*

BOYHOOD FRIENDS   *Neither has ever known a dentist.*

PRESIDENT ABDEN ABDULLAH OSMAN

President Osman comes from a poor family. He was a civil servant in Italian Somaliland. After World War II, Osman went into business and then into politics. His Young Somali Party took a leading part in the agitation for independence.

Today, several parties have seats in the National Assembly, which is a truly representative body. Somalia is governed democratically; its President has shown no dictatorial ambitions.

ABDEN ABDULLAH OSMAN   Osman was born in 1908. When 14, an Italian friend took him under his wing, and among other things, taught him how to type. Later, he served in the Italian Administration. After various political stints, he was elected President of the Somali Legislative Assembly in 1956. Widely respected, especially by the conservative elements, he was elected President of Somali in 1960, when the country became independent.

IN BRIEF

AREA	246,202 square miles, about the combined size of California, Pennsylvania and Tennessee.
TERRAIN	The southern portion of this country, once Italian Somalialand, is much longer than it is wide, and runs parallel to the Indian Ocean. There is an agricultural region between the Juba and Shebeli Rivers. The northern section, once British Somalialand, is much wider. It is bordered on the north by the Gulf of Aden. The main watershed is a mountain range running east-west along the extreme north of the country. The plateau area is in the south.
CLIMATE	Tropical, little variation in annual mean temperature. Periodic winds maintain constant temperature. Two rainy seasons a year.
CAPITAL	Mogadishu (population, 87,000).
POPULATION	1,900,000; about 4,000 Europeans.
ETHNIC GROUPS	Mamitic peoples, divided into two main families, Somali and Sab; many Arabs.
LANGUAGE	Italian, Somali, Arabic, and English are all spoken.
RELIGION	Mohammedanism is the state religion.
DATE OF INDEPENDENCE	July 1, 1960.
FORM OF GOVERNMENT	Constitutional democracy with one-house legislature. President, who is popularly elected, has power to dissolve government, but actual government operations are conducted by Prime Minister and Council of Ministers. Elections are held every five years on basis of universal suffrage. Member of United Nations.
EDUCATION	232 primary schools have 20,077 students, 6 secondary schools have only 855 students. The Higher Institute of Law and

MILKING A CAMEL A camel is milked twice daily and gives approximately the same amount of milk as a cow. The milk is very low in fat content, and quite similar to skimmed milk in consistency. It is used mainly to make cheese. When milking, the man stands on the side of the camel, one knee raised to balance a hollowed-out gourd, into which the milk is run. There are over 16 million camels in Somalia, mostly dromedaries (one-humped camel). Camels are a status symbol, and are, therefore, tended only by the men. The women are consigned to the tending of sheep, goats, and cattle.

Economics, at Mogadishu, had 33 students enrolled in 1958. It is now being expanded, with Italian aid, into Mogadishu University. Outside of the Mogadishu area, an estimated 90 percent of the people are illiterate.

HEALTH FACILITIES

18 hospitals, 21 infirmaries, and 139 dispensaries.

CURRENCY

Unit is somolo (1 somolo = U.S. $0.14).

INDUSTRY

Light industry, processing of some raw materials and food.

CROPS: Corn, sorghum, legumes, cotton, and sesame for domestic use. Bananas and sugar are the cash crops for export.

STOCK: Cattle, goats, sheep, and camels.

FISHING: All fish, caught principally in the Indian Ocean, are for local use.

MINING: Small amounts of limestone, soapstone, alabaster, and marble. Minor exporting, recently begun, includes beryllium, columbite, cassiterite, and mica, mainly from area of former British Somaliland.

TRADE

No international trade figures are available. As of 1960, Italy imported both cash crops entirely, and heavily subsidized the economy.

TRANS-PORTATION

ROADS: 758 miles surfaced; 1,500 unsurfaced, all-weather.

VEHICLES: 2,159 passenger cars; 3,267 commercial vehicles (1960).

WATERWAYS: No natural harbors. Mostly small fishing ports.

RAILROADS: None:

AIR TRAFFIC: 14 airfields.

COMMUNI-CATIONS

Government-controlled postal and telegraph services. Eight towns have telephone service. One local radio station. Two daily newspapers.

SUDAN

Two Cultures and a Cotton Crop

Rudyard Kipling paid memorable tribute to Sudan's crack warriors when he wrote:

> "So 'ere's to you, Fuzzy-Wuzzy
> At your 'ome in the Soudan;
> You're a pore benighted 'eathen
> But a first-class fightin' man."

These warriors were members of the Beja tribe, one of the many sturdy ethnic groups in the Sudan. Sir Winston Churchill, as a young man, fought with Lord Kitchener, in a campaign to put down a Sudanese rebellion—one of the many uprisings that were not completely quelled until 1899.

Today, the Sudanese concentrate their attack on the country's economic problems, directed by the Sudanese "strong man," Lieutenant General Ibrahim Abboud, who was brought to power in 1958 by the armed forces, after the parliamentary democracy failed to solve a strictly non-military problem—the disposal of Sudan's all-important cotton crop.

COTTON—KING OF THE SUDAN

Cotton is Sudan's principal crop, accounting for about 70 percent of the country's exports. From 1899 until 1954, while Sudan (then called Anglo-Egyptian Sudan), was under joint British and Egyptian rule, highest priority was given to the establishment of regional farming developments for the raising of cotton. Attempts were made to use the Nile River and its tributaries to irrigate such new sites.

A prime example is the Jazirah Scheme, dating from the 1920's, located near the confluence of the Blue and White Niles. This development produces the bulk of the nation's cotton and brings in almost half the government's revenue. The land is owned, or leased, by about 30,000 farmers who manage it in partnership with the government through the Jazirah Board. The farmers and the government each receive 40 percent of the annual proceeds, with the remaining 20 percent going to the Board for management expenses. This project is similar to the *Office du Niger* in Mali and follows a pattern that is likely to be repeated in many African areas.

COTTON AND THE MILITARY COUP

The Anglo-Egyptian agreement of 1953 provided for Sudanese self-determination. By December, 1955, Sudan, through her first generally elected parliament, had voted for complete independence. Great Britain and Egypt promptly assented. A parliamentary democracy with contending political parties was set up, but soon ran into difficulties. The government was unable to sell cotton effectively on the world market, and the new republic was soon in a state of financial chaos. As the cotton surplus rapidly accumulated, the economy began to totter.

On November 17, 1958, Lieutenant General Abboud, Commander-in-Chief of the armed forces, seized power and established a military regime with himself at the head. Dissolving the political parties, Abboud's government plunged into the country's tangled economic affairs.

Their efforts were successful. Within a year the accumulated cotton surplus had been sold, and buyers were available for the 1959 crop. In 1960, a bumper crop of more than 650,000 bales was completely sold, bringing in about $75 million. The treasury built up a record foreign exchange reserve of $165 million. Import restrictions, imposed earlier to keep the country solvent when the economy was foundering, have been lifted; the national budget is balanced; national credit is good; and foreign goods of many descriptions are on sale in the shops of Khartoum. The country is enjoying a modest boom.

EXPANDING AND DIVERSIFYING AGRICULTURE

Sudan's marketing problems of 1957 and 1958 gave clear warning to the government of the danger inherent in a one-crop economy. The government started experimenting with other agricultural products.

DESERT HERDSMAN   *Typical Zebeida tribesman has
just brought a herd of camels to sell in the market at Kassala.*

Success in this direction will depend on supplementing the inadequate water supply. This, of course, can be accomplished only through irrigation.

On the Blue Nile, south of Jazirah Scheme, Sudan has constructed the Managil Dam, which has put 600,000 additional acres under irrigation. An even larger project now under way is the construction of the Roseires Dam, which will store enough water to more than double the amount now available. The new project will stabilize the country's water supply, and will place another 900,000 acres under irrigation.

DEVELOPMENT OF INDUSTRY

The Roseires Dam will also furnish abundant hydro-electric power. Sudan will probably have developed sufficient industry to utilize this increased power when it becomes available. The government is currently encouraging the development of light industry in Khartoum, financed through public and private loans.

During 1960 and 1961, 88 industrial enterprises were established, representing a capital investment of $500 million. The products manufactured include such low-priced items as cigarettes, matches, chinaware and kitchen pans. A $20 million loan from the United States Development Loan Fund serves to finance a textile mill outside Khartoum. Cotton fabrics will be produced here for domestic use.

CULTURAL DICHOTOMY

Sudan is composed of two peoples; one represents an African civilization, and the other an Eastern civilization. The central and northern parts of Sudan are inhabited principally by Arab-speaking Mohammedans, who comprise two-thirds of the population. The broad plains of southern Sudan are inhabited by Negroid tribes who speak several

MARKET AT KASSALA   The fuzzy-headed man is from the Hadendawa tribe; the turbaned man from the Zebeida tribe. Both tribes are nomadic and both raise camels for the market.

African languages. There are no less than 100 dialects spoken.

The people of the north have written records which go back 4,000 years to a time when Sudan was a southern extension of the land of the Egyptian Pharaohs. The people of this region have cultural ties to the Middle East, and have more kinship with the civilization of Europe than they have with the civilization of tropical Africa.

On the other hand, the Negroid Africans are highly sensitive to any suggestion of cultural inferiority. To bridge the gulf between these two racial groups will test the wisdom and patience of the country's leaders.

IBRAHIM ABBOUD   Born in 1900, the son of a junior official of the old British administration, Abboud studied engineering at the Gordon Memorial College at Khartoum. Upon being graduated in 1917, he became a cadet in the Military College. In 1949, the British appointed him to the highest military post ever held by a Sudanese. Only as late as 1958, did he enter politics when, as Supreme Commander of the military junta, he engineered a coup to gain control of the government.

UNLOADING LUMBER AT OMDURMAN   Three vessels discharge their loads of lumber and firewood at a wharf on the western bank of the Nile.

NOMADS VISITING KHARTOUM   *Desert nomads visit the capital, at the juncture of the Blue and White Nile. The tribeswomen are heavily veiled. The camels are used for draft as well as for riding.*

UNIVERSITY COLLEGE OF KHARTOUM   *Faculties of arts, science, agriculture, engineering, law, veterinary science, and medicine, serve over 1,000 students in this co-educational institution. Established in 1956; degrees gained here are honored by the University of London.*

IRRIGATION IN THE JAZIRAH DISTRICT   *This region has developed into a great cotton-growing area which has become the mainstay of the Sudan economy. The farmer controls the flow of water to his section of land by working the valve of the irrigation lines.*

POLITICAL PULLS

There is conflict among the Mohammedans as to what attitude is to be taken towards Nasser's United Arab Republic. To many Moslems, the U.A.R. is a powerful magnet. When Sudan became independent, its two major political parties disagreed on this issue. The pro-Nasser party looked toward union with the Egyptian Arabs. The anti-Nasser party felt that Sudan should pursue her own national development independently.

Arab nationalism will continue to be an issue in countries such as Sudan, that have a substantial Moslem population. Though he takes his Islamic creed very seriously, Acting Chief-of-State Abboud has made no move toward union with Egypt.

Abboud is considered pro-Western, but has not hesitated to accept aid from both Russia and the United States.

NATURAL RESOURCES AND EXPORTS

Sudan is a poor country. The average income is something like $75 a year per person.

The country grows peanuts, oilseed, and millet for export. Livestock is part of foreign trade.

Sudan contains a paucity of minerals. There are but fair deposits of iron ore, mica, manganese, and asbestos. Gold has been mined in small quantities for centuries; but oil, in any appreciable quantity, has not yet been discovered.

WAD MEDANI   In this town of 48,000 people, markets like this line the streets. Though women are often the vendors in such street stalls, in the larger towns such as this, men (white garments) are the chief merchants. This market caters to women, offering household wares and personal adornments.

CAMEL VENDORS AT KASSALA   *The turbaned Zebeida tribesmen visit the cattle and camel market at Kassala.*

IN BRIEF

AREA 967,500 square miles; almost one-third the size of continental United States.

TERRAIN Nile River, formed by confluence of Blue and the White Niles near Khartoum, dominates the land. Most of the country is a plain; the northern end is largely desert. Good harbors at Port Sudan and Suakin, on the Red Sea.

CLIMATE In the desert and along the coast of the Red Sea, temperatures exceed 100° most of the year. Rainfall varies from 60 inches annually in the tropical south to almost none in the northern desert.

CAPITAL Khartoum (93,000).

OTHER CITIES Omdurman, 113,600.

POPULATION 11,928,000; about 6,998 Europeans and Americans.

ETHNIC GROUPS 40 percent are Arabs, 20 percent are Nilotic Negroid peoples, and the balance is made up of smaller tribes.

LANGUAGE Arabic is official language, spoken by more than half the population; English is widely known. There are also about 100 local languages and dialects spoken.

RELIGION Mohammedanism is official religion, practiced by two-thirds of the people. The rest are animists, with small numbers of Christians, Hindus, and Jews.

DATE OF INDEPENDENCE January 1, 1956.

FORM OF GOVERNMENT Democratic republic originally. Military dictatorship installed in 1958. Government administered by the Prime Minister and his Cabinet. A bicameral Parliament has a Senate of 50 members and a House of Representatives of 97 members. Member of United Nations and of the Arab League.

EDUCATION 75 percent of males and 95 percent of females are illiterate. However, now 268,000 students in 2,197 primary schools, and 51,000 students in 253 secondary schools. Khartoum University has an enrollment of about 1,000 students.

HEALTH FACILITIES	45 hospitals, plus 660 dispensaries and dressing stations.
CURRENCY	Unit is Sudanese pound (£ 1 = U.S. $2.87).
INDUSTRY	Light industry only, mostly low-priced products for domestic consumption: cigarettes, matches, chinaware, and kitchen pans. Textile mill being built outside Khartoum.
MAJOR PRODUCTS	CROPS: Sorghum, millet, and wheat grown for domestic consumption. Cotton is principal export crop.
	STOCK: Stock raising is a major industry. Cattle, sheep, goats, and camels are owned almost exclusively by nomadic tribesmen, principally raised for domestic use. Some meat, wool, and hides are exported.

MARKET IN OMDURMAN   On the Western bank of the Nile, opposite Khartoum, lies this city of 113,000. The market is a series of open stalls. The single modern vehicle contrasts with the handcart so close to it.

PALACE AT KHARTOUM   Located on the River Esplanade along the Nile, the Republican Palace, a three-storied, stone and brick building with arcaded verandas, stands on the main boulevard of Khartoum. The southern facade of the building overlooks Khedive Avenue, the main business street of the city.

FISHING: Fish from Nile River is staple diet in many areas.

MINING: Large copper reserves appear to exist near Port Sudan, but mining is not yet developed.

TRADE

1960:	EXPORTS	$182,000,000
	IMPORTS	$181,000,000
	DEFICIT	$1,000,000

TRANS-PORTATION

ROADS: No modern roads outside the cities.

VEHICLES: 11,300 passenger; 14,000 commercial (1959).

WATERWAYS: Cargo and passenger port at Port Sudan.

RAILROADS: 2,700 miles of track, linking north and central sections of the country to Port Sudan.

AIRPORTS: One international and thirty-seven minor airfields.

COMMUNI-CATIONS

Postal, telephone and telegraph services and a radio station, all state-owned. Eighteen daily newspapers published in four languages.

L. ALBERT

L. EDWARD

Entebbe

L. VICTORIA

L. RIVU

Bukoba

Musoma

Mwanza

Geita

Moshi

Arusha

Tabora

Tanga

MALAGARASI
R.

UGALLA R.

TANGANYIKA

L. TANGANYIKA

Dar es Salaam

Bagamoyo

RUNGWA R.

GREAT RUAHA R.

Mbeya

Iringa

Kilwa Masoka

Njombe

Lindi

Songea

Mtwara

RUVUMA R.

L. NYASA

TANGANYIKA

Scenic Splendors and the Tsetse Fly

Tanganyika, a large agricultural country, contains over 9,000,-000 inhabitants, composed of over 120 Negro tribes.

The majority of the people are pagans. The Moslems constitute the largest group of adherents to an organized religion. Catholics and Protestants are about equally divided.

Though English is the official language, Swahili is the principal tongue and is spoken by practically everyone. Only half a million Tanganyikans work for wages. Most of the remainder engage in farming.

THE STRANGE MASAI TRIBE

The Masai may well be the most interesting tribe in Africa. Of distinctive physical appearance, the Masai are slender, handsome, tall, and well-made. Many of the men are well over 6 feet, with eyes that are slightly oblique. The finely chiseled nose of the chocolate-colored Masai is almost Caucasian.

Almost all men and women knock out the two lower incisor teeth. They have a tradition that lockjaw was once very common among them, and they say that they find it easier to feed a sufferer through the gap they provide in this way.

The Masai pull out the hair on the bodies of both sexes with iron tweezers. Women shave off the hair of their heads; so do married men. Young unmarried Masai coat their hair with red clay, mutton fat, and dung, and then plait the hair with thin strips of leather, forming it into pigtails. The largest pigtail hangs down the back; another over the forehead, and two others on each side of the head.

Both men and women distend the ears into great loops by piercing the lobes and inserting large discs of wood into the holes. Before marriage, a Masai girl will wind thick iron wire around her legs tight enough to impede the development of her calves.

The nomads of this tribe have long, low houses that are unlike

MASAI WARRIOR *Compulsory military training for youths is the order in this tribe. Each warrior carries a spear and a knobkerrie. Pierced ear lobes, which have been enormously enlarged, carry long earrings.*

MASAI GIRL *The curly hair is thickly plastered with ochre dust. Metal jewelry in great abundance is worn around neck and arms.*

MASAI SHEPHERD *Proud, dignified, and superior, the Masai maintain great herds of cattle which supply their basic diet needs of blood and milk. The blood is obtained by shooting an arrow with a curved head into the jugular vein of the cow, and then draining off the blood in a gourd. A plug of dung is placed over the wound, and the cow recovers. Cows are bled every two weeks or so. Chicken and game are not eaten.*

MARRIED WOMAN *Married women in this tribe have shaved heads. The necklaces that are worn are indicative of the wealth of the matron.*

MASAI DANCE *A pre-battle frenzy, imitating the sound and walk of the lion, is traditional with this tribe of tall, well-built warriors.*

those of any other tribe in Africa. These 6-foot-high dwellings are flat-roofed, and are built on a framework of sticks, out of mud and cow dung. Strong partitions divide the structure into separate apartments. In these huts, the only furniture besides cooking pots are gourds, which are used as milk cans, half-gourds used as cups, and an occasional three-legged stool which has been carved out of a single block of wood.

The Masai do not bury their dead. A corpse is carried outside the village, and simply left on the ground to be devoured by beasts and vultures.

Perhaps their strangest custom is spitting to denote reverence and good will. Newly-born children are spat upon by those who wish to endow the child with good luck. Masai will spit at each other when

RADIO PROGRAM   *Members of the radio broadcasting staff sending a program from the studios in Dar es Salaam.*

BAGAMOYO *A typical street in this town of 5,000.*

they meet, and spit at each other again to say good-bye. To seal a bargain, two traders will spit at each other.

Masai women generally attend to the personal needs of the men, for males consider themselves above the indignity of work.

A LAND OF NATURAL BEAUTY

This fascinating country contains 20,000 square miles of lakes, among which are Lake Tanganyika, and the great, sprawling Lake Victoria—the second deepest lake in the world—a body of water which is about the size of Scotland. Tanganyika comprises an area that is so large that Belgium, France, Switzerland, Holland, and the Federal German Republic could be fitted into it and still leave several thousand square miles left over. Within its boundaries rises Mount Kilimanjaro, Africa's highest mountain, 19,340 feet above sea level, a peak immortalized in a short story by Ernest Hemingway.

OUTDOOR KINDERGARTEN At a primary school in Dar es Salaam, a Tanganyikan teacher instructs a kindergarten class in the elements of writing.

Few nations are so rich in wildlife. In Tanganyika, one can find elephants, giraffes, hippopotamuses, buffalos, lions, leopards, cheetahs, hyenas, wild dogs, one hundred varieties of snakes, and a thousand species of birds.

PRESERVING THE NATION'S HERITAGE

One of Tanganyika's most important responsibilities is preserving the remarkable fauna of the country. Poachers pose grave threats to many species.

Today, preserves have been set up, and hunting is being carefully regulated. It seems likely that the wanton destruction of wildlife has been checked in time.

THE TSETSE FLY

Nearly two-thirds of Tanganyika is infested with the tsetse fly, carrier of sleeping sickness, killer of humans, and transmitter to horses and cattle of the fatal disease called nagana. This dread insect infests large areas of tropical Africa. In Uganda, between 1901 and 1906, roughly 200,000 people died from sleeping sickness.

Sleeping sickness is a disease of the bloodstream and the central nervous system. It is characterized by severe headaches, apathy, emotional disturbance, emaciation; its final phase is coma and death.

This paralyzing insect is the prime target in the medical war against the diseases which ravage tropical Africa. Drugs have been developed that may cure sleeping sickness, or at least arrest its development, if treatment is received promptly after infection. New drugs give some promise of immunity. However, there are different types of sleeping sickness, and some are much easier to treat, or prevent, than others. Controlling the fly itself is difficult. Aerial spraying with insecticide has not been successful. Since it is known that the flies tend to avoid open clearings, sometimes whole areas around native villages have been deliberately laid waste. The complex and difficult fight is continuing; but

WOMEN POLICE   *New recruits are receiving instructions in wireless telegraphy.*

PRISON WITHOUT WALLS   *Kingolwira prison farm, near Morogoro, in the eastern province of Tanganyika, covers 20,000 acres. The prison authorities provide training in useful occupations for 1,200 long-term first offenders so that, on release, they can be useful members of society. One of the first prisons without walls in Africa, the farm is equipped with modern machinery and installations. Most of the farm produce is consumed by the prisoners, but the modern dairy supplies 200 gallons of milk daily to Dar es Salaam. The structure is the granary, with a capacity of 175 tons.*

COFFEE CURING   *Chagga tribeswomen check coffee beans as they leave the automatic sorting machine on conveyor belts at the Moshi coffee-curing works in the northern province.*

doctors believe it will be many years before human beings and livestock in Tanganyika will be free of this curse.

THE USE OF MARGINAL LANDS

Despite its natural wonders, Tanganyika is a poor land; primarily because much of its area is at present unsuitable for raising first-rate crops. Excluding the paramount matter of health, the country's major problem is the effective utilization of its marginal lands. These constitute a vast area in which the soil is poor, and the rainfall relatively sparse and unreliable. Because of insufficient rainfall, much of the central plateau does not enjoy sufficient water for more than half of the year.

After World War II, the problem of turning these marginal lands into more substantial assets lay squarely before the British who were administering the country as a United Nations Trust Territory. A ten-year development and welfare plan was drawn up. The first undertaking was an attempt to grow peanuts. This abortive scheme has become a classic example of ill-advised economic planning.

The soil had not been properly studied; peanuts simply would not grow well in it. The rainfall, sparse and irregular, provided only a fraction of the moisture needed. The existing railways and roads were inadequate for transporting the paltry crops when they were finally harvested.

By 1949, although a large road-building program had been started, it was already too late to help the faltering peanut project.

The developers had miscalculated the efficiency of heavy machinery. On the stony, rutty land, large machines broke down, where small machines would have performed. The lack of trained personnel added a further complication. In 1951, the peanut-growing plan was abandoned. The government, sadder, wiser, and much poorer, turned its efforts to long-range experimentation.

NEW APPROACH TO AGRICULTURE

This more cautious approach is beginning to bear fruit. Primitive methods are slowly being replaced by modern techniques. Farmers are being trained; centuries-old agriculture is being revitalized.

A new approach has been taken to the problem of drought. A team of experts from the Food and Agricultural Organization of the United Nations has surveyed a million acres of the Rufiji River basin. This area of 68,500 square miles is 20 percent of the country. It was estimated that by using the available reserves, somewhere between 5 and 6 million acres could be irrigated. The building of a dam across the Rufiji is now under study.

THE COLORFUL PAST

Tanganyika has a rich history. The country enjoyed trade with Arabia and India before the Christian era; and during the eighth century, Arabs began to settle along the coastland. Trading with China flourished as early as the thirteenth century.

Tanganyika, formerly a German colony, became an English colony after World War I.

POLITICS

Tanganyika became independent on December 9, 1961, and was headed by Julius K. Nyerere, who was named Prime Minister. Nyerere, the scion of a tribal chieftain, is a Catholic and owes his education to Catholic missionaries, who sent him to school at age twelve. He went on to study at Makerere College in Uganda; and he followed this schooling with three years spent in post-graduate work at Edinburgh University. He became a teacher in his homeland, and was soon drawn into politics.

He founded the Tanganyika African National Union, the first mass party in the country, which has since become the leading political force. At the last election, Nyerere's party held 72 of the 73 seats in the

MUSOMA TRIBESMAN   The hair is cut so as to look like a fur hat. The ears have been pierced to make the lobes extend. Metal amulets constrict the muscle of the upper arm.

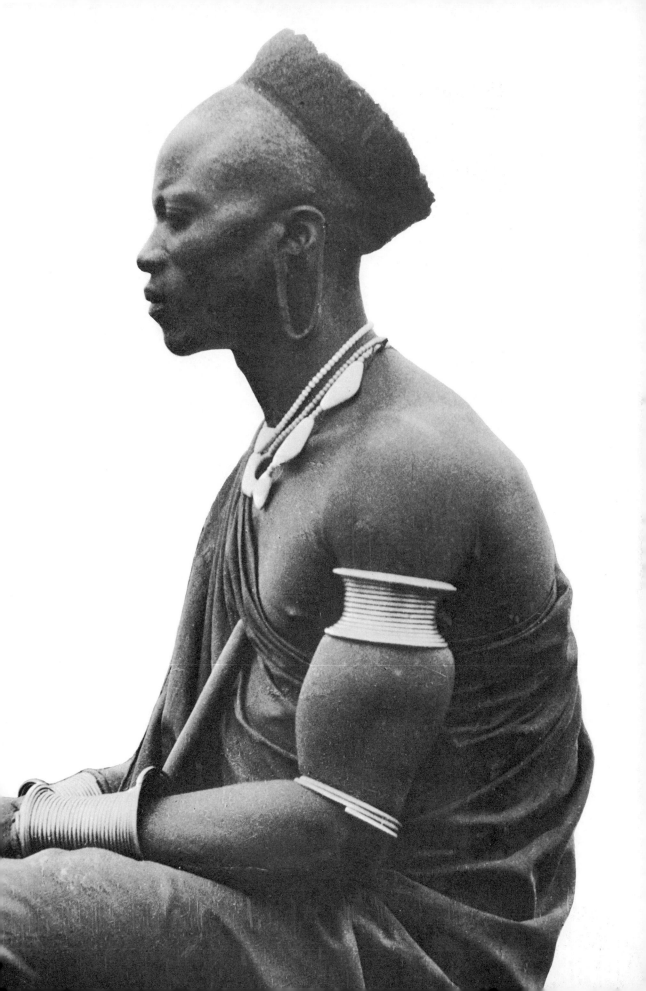

BUILDING NEW HOMES *Both law students and staff of the University College of Dar es Salaam, both white and black, have pitched in, in this self-help project, to mix cement and concrete. They work without pay.*

TO THE MARKET *A woman from the Southern Highlands region brings along her bowl, in which she will carry home some food.*

JULIUS NYERERE Son of Chief Burito of the Zanaki tribe, Nyerere was born in 1921. After gaining a teacher's diploma upon graduation from Makerere University College in Uganda, Nyerere taught at St. Mary's Mission School in Tabora. He was the first student from Tanganyika to go to a British university, and he took his Arts degree at Edinburgh, in 1952.

TOBACCO CO-OPERATIVE Peasants cure their tobacco leaves and then tie them in bundles of 14 leaves. The reed baskets are filled with such bundles, and are then brought to the local co-operative society for further processing and marketing.

legislative council. But Nyerere's policies encountered growing opposition because he was considered too favorable to Britain and to the West. In January, 1962, he was replaced by Rashidi Kawawa, a young Moslem of neutralist views. After Nyerere resigned as Prime Minister, he still retained his post of Secretary General of the dominant party.

AGRICULTURAL CO-OPERATIVES

Tanganyika is the world's largest exporter of sisal, used in making rope. This product accounts for one-third of the total exports. In 1959, the export value of diamonds was $12 million, of gold, $3 million. Lead and tin are also mined. Coffee, tea, and cotton are grown.

One hopeful aspect in Tanganyika's economy is the development of a well-organized co-operative movement. In particular, the Wa-Chagga tribe has found successful co-operatives in several villages for the production and the marketing of the coffee they produce.

SELF-HELP PROJECT *Tanganyikans, united in their great desire to build a prosperous nation, have volunteered through projects such as this, to build new roads, build new dams, construct buildings. The group pictured here includes volunteers from all walks of life: law students, tutors, men, women and children, all working without pay in the project at Magomeni, to build a new road.*

LIP ORNAMENTS *Women of the Makonde in the Newala District are wearing traditional lip plugs. This custom is dying out in Tanganyika.*

389

EDUCATION

Like most of the new nations of Africa, Tanganyika has a severe problem of illiteracy. It is estimated that less than one out of fifteen people can read and write.

Although there has been a rapid expansion of educational facilities

UHURU NA KAZI   In line with President Nyerere's slogan "Uhuru na kazi"— Freedom and Work—Tanganyika has mustered the energies of more than one million volunteers, one in every nine persons in the country. In nine months, Tanganyikans have built 10,000 miles of road, 600 communal farms, 166 schools, 66 dispensaries, 31 clinics, a football field, and two bus stations. Nyerere estimates that the program has saved the country $560,000. More important, this self-help project has brought a new sense of purpose to Tanganyika. By dedicating their energies to the upbuilding of their own country, Tanganyikans have become invested with a sense of identity extending beyond tribal parochialism.

during the last few years, there has been a woeful shortage of teachers and school buildings.

Only 40 percent of the children go to primary school. In 1959, only 4,000 boys and girls were in secondary schools.

In 1961, a university was founded in Dar es Salaam, and began with a law school.

COFFEE PLANTATION Here are ripe Robusta coffee cherries on a plantation in Bukoba, on the shores of Lake Victoria.

DAR ES SALAAM The capital has a population of over 130,000 people, and handles about 70 percent of the country's foreign trade.

IN BRIEF

AREA:
361,800 square miles, almost as large as Texas and New Mexico combined.

TERRAIN
Two extremes of geography within the nation's boundaries, ranging from Mount Kilimanjaro, with its permanent ice cap (19,340 feet above sea level), to the trough-like depression of Lake Tanganyika. A 250-mile coastline, beyond which a rolling plain rises to 5,000 feet, drops sharply on the east but falls gently on the west to the level of lakes in the Great Rift Valley. 20,000 square miles of inland water, including most of Lakes Victoria and Tanganyika; also Lakes Natron, Manyara, Eyasi, and Rukwa. Main rivers are the Panganis (Rivu), Wanu, Rufiji, Great Ruaha, Matandu, Ubemkuru, Lukuledi, and Revuma, all draining the central plateau and flowing into the Indian Ocean; also the Mori, Mara, Kagera, Malagarasi, Songiwa, and Ruyuhu, which feed the great lakes.

CLIMATE
Three zones: tropical in the coastal area with average temperature of 76°, and rainfall of 40 inches; central plateau has low humidity and extreme temperature variations; semitropical mountain areas.

CAPITAL
Dar es Salaam (population, 130,000).

POPULATION
9,238,000; about 22,300 Europeans and 117,300 Asians.

ETHNIC GROUPS
Sukuma, largest of over 120 different tribes ranging from the primitive Tiniga and Dorobo to the comparatively advanced Chagga. Other main tribes are Nyamwezi, Ha, Makonde, Gogo, Haya, Aloof and Masai.

LANGUAGE
English, Swahili, Gujerati, and various tribal tongues.

RELIGION
Majority are pagan. Moslems, next largest group.

DATE OF INDEPENDENCE
December 9, 1961.

FORM OF GOVERNMENT
Constitutional democracy. National Assembly of 71 members, elected for 3 years. Premier is chief of state and leader

SUKUMA WITCH DOCTORS *The Sukuma people constitute the largest tribe in Tanganyika, numbering about one and one-quarter million people. The men of this tribe wear cow skins on which the hair is permitted to remain. They scrape off a part of their own hair at the crown of the head, and sometimes they cover the bare spot with cuts and gashes, which they believe will provide a sovereign cure for headaches. They pull out the hair of their eyelashes, eyebrows, and beards with tweezers, and they file their teeth sharp to ward off evil spirits. The witch doctors wear a headdress of feathers and a large spread of horns. Numerous coils of metal rings are wound around the legs. The tribesmen account the decorated gourds and the iron axes as instruments which, along with incantations, can weave potent spells.*

of majority party. Member of United Nations.

EDUCATION	In 1960, 386,267 students were enrolled in 3,137 primary schools; 11,283 students in 66 secondary schools. University opened in Dar es Salaam, 1961.
HEALTH FACILITIES	In 1956 there were 46 government hospitals, 7 special hospitals, 20 dispensaries, and 227 maternity and child-care centers. Many missions and industrial firms have health facilities.

CURRENCY	Unit is the East African shilling. (1 shilling=U.S. $.14).

INDUSTRY Some light industry, primarily processing raw materials, and food. Some manufacture of machinery, steelwork, paints and varnishes, soap, and furniture.

CROPS: Sisal, cotton, and coffee for export; rice, sugar, tea, tobacco, wheat, cashew nuts, sesame, cassava for domestic use and export. Forest products (resins, oils, woods).

STOCK: Cattle, sheep, goats, poultry, and pigs.

FISHING AND HUNTING: Fresh- and salt-water fish for domestic use and export. Government receives substantial income from the sale of game licenses and trophies.

MINING: Diamonds, copper, gold, silver, gypsum, lead, mica, salt, tin, tungsten, and coal.

TRADE

1960:	EXPORTS	$153,507,200
	IMPORTS	82,664,400
	SURPLUS	$ 70,842,800

MAJOR IMPORTS: Transport equipment, machinery, petroleum products, textile goods, maize, rice and chemicals.

MAJOR EXPORTS: Agricultural products (*see* Crops), seeds, hides and skins, beeswax, metaliferous ores, fresh and cured meats, diamonds.

TRANS-PORTATION ROADS: 3,000 miles territorial; 4,400 miles local; 10,000 district routes (not surfaced).

VEHICLES: 23,000 passenger cars; 9,000 commercial vehicles.

WATERWAYS: Navigable routes on Lakes Victoria and Tanganyika, and on the Rufiji River.

RAILROADS: Central Railway, 1,103 miles of track. Tonga line, 273 miles of track.

AIR TRAFFIC: 51 airfields; 13 equipped with navigational aids.

COMMUNI-CATIONS Tanganyika Broadcasting Company is a national network. All major cities have telephone service and post offices.

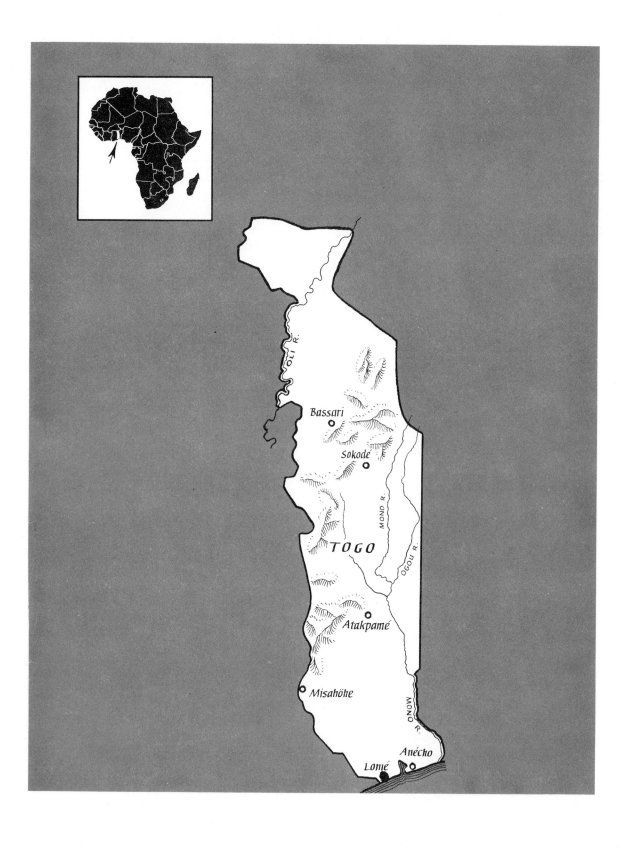

TOGO

Balkanization in Africa

The republic of Togo is only 124 miles across at its widest point. Its coastline on the Gulf of Guinea extends only 32 miles. Smaller than West Virginia, Togo has an area of roughly 22,000 square miles.

Togo illustrates certain features inherited from the days of colonialism, operative in the current geographical and cultural situation of many African nations. Togo's boundaries result from historical accident rather than from rational factors based on either geography or ethnic characteristics. This capricious boundary-making has resulted in the balkanization of large sections of Africa. Parts of the continent are divided into extremely small states, many without resources for a strong economy.

Such countries are subject to strong tensions when one ethnic group has been arbitrarily split among several states. Once begun, the process of balkanization is hard to reverse. In fact, full federation of two or more states for mutual economic betterment and cultural unity is extremely difficult to accomplish.

THE COMING OF THE EUROPEANS

Between the twelfth and the fourteenth centuries, the Ewe people, one of Togo's three main ethnic groups, came to southern Togo and to adjoining Ghana from the Niger Valley. This migration, as will be seen, had important consequences in the twentieth century.

During the fifteenth and sixteenth centuries, Portuguese sailors landed on the Togo coast to raid for slaves. The Ewe people were among their earliest victims. At the same time, the Portuguese established small trading stations on the coast and on adjacent shores to provision their ships. Centuries later, these insignificant trading stations were to have an important impact on the crop-growing and international-trade patterns of these countries. In Togo, the Portuguese introduced the growing of cassava, coconuts, and corn, all of which are now part of the

*OUTDOOR EDUCATIONAL MEETING   Mrs. Eunice Adabunu,
Vice-Chairman of the Union of Women of Togo, leads an outdoor meeting in Lomé to advise women on hygiene, care of the family, and social
conduct. Local chapters of the Union are being set up throughout the
country.*

domestic economy. (Most of the cassava is exported.)

In the nineteenth century, with the rise of colonialism, France
and Germany both established trading posts on the Togo coast. The
French established themselves near Lomé, now Togo's capital and only
sizable city. The Germans moved faster and more systematically; they
acquired part of Togo as an African colony in July, 1885. Dr. Gustav
Nachtigal, the famous German explorer, whose exploits were important
in setting the boundaries of several African states, had earlier made a
treaty with the chief of the village of Togo, on the north shore of Lake
Togo. On the basis of this treaty, the Germans established a protectorate
over the small enclave, and applied the name of the village to the entire
territory.

THE BOUNDARY PROBLEM

Meanwhile the British and the French were active in three areas then known as the Gold Coast Colony, Ashanti, and the Northern Territories, all now part of the Republic of Ghana. The Volta River would have formed a reasonable and natural boundary between Togo and Ghana, but jealousy among the representatives of the three European powers ignored geography, logic, and the human factor. A boundary was drawn between Togo and the Gold Coast which followed the course of the Volta River for a short distance along Togo's northern areas. The boundary then left the river and meandered irrationally to the east. Togo's border with Dahomey was determined by a similar process of treaty-making with local chiefs, after the usual bickering between Germany and France.

This irresponsible, unrealistic settlement had two consequences. First, Togo lost its natural boundary of the Volta River. Second, the Ewe people and several of the smaller tribes were indiscriminately split up among three countries: the Gold Coast, Togo, and Dahomey.

The baleful results of such political stupidity bear heavily on the

ELEMENTARY SCHOOL   *Scene at Ecole Normale d' Atakpamé.*

new states that are heirs to this capricious map-making. Most states have found that such boundaries pose severe and continuing obstacles to the development of a stable national culture. Arbitrarily divided ethnic groups hinder political stability by their demands for reintegration. Growth, based on cultural unity and sufficient land, is impossible.

THE COLONIAL PERIOD AND ITS AFTERMATH

As colonizers, the Germans were meticulous, methodical, and by no means utterly malevolent. Having secured recognition from France and Britain of its claim to Togo, Germany extended its control to the north, built roads and railroads, set up administrative machinery, and developed the rudiments of economic and educational institutions.

Some of the Ewe lads who were educated in German schools have now become the leaders of the country. In pre-Hitler days, the Germans

STATION AT ATAKPAMÉ   The train has just come in. The little girl with a tray on her head is about to offer peanuts for sale. The man in the striped shirt is a member of the Moslem Haoussa tribe, whose everyday attire is a cotton cap, long shirt and trousers, and open sandals. The train, which runs from Lomé, the capital, to this town, is a Diesel-engined autorail.

TOGO WOMEN ON PARADE   After independence, a group of Togo women formed a non-political organization for the protection of children, and the education and emancipation of women. "The Union of Togo Women" was founded by Dina Olympio, widow of the late Sylvanus Olympio. She is President of this organization, which has about 600 members in Lomé, and maintains other branches throughout the country. The Union has organized a program of free lectures, and combats illiteracy by giving lessons to women in English, French, and the Ewe language.

did not indulge in race discrimination; and in 1914, when German rule over Togo came to an end, the population included several hundred offspring of German-Togolese unions.

The First World War brought about major shake-ups in the colonial structure in Africa, particularly in the German colonies. French and British military units, from the Gold Coast on one side, and Dahomey on the other, descended on German Togo in August, 1914. After the war, the two allies obligingly divided up the country. They subsequently agreed to place it under mandate of the League of Nations; for the most part, under French administration.

The next great upheaval came after the Second World War when the mandates of Britain and France were transferred to the U.N.

INDEPENDENCE ACHIEVED

But the old days of colonialism were gone forever. The Ewe people who had lived in the area for eight centuries, began to clamor for the unification of their tribes, and they found a ready forum in the Trusteeship Council of the United Nations. From 1947 to 1956, the question was debated periodically. Finally, in May, 1956, a plebiscite was held in British Togoland, under United Nations supervision. The majority voted to integrate that area with neighboring Gold Coast. Consequently, when the Republic of Ghana was formed out of the Gold Coast, the new country absorbed British Togoland. The Ewe people were deeply resentful, and have been agitating for reunification ever since.

In 1958, French Togoland, through a referendum held under the new French constitution, chose full independence within the French Community. On April 27, 1960, Togo became a sovereign nation.

SYLVANUS OLYMPIO

Before independence, the very able spokesman for Togo on the world scene was Sylvanus Olympio, late President of the Togo Republic. A member of the Ewe tribe and a Catholic by religion, he attended a German school, when Germany was the ruling colonial power. During the British mandate, he continued his studies at the London School of Economics and Political Science. He then returned to Togo; and in time, he became a successful businessman. During this period, he strove to develop Togo nationalism; and in 1941, he founded the Committee of Togo Unity.

The Vichy Government had him arrested; and the post-war French Government did everything in its power to hamper his political activities. When, on one occasion, he came to New York to present his plea for Togo at the U.N. Assembly, he was confined by the U.S. State Department, through French insistence, to the actual premises of the U.N. Building. Later, his visa was extended to include Manhattan, between 23rd and 96th Streets.

Olympio was considered one of the foremost statesmen of West Africa. His was a voice which was accorded respect at international conclaves. When he was assassinated in January of 1963, the free world was shocked, and his loss publicly deplored by President John F. Kennedy of the United States.

A TINY ECONOMY

In some respects Togo is relatively well advanced. Its assets include 300 miles of railroad, 900 miles of roads passable in all weather, 1,560 miles of telegraph lines, and 819 miles of telephone lines.

But Togo will have to overcome many difficulties to offset her small size. The principal cash crops are infinitesimal on the world market—it exports only 5,000 tons of cocoa and 4,000 tons of coffee each year.

Deposits of chromite, iron ore, and bauxite are not large; but there are major deposits of phosphate, and it is hoped that the exploitation of these deposits may work a fundamental change in the economy of Togo.

Togo has made a good start toward economic stability. The extraction and processing of phosphates is under way, and their exportation began early in 1961. But Togo as a geographical entity remains a victim of early caprice. The mistakes of its early masters have endowed the present leadership with a heavy legacy of very severe problems.

IN BRIEF

AREA	22,000 square miles, about size of West Virginia.
TERRAIN	Narrow strip of land, 124 miles wide and 372 miles long, extending from Gulf of Guinea to Upper Volta. Coastline is only 32 miles long. Atakora Mountains cross Togo southwest-northeast, averaging 2,300 to 3,300 feet high. Plains area in the north, through which runs the Oli River.

SYLVANUS OLYMPIO
The late President in native
costume. He was assassinated
in January of 1963, by dissi-
dents of the Togolese Army be-
cause he had refused to build
up the country's tiny military
forces.

CLIMATE	Typical of central tropical Africa. Rainy season lasts from May to October. Annual rainfall ranges from 40 inches in the north to 70 inches in the south. Average temperature in the low 80's; average humidity ranges from 45 percent in the north to 95 percent in the south.
CAPITAL	Lomé (population, 78,000).
OTHER CITIES	Tanga, 39,000.
POPULATION	1,440,000; about 1,200 Europeans.
ETHNIC GROUPS	Voltaic people dominate the north; tribes of the Benin group, including the Ewe people, are principal groups in the south.
LANGUAGE	French is official language. Nearly 50 native languages and dialects are spoken.
RELIGION	Largely animist. About 80,000 Christians and 30,000 Mohammedans in the northern areas.
DATE OF INDEPENDENCE	April 27, 1960.
FORM OF GOVERNMENT	Parliamentary democracy. Chamber of Deputies of 46 members is popularly elected for six-year terms. Prime Minister, who leads a coalition of parties in Chamber, appoints Council of Ministers. Member of French Community and United Nations.

EDUCATION	In 1959, about 39 percent of school-age children were enrolled in schools. No universities.
HEALTH FACILITIES	In 1959, there were 13 hospitals and 13 maternity centers, plus 107 rural dispensaries. The country's public health medical staff at that time consisted of 16 doctors, 4 pharmacists, 1 dental surgeon, and 324 nurses.
CURRENCY	Unit is the French Community franc (247 francs = U. S. $1.00).
INDUSTRY	A few light industries for processing agricultural products, plus various native handicrafts.

CROPS: Yams, millet, and sorghum for domestic consumption; cocoa, coffee, cassava, palm oil, peanuts, and copra for export.

STOCK: Cattle, sheep, goats.

FISHING: Important along the coast; small amounts exported to Ghana.

MINING: Prospecting is in process. Iron ore, chromite, and bauxite have been discovered, but are not easily accessible. Major deposits of phosphate near Lake Togo.

TRADE

1960: IMPORTS	$26,000,000
EXPORTS	$15,000,000
DEFICIT	$11,000,000

MAJOR IMPORTS: Cloth goods, petroleum products, tobacco, automobiles, machinery, and industrial goods.

MAJOR EXPORTS: Agricultural (*See* Crops).

TRANS-PORTATION

ROADS: 427 miles surfaced.

VEHICLES: 1,212 passenger cars; 2,931 commercial vehicles (1959).

RAILROADS: 300 miles of track.

AIR TRAFFIC: International airport at Lomé.

COMMUNI-CATIONS

Only broadcasting station is government-owned Radio Lomé. 1,560 miles of telegraph and 819 miles of telephone lines. Three daily newspapers and twelve other publications.

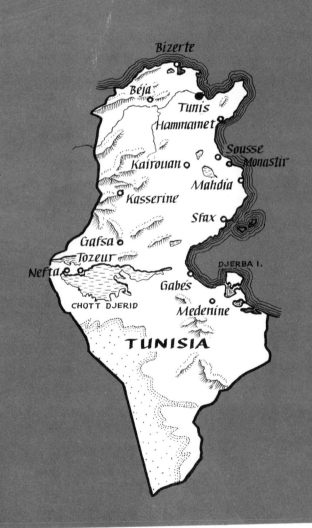

Bizerte

Béja

Tunis

Hammamet

Sousse
Monastir

Kairouan

Mahdia

Kasserine

Sfax

Gafsa

Tozeur

DJERBA I.

Nefta

Gabes

CHOTT DJERID

Medenine

TUNISIA

TUNISIA

Cultural Revolution in Islam

In 1956, after years of bitter struggle, Tunisia finally gained full independence from France.

Sweeping social and economic changes have been wrought by the dynamic government of President Habib Bourguiba. These have affected the very fabric of Tunisian existence.

RADICAL REFORMS OF NEW REGIME

Polygamy has been outlawed. Land reforms have been instituted. Women have been granted equal status—a radical move for a Moslem nation. Education, powerfully stimulated in the process, has moved from religious to state control. Courts of justice have also come under government jurisdiction. Begging has almost entirely been eliminated. New housing construction has increased. Soil conservation and irrigation projects have been initiated. Exports have increased. Farming and livestock-raising methods have been greatly improved. Tourism and foreign investment have been encouraged.

NEW NAMES FOR TUNISIANS

Other changes have been more subtle, but no less important in their long-range effect. A law now requires Tunisian peasants to have a given name and a surname, in contrast to the ancient Islamic practice by which a child was given a long series of given names indicating ancestry (for example, Mohamed ben Ahmed ben Mohamed, and so on). This is not a dollar-and-cents change, but a change which assures each man an individual identity and increased self-respect—crucial factors for twentieth-century living.

Militating against these efforts toward progress are other, older problems: overpopulation, poverty, lack of power resources, lack of water.

THE POPULATION PROBLEM

Tunisia is one of the most prolific nations in the world. There are 45,000 new mouths to feed each year. The birth rate of Tunisia is almost three times that of Italy, a country traditionally regarded as having a high birth rate. Tunisia has one of the youngest populations in the world: 50 percent of the people are under nineteen.

This staggering population growth is the cause of Tunisia's inability to provide a livelihood for all its citizens. The national output of goods and services increases, but the number of people among whom these goods and services are to be divided increases at an even faster rate.

Severe unemployment has resulted: the rate varies from 9 to 80 percent, depending on geographic location and agricultural conditions. Despite prodigious efforts by the government, the standard of living has been declining.

On March 6, 1962, Bourguiba declared that the key to solving the economic problems of Tunisia was birth control. The open recognition by this popular leader of the need for changing an attitude so deeply ingrained in the people may introduce a new era.

LACK OF POWER RESOURCES

Despite some great natural advantages, Tunisia lacks one of the basic requirements for a healthy industrial economy: a cheap source of power. There is no coal; there are no certain oil reserves; and there is no appreciable source of hydro-electric power.

Some progress is being made in developing power resources. In the southern part of the country, prospecting for oil continues at a fast pace. Results are still inconclusive, but French discovery of huge oil fields in the Sahara, near Tunisia, has raised hopes. Much of this oil will be

INTERIOR OF TUNISIAN HOUSE   This beautiful mosaic fountain, when running, lends an air of coolness to the open inner court,which is typical of Arabic architecture in this area. Elaborate tilework and grilled wrought iron,grace upper-class Tunisian homes.

THE RIBAT FORTRESS AT MONASTIR *This fortress was once a monastery; hence the name of the town, Monastir. At the end of the eighth century, the building was rebuilt by the Arabs as a fortress to defend the shores from sea raids. The mosque, the low, flat structure to the right of the Ribat, has the characteristic square-towered minaret of this region. On the island opposite the beach, a new café for tourists has recently been erected, and can be reached by a modern causeway.*

carried, via a new pipeline, into the Tunisian port of La Skhirra, on the eastern coast.

The problem of water supply is nation-wide. There is very little rain in the southern regions, and only variable amounts in the north.

CROSSROADS OF HISTORY

Tunisia is small, but it is strategically located. Its 745 miles of coastline can dominate the Mediterranean Sea. At its closest point to Europe, Tunisia is only 86 miles from Sicily.

In ancient times, Tunisia did, indeed, dominate the Mediterranean. Known as Carthage, it rivaled ancient Rome until defeated by its arch foe during the Punic Wars. Hannibal brought his army and his elephants across the sea to attack Rome in one of the great military campaigns of history; but Carthage was ultimately crushed, and became a key possession in the Roman Empire in 136 B.C.

Some fine relics of Carthaginian days are to be seen today in the Bardo Museum located in the environs of Tunis. Here, too, one may view an unrivalled collection of Roman mosaics.

Ancient Carthage was referred to as the "granary of Rome," as its lush wheat fields provided grain for its conquerors. This ancient ability to export grain has caused the leaders of Tunisia to believe that the country's agricultural desolation has resulted from man-made ravages rather than from natural causes. Tunisians confidently hope that, just as the ancient Roman aqueducts made the land rich and fruitful, so modern irrigation projects can turn the land once more into a garden.

TUNISIAN WOMEN VOTING *Independence Day, March 29, 1957, brought unprecedented freedom to Tunisian women: for the first time in history, women cast their ballots in an election. Note the range of formality—the black khamas (veils) at the right, the white khamas at the left, and the informal European dress of the younger generation sitting at the table.*

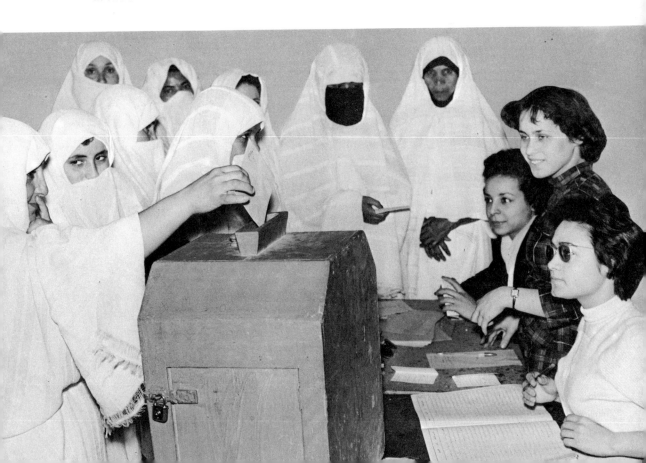

During its long history, Tunisia has been controlled by many powers: Punic (Carthaginian), Roman, Arab, Spanish, Turkish, and then French. In 1881, France set itself up as a governing body declaring Tunisia to be a protectorate. The French turned over about 10 percent of the most productive lands to Europeans for colonization.

In 1907, the Young Tunisian Party was founded from which sprang the roots of the independence movement. In 1934, the Neo-Destour (New Constitution) Party came into being; its avowed purpose was emancipation from French rule; its leader was a young lawyer and journalist named Habib Bourguiba. The political history of Tunisia from that time on can, for the most part, be followed in the career of that one colorful and exciting figure.

HABIB BOURGUIBA

Unlike most of the new nations of Africa, Tunisia has a well-developed middle class which has strong cultural ties to Europe. It is this group that is leading the country's fight for progress.

Bourguiba was born in 1903, the son of a middle-class citizen. Of modest social origin, he studied law in Paris and received a degree in political science at the Sorbonne. He practiced law in France, married a Frenchwoman, and returned to Tunis in 1927 to become a journalist.

Bourguiba took the lead in the struggle for independence. He is a gifted orator in both Arabic and French. He was jailed and exiled several times; and once, he was in peril of execution. His personal experiences, adventures, deliverance, and success read like a movie thriller.

In 1956, France finally gave way. In 1957, Tunisia abolished its monarchy, and elected Bourguiba as its first President.

Bourguiba rules with a strong hand, but he has nevertheless maintained a considerable measure of democratic freedom in Tunisia.

THE CASBAH   *The mesh-like objects hanging from the ceiling in front of a shop are kemamas, camel muzzles, which are made of tough grasses. Women tourists in Tunis buy them to use as handbags.*

HABIB BOURGUIBA Head of the Neo—Destour (New Constitution) Party, he became the first President of Tunisia on July 25, 1957.

ROMAN COLOSSEUM The remains of a full-scale Colosseum built by the Romans, sometime between the 1st century B.C. and the 1st century A.D., rises above the city of El Djem. The Tunisian Colosseum is better preserved than the one in Rome. El Djem is currently being explored in great detail by archaeologists. Underground tunnels run for many, many kilometers from the theater to the sea. During construction, these underground thoroughfares were used in hauling stone and marble, which had been transported to Tunisia in ships from Rome.

THE EUROPEAN COMMUNITY

Tunisia is an Arab nation; over 90 percent of its people are Arabic or Berber stock. Although French is still used for administrative and commercial purposes, Arabic is the official language.

The European population has been reduced by the departure of officials and tradesmen. This community consists of roughly 90,000 French, and 50,000 Italians. There are a considerable number of Maltese. Most Europeans are Roman Catholics.

European residents believe the political climate has taken a turn for the worse, following Tunisia's abortive attempt to seize the French air and naval base at Bizerte in the fall of 1961. Europeans have definitely found it more difficult to earn a living. Italian taxi-drivers can no longer obtain work permits.

ARTESIAN WELL The recent discovery of important underground water resources near Gafsa will permit the cultivation of more than 60,000 acres of what has been a completely desert area.

REFORMS FOR CITY AND COUNTRY

The capital and largest city in Tunisia is Tunis, the center of industrial activity, with a population of 695,000. Other major urban centers are Sfax (65,000), Sousse (48,000), and Bizerte (44,000).

An extensive re-development program is under way in Tunis to provide better living facilities. The city has suffered from classic urban overcrowding resulting from increased industrialization. Slums have sprung up as peasants have come in great numbers from agricultural areas seeking employment. The government hopes that within a few years the gainfully employed residents of these slums will be relocated to suitable housing now under construction, and that the unemployed will be sent back to the countryside.

The population of the south and central semi-arid steppes consists largely of semi-nomads and camel drivers. The people in the inland area dwell in huts and inhabit small villages. They live by primitive farming. A gradual process of agricultural reform has been instituted by the government, the purpose of which is to improve the farming methods among these illiterate peasants. Agricultural reform is of crucial importance. More than 70 percent of the people are engaged in agriculture; yet only one-third of the national income derives from this activity. Antiquated methods of cultivation, as well as the crippling lack of water, account for this meager production.

Four main categories provide the agricultural wealth: cereal grains, fruit trees and grape vines, olive trees, and date palms. All of these crops are, to some degree, exported; they also form the basis for the many small food-processing industries within Tunisia, most of them concentrated in Tunis.

INDUSTRY AND TRADE

The manufacture of olive oil is of particular significance in Tunisia. There are over 2,000 olive oil factories in the nation, producing between 70,000 and 130,000 tons annually. Other food-processing industries of importance are spaghetti making, wine making, and the canning

POTTERY MAKING *Manufacture of pottery is at the handcraft level. One of the men is treading a batch of clay into a workable consistency. Drying and storing facilities are primitive. Note the heavy block wheels on the donkey cart.*

of sardines caught by the very active fishing fleet of Tunisia.

Tunisia relies heavily on its almost unlimited resources of phosphates, which account for 30 percent of the total volume of exports. At one time Tunisia produced almost half of the world's supply; today the nation ranks fourth—behind the United States, Russia, and Morocco —producing over 2 million tons annually.

There is no real heavy industry in Tunisia. Many small, new industries are emerging, however, and the government hopes that in a not too distant future these will at least meet Tunisia's own requirements, eliminating the need to import manufactured goods.

The economic situation at the end of 1960 is quite dismal. The country suffers from a huge annual trade deficit. In 1960, the excess of imports over exports amounted to more than $70,000,000.

In July, 1962, Tunisia negotiated a pact with Italy for a loan of $10 million. A few days later, the United States promised up to $180 million in aid to Tunisia for a three-year development program; in mid-August, 1962, a Peace Corps group was on its way from America.

POLITICAL ORIENTATION

Now that Algeria has achieved independence, the way is clear for the possible forming of the Maghreb, a union of North African countries —Tunisia, Algeria, and Morocco. The formation of this political union is a dream long cherished by North African statesmen.

Politically, Tunisia is a member of the Arab League, and shares with that group an antagonism toward Israel. For a time, strained and even hostile relations existed between Tunisia and Egypt, but these relations are now on a more cordial basis.

RUE DE LA CASBAH   This street in Tunis, narrow and paved with block-brick, is flanked by splendidly ornamented structures.

IN BRIEF

AREA
48,300 square miles, about the size of Michigan.

TERRAIN
745-mile coastline on two sides, with most Tunisian cities located on or near the coast. The Atlas Mountains divide the country into a well-watered north and an arid south. In the north are the Khroumirie and Binzart River valleys. The extreme south is part of the Sahara Desert.

CLIMATE
Temperatures are moderate along the coast; frequent rains occur during the October to April winter season.

CAPITAL
Tunis (population, 695,000).

POPULATION
4,168,000; about 140,000 Europeans.

OTHER CITIES
Sfax, 65,000; Sousse, 48,000; Bizerte, 44,000.

ETHNIC GROUPS
Over 90 percent of Arab and Berber descent.

LANGUAGE
Arabic is the official language, although French is also used in official and commercial communications.

RELIGION
About 90 percent Mohammedan.

DATE OF INDEPENDENCE
March 29, 1957.

FORM OF GOVERNMENT
Constitutional Islamic Republic. The President, who must be a Moslem, is elected for five years. A National Assembly of 90 members is elected for a similar term at the same time. The President may rule by decree in emergencies. Member of the United Nations.

EDUCATION
Compulsory and free, but illiteracy is still relatively high; concerted government actions are being undertaken to extend education. In 1959-1960, 370,362 pupils attended pri-

CAMEL AT WORK   This animal has been used for time on end to draw water from desert wells. The working camel is generally muzzled because he has a tendency to unexpectedly bite.

mary schools; in 1958, 25,000 students attended secondary schools. The proportion of girls in school remains small, but is growing. Five institutions of higher education have a combined enrollment of 2,500 students. The Institute of Higher Education is the nucleus for a projected national university.

HEALTH FACILITIES

64 hospitals provide 10,539 hospital beds. Free medical care is provided for the majority of the population. There are many rural dispensaries; also 14 health education centers. The government places emphasis on expanding its health facilities.

CURRENCY

Unit is the Tunisian dinar; the government controls the exchange rates. (One dinar = U. S. $2.38).

INDUSTRY

Modest degree of industrial development, including manufacturing of superphosphates and processing of lead, cement, and building materials. A state-owned plant processes tobacco. Handicraft industry employs one-sixth of the population.

CROPS: Wheat, barley, olive oil, wine, and dates, both for domestic consumption and export.

STOCK: Substantial herds of sheep, goats, cattle, and camels. Sheep raising is given priority for potential export of wool and meat.

HOTEL MIRAMAR   Roughly 40 miles from Tunis, this luxurious hotel at Hammamet on the Mediterranean, contains 108 rooms. Rates range from $7.00 to $11.00, per person, including meals. The hotel provides many facilities, including a swimming pool and canoes for surf-sailing.

MONASTIR   Scene along the shore line.

FISHING: 13,000 fishermen along the coast provide fish both for domestic consumption and export.

MINING: Extensive deposits of phosphate, some of which are processed (for example, into superphosphates) as well as mined. Iron, lead, and zinc deposits are widely scattered. Considerable oil prospecting.

TRADE

1960: IMPORTS $191,000,000
      EXPORTS $120,000,000
      DEFICIT $71,000,000

MAJOR IMPORTS: Petroleum products, cloth, machinery, clothing, and motor vehicles.

MAJOR EXPORTS: Wines, olive oil, wheat, phosphates, iron ore, dates, lead and lead alloys.

TRANS-PORTATION

ROADS: 9,154 miles, all-weather, connect the major cities.

VEHICLES: 37,800 passenger cars; 17,000 commercial vehicles.

WATERWAYS: Excellent harbor at Tunis. The small Tunisia-owned merchant fleet operates between Tunis and France.

RAILROADS: 1,725 miles of track, now nationally owned.

COMMUNI-CATIONS

Well-developed, government-owned telephone and telegraph systems link the major cities. Radio Tunis is government-owned. Newspapers: 9 daily and 14 weekly.

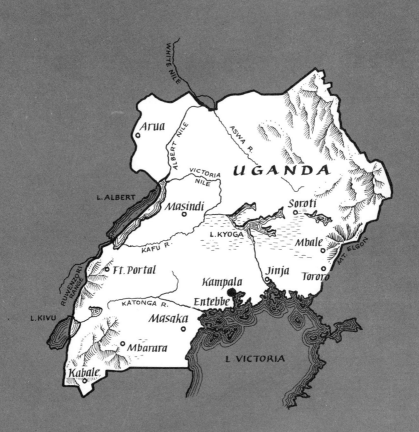

UGANDA

Fairyland of Africa

"Uganda is a fairy tale." So wrote Sir Winston Churchill. And indeed, travelers to Africa account this country as the gem of the continent. Everyone is entranced by this emerald-green land of pleasant vistas and charming cities.

Most of Uganda occupies a high plateau, 4,000 feet above sea level. Although astride the equator, Uganda enjoys a mild climate with a temperature that ranges from 60 to 85 degrees. In the lowland jungle areas, heat and high humidity are prevalent, and rainfall is frequent.

Situated in East Central Africa, Uganda is about the size of Oregon, roughly 93 thousand square miles in area. Lake Victoria forms its southeastern border, and the Ruwenzori Mountains, the famous Mountains of the Moon, separate it from Congo (Leopoldville) on the west.

THE SOURCE OF THE NILE

The Mountains of the Moon seemed legendary but the magic of the name fascinated explorers who struggled to reach the mysterious peaks. It is known today that these mountains are but an indirect source of the Nile. Most of the water drains to Lake Nyassa, Lake Tanganyika, and Lake Victoria. A major source of the Nile was discovered at the northeast corner of Lake Victoria, where it leaves that deep and wide body of water in cataracts and tributary streams.

THE OWEN FALLS HYDRO-ELECTRIC PLANT

In this area, at Owen Falls, the British built Uganda's major hydro-electric plant, tapping one of the largest sources of water power in the world. In 1960, this plant generated 150,000 kilowatts, enough to meet Uganda's needs and to supply neighboring Kenya; yet the plant uses less than five percent of the available water power. A second plant is in the planning stage.

MISSIONARIES, MOSLEMS, AND THE SLAVE TRADE

In 1862, the English explorer, John Speke, was among the first Europeans to reach Uganda. For about 30 years, the contacts with the West were mainly through English and French missionaries. Arab slave traders had long exploited this region. The English missionaries actively opposed the slave trade; and in 1888, the Arabs burned many of the missions and dominated the native kingdom. By 1892, the country was under control of the British East Africa Company; and in 1894, Great Britain proclaimed a protectorate over Uganda.

A COLONIAL EXPERIMENT

Great Britain pursued an unusual policy in Uganda: no Europeans were allowed to own land. The land remained in the possession of the Buganda, a powerful native tribe with its own kingdom, and of the other powerful tribes that form the kingdoms of Unyoro, Ankole, and Toro.

This policy has kept down the number of immigrants. Lands and estates are primarily owned by Africans. Today, of the 6,000,000 inhabitants, only 11,000 are Europeans. But all the towns in Uganda are creations of the Europeans and the Asians. These urban developments have grown around administrative centers. All the foreigners in Uganda are either civil servants, missionaries, technicians, teachers, or representatives of commercial firms.

The business of the country is largely in the hands of the 80,000 Asians, many of whom have been in Uganda for two or three generations.

KAMPALA, CAPITAL AND EDUCATIONAL CENTER

Kampala, the capital, a city of fine streets and skyscrapers with a population of 47,000 people, is accounted as one of the most handsome cities in Africa.

Located here is Makrere University College, with studios and classes in art and sculpture, and an outstanding library. The city is graced with three religious structures of architectural magnificence: a mosque, a Church of England cathedral, and a Roman Catholic cathedral.

KAMPALA Capital of Uganda and principal business center, Kampala is a city of 47,000 inhabitants. Built on a series of seven hills, this city of modern skyscrapers and fine architectural edifices is one of the most handsome municipalities on the continent. The Parliament Buildings can be seen in the center of the picture.

The Uganda Museum in Kampala is unique. The attendants are also musicians; and at regular times they demonstrate the musical instruments of Africa.

UGANDA'S NATIONAL PARKS

Two of the finest parks in all Africa are located in this country. The Queen Elizabeth National Park is an animal sanctuary where one can see water-buck, lion, leopard, cheetah, water hog, hippo, pelican, and immense herds of buffalo. Some of the roadmarks read, "Elephants have right of way."

Murchison Falls National Park is replete with scenic wonders. For the ornithologist, this bird haven is a dream come true; the fantastic variety of bird life is quite unbelievable.

And then there is the Ituri Forest, peopled by Pygmies, whose ways

KARAMOJO WOMAN   This young married matron wears earrings made of copper and aluminum wire. Her necklace consists of loose rings of copper and iron wire. Just before her wedding ceremony, according to custom, her ear ornaments and necklace were presented to her by the bridegroom's mother. The type of jewelry is dictated by the tribal taboo against a bride wearing beads.

KARAMOJO TRIBESMAN   This man of the Karamojo region wears lip and ear ornaments made of aluminum. When he was deemed to reach manhood, his long hair was molded into two buns, one on top of his head, and the other at the back. Colored clay was used to work the strands into patterns. Metal eyelets were inserted into the bun at the back in which he may, after obtaining permission of the elders, wear ostrich feathers. At such time, he is considered to be of marriageable age. The arm shows traditional designs made by lacerating the skin. Ashes are rubbed into the open wounds of the cuts to raise the decorative welts.

PYGMY The Ba Mbuti Pygmies of the Ituri region average 4 feet, 4 inches in height, and are not a degenerative human type. They have a characteristic body odor, which differs from both light and dark humans. Twenty-five thousand Pygmies live in this region, and hunt with bow and arrow. They maintain some kind of feudal system, in which groups hunt for a master who, in return, pays his hunters with food, mostly plantains. Pygmies are monogamous.

TESO WOMAN This old woman is carrying a basket of new cotton picked from her small plot. She will spin the cotton in her hut.

are full of enchantment. Here one can meet these strange primitives and observe them at first hand.

TRIBAL LOYALTY VERSUS THE STATE

There are more than twenty different tribes in Uganda. The Buganda, representing one-sixth of the population, is the largest, and most prosperous tribe; culturally, it is the most advanced.

For centuries, the Buganda have had their own king, called the Kabaka. The Buganda, who agitated for tribal control of the state, were opposed to democratic government and equal representation for minority tribes, since this would decrease their power.

KIBULI MOSQUE   This architectural showpiece of Kampala is one of the finest examples of Moorish architecture in Africa.

RELIGION AND POLITICS

Religion and politics have been closely connected in Uganda. The natives called the Catholics *Wa-Franza*,(the French); and they called the Protestants *Wa-Ingrezi*,(the English). Today, the population of Uganda consists of 1.8 million Catholics, 800 thousand Protestants, and 1 million Moslems. The remainder of the people are adherents of primitive religions. The Catholics control politics. The cabinet, formed after the 1961 elections, included 6 Catholics, 3 Protestants, and 1 Moslem.

However, for all its democratic forms, Uganda's politics are dominated by one man: the Kabaka of Uganda, Mtesa II, also called by his Christian name of Frederick. This powerful figure was educated at Cambridge, in England, and served as an officer in a British guard regiment. In 1953, the British exiled him from his native land because he blocked the way towards the establishment of a democratic Uganda by insisting that the privileged position of the Buganda tribe over the other natives be maintained. After his return from exile, he proved more than

a match for the several democratic parties which had established themselves under British sponsorship. When independence was discussed,
the Kabaka managed quite well to hold his own, with the result that the
new country is still very much under his personal control.

*PRACTICAL LESSON   Young Africans at the
Gayaza Primary School are learning a lesson in
shopping. They use sugar cane, bananas and
gourds for merchandise. The signs are in Swahili.
All the children wear school uniforms. All are
barefoot.*

Uganda is a constitutional democracy. It is governed by a National Assembly composed of eighty-two members, of whom twenty-one are Buganda. In the face of divisive tribal interests, the Assembly may face problems in pursuing the national interest.

ZEBRAS AT A POOL *In the plains of Lake Victoria, zebras abound. They are killed by natives for food, and for their hides which are made into leather. The species is also subject to decimation by big game hunters.*

QUEEN ELIZABETH NATIONAL PARK   *A hippopotamus family at ease.*

QUEEN ELIZABETH NATIONAL PARK   *The topi has a glossy purplish-brown coat which is silky in appearance.*

BUILDING A HOME   *In Kigezi, the Bakiga tribe are building new homes on land given to them by the government for resettlement. A new home is half-built by the time the women and children arrive. The men drive sticks in the ground, lash them together with withes, and put a straw roof on top. The women bring clay, mix it with water, and spread the impromptu plaster on the skeleton walls. After it dries, the surface is smoothed with wet hands. Such a house lasts for ten years or so.*

A FAVORABLE TWO-CROP ECONOMY

Uganda has had a favorable trade balance for many years. Coffee and cotton account for seventy percent of its exports. Copper is also a valuable export. In 1960, exports totaled $116,446,000; imports $72,-800,000. Uganda has received good prices for bumper crops, season after season. But the average annual income, $67 per person, is low even by African standards.

EDUCATION A MAJOR CONCERN

Under British administration, education was the largest item in the budget. The new state is apparently continuing this emphasis. In 1960, local provincial governments allotted as much as 35 percent of their budget to education.

Nevertheless, illiteracy, still widespread, hinders industrial growth and is a factor in keeping the per capita income low. Many primary schools were built during the last decade; and approximately 43 percent of school age children were enrolled in 1960. But secondary schools were neglected; and only about one percent of high-school-age children attended high school in 1960.

PALACE OF THE KABAKA   This handsome-looking building, built in 1908, has both electricity and plumbing, two facilities which are quite unusual for a building erected in Africa at the beginning of the century. The first floor contains state rooms, offices for secretaries, and a large reception room. The upper story contains six rooms, used as living quarters by the Kabaka and Princess Irene, his well-educated and attractive wife. Numerous servants attend the Kabaka. They wear long, white, cotton gowns and prostrate themselves before the presence of their King. The duties of these functionaries are traditional, and are handed down from father to son, and mother to daughter. Functions are severely regulated by protocol and are performed by designated clans, whose duties do not change from generation to generation. The Buffalo Clan have always been carriers. In the past, they carried the Kabaka on their backs. Now they drive his automobiles. Other clans only handle his food, and still others prepare his drinks. On the well-ordered grounds, which contain magnificent lawns and shrubs, there is one spot on which burns the Kabaka's Sacred Flame, to be extinguished only at his death.

THE POPULATION EXPLOSION

Between 1948 and 1961, the population of Uganda rose from 4 million to 6 million. At the present rate, the population is expected to double in thirty-two years. Agriculture will have to be very greatly expanded to meet food needs.

THE FUTURE AND THE CHALLENGE

Uganda has established economic agreements and a common market with Kenya and Tanganyika. The three countries use a common currency.

NATIONAL ASSEMBLY COMPOUND   These buildings at Kampala, erected in 1960 under British supervision, constitute the government center. The Parliament of Uganda, consisting of 82 popularly elected members and 9 special members, meet in the National Assembly building, a chamber modeled along the lines of Britain's House of Commons. The buildings shown here can be seen in perspective in the picture on page 427.

SPEKE ROAD   This street in Kampala is named after the Britisher who discovered Uganda in 1862.

In spite of Uganda's relative prosperity, it faces many tasks: education must be expanded; new roads are needed; and industrialization must be accelerated. British aid will be essential; but Uganda's future depends largely on its tribal leaders whose wisdom, in rising above conflicting tribal loyalties, can alone make Uganda a true nation.

IN BRIEF

AREA	93,981 square miles; about the size of Oregon.
TERRAIN	Most of the country lies on a 4,000-foot plateau. Western border of the country with the Congo is formed by Ruwenzori Mountains, with peaks over 16,000 feet high.
CLIMATE	Hot and wet. Rainfall 40 to 50 inches per year in most of the country. Daily temperature range—60° to 85°.
CAPITAL	Kampala (Population: 47,000). When a British protectorate, the capital was Entebbe.

POPULATION   6,538,000; about 11,000 Europeans and 80,000 Asians and other non-Africans.

ETHNIC GROUPS   Bantu and Nilotic. Over twenty different tribes in the country. Most important are the Buganda, about one-sixth of the total population. Other tribes are the Iteso, the Basoga, the Lango, the Acholi, the Batoro, the Banyoro.

LANGUAGE   Official language is English, but most people speak one of the African languages: Swahili, Bantu, Sudanic.

RELIGION   Animists, Moslems, Christians.

DATE OF INDEPENDENCE   October 9, 1962

FORM OF GOVERNMENT   Constitutional democracy. Individual states have great amount of local autonomy. Most important province, the Kingdom of Buganda, is a constitutional monarchy. National Assembly of 82 members elected every 5 years.

EDUCATION   In 1960, 346,000 children, about 43%, were enrolled in primary schools. Only 1% of children of high school age were enrolled in secondary schools. One university, the University College of East Africa (Makerere) located at Kampala; 27

teacher's colleges for primary school teachers turn out approximately 600 teachers a year.

HEALTH FACILITIES
375 registered nurses. Major disease is malaria. Uganda has 517 doctors, about 1 for every 13,000 persons; over 2½% of the population receives hospital treatment. Sleeping sickness is rare.

CURRENCY
Unit is Uganda pound. (£1 = U.S. $2.80).

INDUSTRY
Processing of cotton and sugar. Also a cement factory, a copper mine and smelter, breweries, cigarette factories.

CROPS: Cotton and coffee are chief exports; sugar, tea, and cocoa have been introduced.

STOCK: A growing cattle industry.

FISHING: Mostly for domestic use; from the western lakes.

MINING: Some copper.

TRADE

1960:	EXPORTS	116,446,000
	IMPORTS	$ 72,800,000
	SURPLUS	43,646,000

MAJOR IMPORTS: Manufactured goods.

MAJOR EXPORTS: Coffee, cotton, copper.

TRANS-PORTATION
About 13,000 miles of roads; 445 surfaced; 38,000 motor vehicles. Entebbe has a fine airfield, used for international flights. There are 580 miles of railroad.

RUWENZORI LODGE   This hotel at Mutwanga is the jumping off point for expeditions bound for the Ruwenzori mountain range, known as the "Mountains of the Moon." Located on the equator, these fabulous mountains are capped with glaciers and snow fields. This luxurious hostelry accommodates 24 tourists.

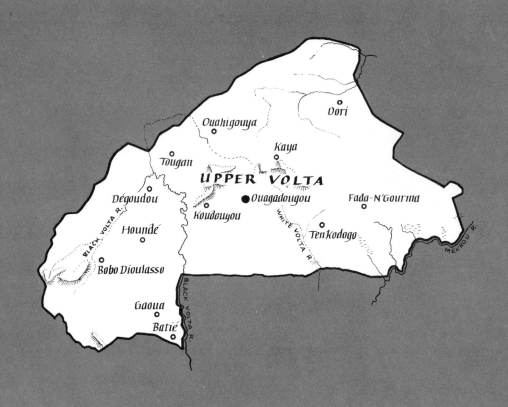

Dori

Ouahigouya

Kaya

Tougan

UPPER VOLTA

Dégoudou

● Ouagadougou

Fada-N'Gourma

Koudougou

Hounde

WHITE VOLTA R.

Ten Kodogo

BLACK VOLTA R.

Bobo Dioulasso

Gaoua

BLACK VOLTA R.

Batié

MEKROU R.

UPPER VOLTA

A Proud Tribe in an Arid Land

A landlocked country of 105,811 square miles, Upper Volta is slightly smaller than the state of Arizona. The country has a population of a little more than 3,500,000 people.

Upper Volta has no important export crop. Purchasing power and living standards are low; illiteracy runs more than 95 percent; education is feeble.

The country has an unfavorable balance of trade, and must rely on grants from FAC to make up its deficit. (*See chapter on Cameroun.*)

THE MOSSI TRIBE

The history of Upper Volta is largely the history of the remarkable Mossi people whose origins are shrouded in legend. They probably came from the Sudan in the 11th century, during which the Moro Naba, Emperor of the Mossi, established his throne at Ouagadougou. Today, Ouagadougou is the capital of Upper Volta.

Symbolizing the sun, the Moro Naba was surrounded by a great court of attending dignitaries. Protocol was as elaborate as that in the court of Louis XIV of France. Every activity was—and to some extent still is—subject to the strictest etiquette.

Today, one of the principal attractions of Ouagadougou is the palace of the Moro Naba, and the rituals which take place on the palace grounds every Friday morning at 7:00. A great horde of the Mossi people comes to pay allegiance to the king; and elaborate ceremonies, with pomp and protocol, give ample evidence of the high regard in which the Moro Naba is held. The present Moro Naba traces his ancestry back through a dynasty of forty-seven predecessors.

The Mossi were able to resist Mohammedanism; and to this day, this people remains a strong enclave of animist belief, surrounded by a predominantly Moslem world. The Mossi were vigorous soldiers and empire builders; but by the end of the 19th century, they accepted

French rule rather than risk being conquered by other neighboring tribes.

More than 1.7 million strong, the Mossi make up almost half the population of Upper Volta. They live in the central region of the country; and for the most part, make their living by farming. Their society is family-centered; parents and their adult offspring make up the larger family unit, who occupy a group of huts surrounding a small court.

ECONOMIC HARDSHIPS

Consumer goods are so scarce that Ouagadougou has become one of the world's most expensive cities in which to live. In September, 1961, a small bar of soap cost $0.42, a tube of toothpaste, $1.12, a newspaper, $0.20, and a soft drink, $0.48. Electric bills can easily amount to $85 a month, and a medium-sized apartment rents for as much as $400 a month. At these prices, most consumer articles cannot be purchased by native citizens and are bought only by members of the diplomatic community. To make at least some of the goods available to Africans, the government has established a non-profit cooperative which sells consumer goods at considerably lower prices.

To bolster the economy, Upper Volta has entered into a customs union with Ivory Coast, Dahomey, and Niger. This agreement reduces tariffs among the four nations; and provides Upper Volta with outlets for surplus meat and livestock that might otherwise be left unsold in the international market.

PROSPECTS FOR A VIABLE ECONOMY

Only the exploitation of mineral deposits will surmount the major hurdles. Because the climate and soil are not favorable to large-scale agriculture, mining of ores is the nation's best hope. As yet, little prospecting has been done, but it seems likely, in view of the geological similarity with Ghana and Ivory Coast, that the country's mineral resources will prove to be a sufficient base for a developing economy. Some gold has been mined in Upper Volta, and large manganese deposits have been discovered at Kiere, only eight miles from the railroad line connecting Ouagadougou with the sea via the port of Abidjan.

STREET ARTISAN *Using the traditional process of making jewelry and statuettes, this workman in Ouagadougou modernized only to the extent of a wrist watch, works his craft for all to see.*

Erosion, primitive agricultural methods, and poor strains of live-stock have all kept the country in a depressed condition. The government is using the funds available from FIDES (FAC) to concentrate on agricultural development.

It is also hoped that cash crops can be developed for the export market. In colonial days, little was done along these lines. In fact, the French had doubts that Upper Volta could ever create a viable economy of its own. It was these doubts that led to the 1932 partitioning of Upper Volta among the surrounding colonies of Niger, Sudan, and the Ivory Coast. However, this created more problems than it solved, and the agitation of the Mossi for a nation of their own provided the final argument for reunification.

LIVESTOCK FOR EXPORT

Like Chad, Upper Volta's principal wealth is in its livestock. It is one of the great cattle areas of Africa. In addition to 1.5 million head of cattle, the country has 2.5 million sheep and goats, 280,000 horses and donkeys, and 31,000 hogs. Exporting animals on the hoof—70,000 cattle

HOME CHORES   *The woman is climbing a home-made ladder made from a palm trunk. She has taken the grain and the fruit handed to her by her companion, and is about to spread these out to dry on the roof of her dwelling. The woven palmyra curtain on the left serves as the door to her home. The mud walls of the house have been crackled by the intensity of the sun. The thatched hut is used for storage. Wine is made from the clustered gourd-like fruit, suspended on a pole. The palmyra that abounds in this area also yields sugar. Two tree trunks in the right foreground support a portico, used mainly for storage.*

and 170,000 sheep a year—represents more than half the total value of exports from Upper Volta. It is interesting that most of this goes to neighboring countries of the customs union, rather than to Western Europe or America. This trend appears to be increasing, and it seems likely that a greater percentage of the trade of all African nations will be trade among themselves.

FORESTATION PROGRAM

Upper Volta has no real forests. A program of forestation has been undertaken that should prevent further dessication of the soil. By preventing rainfall from draining away, the trees will greatly help farming in arid areas.

Upper Volta's principal task is to outwit nature. The land has been so poorly endowed, compared with other nations of tropical Africa, that her problems are immensely more complicated. But Upper Volta has one advantage: her transportation system is unusually good.

YAMÉOGO AND FOREIGN POLICY

President Maurice Yaméogo, a Mossi, is a Catholic. Before he entered politics, he was a nurse by profession and took part in the important campaign against sleeping sickness.

Yaméogo was one of the lieutenants of Houphouët-Boigny. He seems to be alternately attracted by Houphouët-Boigny and Kwame Nkrumah; and the foreign policy of Upper Volta has fluctuated accordingly between that of Ivory Coast and that of Ghana.

IN BRIEF

AREA	105,811 square miles, slightly larger than Colorado.
TERRAIN	Upper Volta is landlocked, with four main rivers — the Black, White, and Red Voltas, and their principal tributary, the Sourou, all flowing southward to join in Ghana. Land is largely semi-arid plateau, most of it poorly suited to cultivation.
CLIMATE	Northern part has high temperatures, with low humidity, and little rain. In March, average temperature in Ouagadougou is 106°. In the south, a rainy season lasts from May to October, but rainfall is modest, ranging from 29 to 44 inches.
CAPITAL	Ouagadougou (population, 63,000).
OTHER CITIES	Bobo Dioulasso, 50,000.
POPULATION	3,635,000; about 6,000 Europeans.
ETHNIC GROUPS	Mossi, numbering about 1.7 million, live chiefly in the central part of the land. Mande, Fulani, and Hausa are other major groups. Numerous other smaller tribes.
LANGUAGE	French is official language. Numerous dialects of the Sudanic family of languages are spoken.
RELIGION	About 600,000 Mohammedans and 100,000 Christians. Remainder are animists.
DATE OF INDEPENDENCE	August 5, 1960.
FORM OF GOVERNMENT	Constitutional democracy. The President and a 75-man one-house assembly are elected every 5 years. Council of Ministers is appointed by President. Member of French Community and United Nations.

MOSQUE AT BOBO DIOULASSO   In this town of 50,000, the design of the mosque follows the local pattern of baked earth reinforced with wooden beams.

MAURICE YAMÉOGO Born in 1921, a member of the Mossi tribe, he received the equivalent of a high school education and then became a civil servant. He was elected to the Presidency in 1959. In 1960, he banned the major opposition party, and arrested most of its leaders. He is definitely oriented toward the West, primarily because of financial aid from this source.

WOMEN OF OUAGADOUGOU Mossi women from villages near Ouagadougou are returning from the market where they have been selling dolo—a light alcoholic drink made from sorghum. The beverage was contained in the terra-cotta jugs they are carrying, and dispensed from the hollowed gourd seen atop one of the jugs. The hair of these women is plaited in tiny braids and wound around the head. The hair looks as if it is cut, but has not been cut, for Mossi women cut their hair only during a period of mourning.

EDUCATION	In 1959, 23,777 pupils enrolled in 185 elementary schools, and 809 in 2 secondary schools. About 600,000 children of school age do not attend school. No universities.
HEALTH FACILITIES	In 1959, 64 doctors, 4 pharmacists, 2 hospitals, 26 medical centers, 41 maternity dispensaries, and 144 other dispensaries.
CURRENCY	Unit is French Community franc (247 francs = U.S. $1.00).
INDUSTRY	Local processing plants for crops and raw materials. Handicrafts are well developed.

CROPS: Mostly subsistence farming, including sorghum, millet, and corn. Cotton, peanuts, and sisal are grown for export.

STOCK: Stock raising is chief economic activity. Large herds of cattle, sheep, and donkeys are kept mostly by nomadic and semi-nomadic tribes.

FISHING: Small amount, used mostly for export.

MINING: Prospecting is in process and looks favorable; small quantities of a number of minerals have been found, but commercial exploitation not yet begun.

TRADE

1958:	IMPORTS	$7,000,000
	EXPORTS	4,500,000
	DEFICIT	$2,500,000

MAJOR EXPORTS: Livestock; karite (vegetable oil).

MAJOR IMPORTS: Transport equipment, textiles, machinery, fruits and vegetables, sugar, and pharmaceuticals.

TRANS-PORATION

ROADS: 2,940 miles all-weather.

VEHICLES: 650 passenger cars; 2,200 commercial vehicles (1957).

WATERWAYS: None.

RAILROADS: 300 miles of track, connecting with Ivory Coast and Niger.

AIR TRAFFIC: International airports at Ouagadougou and Bobo Dioulasso; some 30 smaller fields.

COMMUNI-CATIONS

About 1,300 telephones; all but 50 in Ouagadougou and Bobo Dioulasso; two radio stations; no daily newspapers.

GLOSSARY

ARAB A member of a number of Semitic peoples who were originally inhabitants of the Arabian peninsula. Early in the seventh century, the Arabian groups were united by Mohammed, founder of the religion of Islam. The Arabs then spread to other parts of the world, including North Africa. There are an estimated fifty million Arabs in Africa.

BANTU A family of Negroid peoples, who speak over 300 languages which derive from the same root structure. The Bantus are found in Africa, south of Cameroun and Kenya. They are considered to be a cross between Negroes and Hamites. There are an estimated eighty million Bantu in Africa, among which some of the important tribes are the Zulu (Union of South Africa), the Kikuyu (Kenya), the Bakongo and the Baluba (Congo Leopoldville).

BERBERS A Caucasoid people of North Africa, closely related to southern Europeans. They are the oldest known inhabitants of North Africa. They are predominant in Morocco, and also form a substantial part of the population of Algeria, and have spread southwards across the Sahara. There are an estimated fifteen million Berbers in Africa.

BRAZZAVILLE BLOC A group of twelve African states of pro-Western orientation—all of them former French colonies—which met in December, 1960, at Brazzaville, capital of Congo (Brazzaville), and formulated a common political policy. Members of the Brazzaville Bloc are: Senegal, Mauritania, Ivory Coast, Upper Volta, Dahomey, Niger, Cameroun, Chad, Central African Republic, Gabon, Congo (Brazzaville), and the Malagasy Republic.

BRITISH COMMONWEALTH A term used since World War II to describe the countries associated with Great Britain—independent Dominions, British colonies, and countries under British protectorate. Originally used to embrace only the "White Dominions" inhabited by Caucasians (Canada, Union of South Africa, Southern Rhodesia, Australia, and New Zealand), the term now includes all countries associated with Britain, whatever the race, language, color or degree of self-government of their inhabitants. The African countries included in the British Commonwealth are: Gambria, Sierra Leone, Ghana, Nigeria, Kenya, Uganda, Tanganyika, Zanzibar, Nyasaland, Northern Rhodesia, Southern Rhodesia (three members of the Central African Federation), Basutoland, Swaziland, and Bechuanaland.

BRITISH EMPIRE A term formerly used to describe Great Britain, together with all its colonies and protectorates. This is now referred to as the British Commonwealth.

CASABLANCA BLOC A group of five African states—Egypt, Morocco, Guinea, Mali, and Ghana—which met at Casablanca (Morocco), in 1961, and formulated a common policy of neutralism (non-alignment with either East or West). Libya and Algeria were represented at the Casablanca conclave, but have not joined the Bloc.

453

GLOSSARY

CAUCASIANS One of the three main racial divisions of humanity; the other two, being Mongolians and Negroes. Caucasians are sub-divided into three main groups, based on families of language: Indo-Europeans, Semites, and Hamites.

COLD WAR A term coined by Walter Lippmann, an American journalist, to describe the non-shooting conflict between the Western powers and the Soviet Bloc—a conflict fought through diplomatic maneuver, economic pressure, espionage, hostile propaganda, and military support of nations deemed friendly—all without actual engagement of arms.

COUNCIL OF THE ENTENTE A confederation, formed in 1959, by four West African republics—Ivory Coast, Upper Volta, Dahomey, and Niger—to establish closer economic and political links between these countries. A customs union of the four states was established, and a solidarity fund to provide financial assistance to any member state that needs economic support was set up. The intention of these countries is to coordinate their policies in the fields of taxation, public administration, labor legislation, public works, transportation, and communications.

CREOLE A person of mixed French and Negro, Portuguese and Negro, or Spanish and Negro descent, speaking a dialect which is an admixture of European and native elements. Such a dialect is also called *Creole*. In Sierra Leone, the original settlers, who were freed slaves, are called *Creoles*.

F.A.C. The initials of the *Fonds d'Aide et Co-operation* (Aid and Co-operation Fund), formed in 1958 by the government of the *French Community*. Its purpose is to aid the development of the former French colonies. It replaced the F.I.D.E.S. of the French Union.

F.I.D.E.S. The initials of the *Fonds d'Investissement et Developpement Social* (Investment and Social Development Fund), organized after World War II by the French Union to provide developmental aid to its non-European territories. After 1958, F.I.D.E.S. was replaced by F.A.C.

F.L.N. The initials of the *Front de Libération Nationale* (National Liberation Front) set up by the Algerian rebels against France, in 1954, to unify their political and military efforts. The chief leaders of the F.L.N. are Ferhat Abbas and Ahmed Ben Bella.

FRENCH COMMUNITY A term used, since 1958, to describe France, its overseas territories, and eleven independent republics which were formerly French colonies in Africa. The African members of the French Community are: Algeria, French Somaliland, Ivory Coast, Gabon, Congo (Brazzaville), Upper Volta, Dahomey, Chad, Mauritania, Senegal, Central African Republic, Niger and the Malagasy Republic.

FRENCH UNION A term used after World War II to describe metropolitan

GLOSSARY

France and all the overseas territories under its control, excepting the protectorates of Morocco and Tunisia. The French Union was replaced after 1958 by the *French Community*.

FULANI   A West African people of the Hamitic race, who also have a Negroid strain. They form the ruling class of Northern Nigeria. There are an estimated two million Fulani in Africa. This group of people are also known as the Fulbe and the Peul.

GHANA-GUINEA-MALI UNION   A federal union proclaimed in 1958 by the heads of the states of Ghana and Guinea, with the aim of achieving complete political and economic union. These two countries were joined in 1960 by Mali. However, because of the geographical separation of the member states, there has been little effective functioning.

HAMITIC   One of the three main subdivisions of the Caucasian race. They speak a family of languages, which includes ancient Egyptian (extinct), Berber, Somali, and Tuareg. The Hamites are highly variable in appearance. Most of these peoples are Moslems. There are an estimated fifty million Hamites in Africa.

HAUSA   A Negroid people of the Sudan with a Hamitic strain. They are found chiefly in the region between Lake Chad and the Niger River. There are an estimated four million Hausa in Africa. The Chad language of the Hausa is widely used in West Africa as a language of trade.

I F A N   The initials of the *Institut Français de l'Afrique Noire* (French Institute of Black Africa), created by the French at Dakar as a research and teaching center for their African colonies.

INTERNATIONAL MONETARY FUND   A fund set up at the Bretton Woods (New Hampshire) Conference of 1944, to provide loans to governments and to act as a clearing agency for dealings between governments.

LEAGUE OF NATIONS   An international organization of affiliated sovereign states formed after World War I for the purpose of maintaining peace. Under the aegis of the League of Nations, a number of countries were individually administered by designated powers as League mandates, or Trust Territories. The League ceased operating at the outbreak of World War II. At the end of World War II, it was succeeded by the United Nations.

MONROVIA BLOC   A group of twenty African states of pro-Western orientation, who met in 1961 in Monrovia, the capital of Liberia, to formulate common political policy. This group was composed of the twelve members of the Brazzaville Bloc, plus the following eight countries: Nigeria, Liberia, Libya, Ethiopia, Somalia, Togo, Tunisia, and Sierra Leone.

NEGROES   Negroes, sometimes referred to as "Blacks," are one of the three main racial divisions of humanity, the other two being Caucasians and Mongolians.

455

GLOSSARY

NEGROID An adjective applied to peoples (e.g., the Hausa), who have some of the racial features of Negroes.

NEW EURAFRICAN ASSOCIATION An economic association, to be formed between eighteen independent African states—all former colonies of France, Belgium, and Italy—acting as a group, and between the European Common Market. Negotiations commenced at Brussels in the winter of 1962. Should these efforts be brought to fruition, the eighteen African states would be nominated as associate members of the European Common Market, and treated accordingly.

NILO-HAMITES A group of East African pastoral peoples, including the Masai.

NILOTIC PEOPLES A group of peoples who live in the region drained by the Nile River (e.g., the Dinka and the Shilluk). They are mainly Hamitic, but have some Negroid features.

OFFICE DU NIGER A French authority, established in 1932, to regulate and develop the Niger at its delta. The chief beneficiary of this project has been the Republic of Mali.

RAIN FOREST A tropical woodland in which there is an annual rainfall of at least 100 inches. The forest is dense, exuberant, and characterized by lofty, broad-leaved evergreens which form a continuous canopy of greenery. In the equatorial rain forest, there is an almost complete absence of low-growing, ground-rooted plants. In Africa, the rain forest covers most of the basin of the Congo River. Some tribes who live in the forest are the Ashanti (Ghana), the Bakongo (Congo Leopoldville) and the Pygmies.

SEMITIC A group of peoples who speak any one of the Semitic languages. The Semitic peoples are one of the three main sub-divisions of the Caucasian race. Originating in Southwest Asia, the Semitic peoples spread to North Africa. The main Semitic languages are Babylonian, Phoenician, Aramaic (all extinct), and Arabic, Hebrew, and Amharic (Ethiopic).

SOVIET BLOC A group of countries which, since World War II, have been under the hegemony of the Soviet Union. The Soviet Bloc is sometimes referred to as the *Eastern Bloc,* as opposed to the *Western Bloc,* led by the United States.

SUDANESE A term used to describe: (1) the inhabitants of the Republic of Sudan; (2) the inhabitants of the former French colony of Sudan, now the Republic of Mali; (3) the inhabitants of a vast region called *the Sudan,* which stretches between the Sahara and the western rain forests.

SUDANIC Any one of the languages, neither Bantu nor Hamitic, spoken in a belt extending from Senegal to southern Sudan.

SWAHILI A Bantu-speaking people of Zanzibar and of the adjacent coast. Their language, Swahili, has now incorporated many Arabic and European elements, and is now the language of

GLOSSARY

trade and government over much of East Africa and the Congo. Swahili is spoken by several million people.

TROIKA SYSTEM A proposal made by the Soviet Union to replace the secretary-general of the United Nations by an administrative committee of three men: one nominated by the Soviet Bloc, one nominated by the Western Bloc, and one nominated by the neutral countries.

TUAREG A Hamitic people with a slight Negroid strain. They live in the central and western Sahara, and along the middle Niger. There are an estimated 350 thousand Tuareg in Africa. The Hamitic speech of the Tuareg is considered to be of great purity. The Tuareg are Moslems. They are generally tall, with Mediterranean features; occasionally, some are light-haired.

UNION OF CENTRAL AFRICAN REPUBLICS A confederation formed, in 1961, by Chad, Congo (Brazzaville), and the Central African Republic to establish closer economic and political links between these three countries.

UNITED NATIONS An international organization, with headquarters in New York, formed, in 1945, at San Francisco to replace the League of Nations. The League of Nations mandates became United Nations Trust Territories. All the independent countries of Africa are members of the United Nations. On January 1, 1963, the United Nations had a membership of 110 nominal states.

WORLD BANK A term which includes both the International Bank for Reconstruction and Development set up by the Bretton Woods Conference of 1944, and the *International Monetary Fund*. The World Bank makes loans to governments for developmental purposes.

WORLD WAR I A general conflict involving most of the powers of the world. The Central Powers consisted of Germany, Austria-Hungary, Bulgaria, and Turkey. The Allies consisted of the United States, Great Britain, France, Russia, Belgium, Serbia, Greece, Romania, Montenegro, Portugal, Italy, and Japan. War began on July 28, 1914, and lasted until November 11, 1918. The Allies were victorious.

WORLD WAR II A general conflict involving most of the powers of the world. Germany, with its chief allies of Italy and Japan, was opposed by the United States, Great Britain, France, and Russia, with which were allied many smaller nations.

COMPARATIVE STATISTICS

COUNTRY	AREA	POPULATION	DENSITY PER SQUARE MILE	PERCENT OF ILLITERACY	NUMBER OF CINEMAS
ALGERIA	855,000	11,000,000	12.8	82	358
BURUNDI	10,747	2,220,000	204.7	90	1
CAMEROUN	166,796	4,097,000	24.3	90	11
CENTRAL AFRICAN REPUBLIC	238,224	1,227,000	5	95	3
CHAD	495,794	2,675,000	5.4	95	4
CONGO (BRAZZAVILLE)	132,047	795,000	6	95	9
CONGO (LEOPOLDVILLE)	905,381	14,150,000	15.6	63	8
DAHOMEY	44,696	1,935,000	43.4	95	3
GABON	103,088	440,000	4.3	95	3
GHANA	91,863	6,691,000	72.7	75	62
GUINEA	95,000	3,000,000	31.6	90	16
IVORY COAST	124,503	3,267,000	26.2	95	17
LIBYA	679,358	1,195,000	1.8	90	28
MALAGASY REPUBLIC	227,800	5,298,000	23.2	67	21
MALI	464,874	4,100,000	8.8	95	17
MAURITANIA	419,230	656,000	1.6	95	1

NUMBER OF DOCTORS AVAILABLE	PASSENGER AUTOMOBILES AVAILABLE	MILEAGE OF SURFACED ROADS	PER CAPITA ANNUAL INCOME	COUNTRY
1 for every 6,000 persons	1 for every 65 persons	8,000	$115	**ALGERIA**
1 for every 48,900 persons	1 for every 1,220 persons	3,000	$20	**BURUNDI**
1 for every 37,600 persons	1 for every 490 persons	350	$40	**CAMEROUN**
1 for every 38,350 persons	1 for every 220 persons	1,350	Under $100	**CENTRAL AFRICAN REPUBLIC**
1 for every 78,760 persons	1 for every 600 persons	188	$280 (Fort Lamy)	**CHAD**
1 for every 16,230 persons	1 for every 85 persons	238	$355 per family	**CONGO (BRAZZAVILLE)**
1 for every 20,100 persons	1 for every 420 persons	21,000	$43 for Africans	**CONGO (LEOPOLDVILLE)**
1 for every 46,950 persons	1 for every 360 persons	343	*	**DAHOMEY**
1 for every 8,625 persons	1 for every 100 persons	191	$53	**GABON**
1 for every 35,980 persons	1 for every 380 persons	1,645	Nearly $200	**GHANA**
1 for every 47,620 persons	1 for every 310 persons	1,550	Under $100	**GUINEA**
1 for every 32,670 persons	1 for every 220 persons	520	Under $100	**IVORY COAST**
1 for every 7,970 persons	1 for every 70 persons	1,000	*	**LIBYA**
1 for every 27,170 persons	1 for every 340 persons	1,100	$119	**MALAGASY REPUBLIC**
1 for every 77,360 persons	1 for every 260 persons	1,761	Under $100	**MALI**
1 for every 29,820 persons	1 for every 660 persons	none	$28	**MAURITANIA**

459

COMPARATIVE STATISTICS

COUNTRY	AREA	POPULATION	DENSITY PER SQUARE MILE	PERCENT OF ILLITERACY	NUMBER OF CINEMAS
MOROCCO	171,583	11,600,000	67.6	85	148
NIGER	458,995	2,800,000	6.1	95	2
NIGERIA	339,169	35,752,000	105.4	85	52
RWANDA	10,169	2,600,000	255.6	90	1
SENEGAL	77,401	3,140,000	40.5	95	51
SIERRA LEONE	28,000	2,500,000	89.3	90	3
SOMALIA	246,202	1,900,000	7.7	90	3
SUDAN	967,500	11,928,000	12.3	90	34
TANGANYIKA	361,800	9,238,000	25.5	90	36
TOGO	22,000	1,440,000	65.5	90	1
TUNISIA	48,300	4,168,000	86.3	40	65
UGANDA	93,981	6,538,000	69.6	70	14
UPPER VOLTA	105,811	3,635,000	34.3	95	5

FOR COMPARISON

UNITED STATES	3,615,211	182,953,000	50.6	2.2	11,355
PORTUGAL	35,599	9,130,410	256.5	35	437

NUMBER OF DOCTORS AVAILABLE	PASSENGER AUTOMOBILES AVAILABLE	MILEAGE OF SURFACED ROADS	PER CAPITA ANNUAL INCOME	COUNTRY
1 for every 6,360 persons	1 for every 100 persons	8,072	$320	**MOROCCO**
1 for every 107,700 persons	1 for every 680 persons	1,117	Under $100	**NIGER**
1 for every 43,650 persons	1 for every 1,480 persons	4,000	Less than $90	**NIGERIA**
1 for every 57,780 persons	1 for every 1,450 persons	3,000	$20	**RWANDA**
1 for every 57,090 persons	1 for every 225 persons	450	Under $100	**SENEGAL**
1 for every 69,450 persons	1 for every 4,845 persons	2,900	$70	**SIERRA LEONE**
1 for every 126,670 persons	1 for every 950 persons	758	Under $100	**SOMALIA**
1 for every 47,700 persons	1 for every 1,055 persons	negligible	$75	**SUDAN**
1 for every 18,330 persons	1 for every 400 persons	7,400	$56	**TANGANYIKA**
1 for every 57,600 persons	1 for every 1,185 persons	427	Under $100	**TOGO**
1 for every 7,600 persons	1 for every 110 persons	9,154	$127	**TUNISIA**
1 for every 13,000 persons	1 for every 170 persons	445	$67	**UGANDA**
1 for every 56,900 persons	1 for every 5,590 persons	2,940	Under $100	**UPPER VOLTA**

F O R   C O M P A R I S O N

NUMBER OF DOCTORS AVAILABLE	PASSENGER AUTOMOBILES AVAILABLE	MILEAGE OF SURFACED ROADS	PER CAPITA ANNUAL INCOME	COUNTRY
1 for every 840 persons	1 for every 12 persons	2,000,000	$2,242	**UNITED STATES**
1 for every 1,335 persons	1 for every 37 persons	9,000	$209	**PORTUGAL**

*Figures not available.

INDEX

INDEX

INDEX

INDEX

INDEX

INDEX

INDEX

INDEX

INDEX

INDEX

INDEX

472

INDEX

INDEX

INDEX

INDEX

INDEX

INDEX

INDEX